Edward MacLysaght

IRISH LIFE
IN THE
SEVENTEENTH CENTURY

This is the standard work of Irish social history during the period associated with Owen Roe O'Neill, Oliver Cromwell, Oliver Plunkett, Patrick Sarsfield, King James II and William of Orange. The seventeenth century was one of transition from the almost medieval to the early modern world. In the Ireland of this period nationalism had so developed that the clans were now at one in their opposition to the English. Within this development Dr MacLysaght analyses the social and cultural range of the Irish family and individual — looking at everyday life in city and country, travel, the class structure, sports and recreations. In many respects this is the most interesting period in Irish history; this very readable account does it justice.

Dr Edward MacLysaght is a former Chairman of the Irish Manuscripts Commission. As an author he is best known for books on social history and family history. His *Surnames of Ireland* is an established best-seller.

LANDING OF KING JAMES II AT KINSALE

(Reproduced from an engraving in the National Gallery of Ireland by kind permission of the Governers)

EDWARD MacLYSAGHT

MA DLitt MRIA

IRISH LIFE IN THE SEVENTEENTH CENTURY

IRISH ACADEMIC PRESS

TECHNICAL AND LEGAL INFORMATION

First edition 1939; second enlarged edition 1950; reprinted with corrections and additional bibliography 1969; now reprinted with the omission of appendices and bibliography. This edition is published by Irish Academic Press Limited, 3 Serpentine Avenue, Dublin 4. Printed in England by Billing and Son Limited, Guildford.

ISBN 0 7165 2342 6   paperback edition
ISBN 0 7165 2343 4   cased edition

CONTENTS

LIST OF ILLUSTRATIONS

PREFACE

This edition of *Irish Life in the Seventeenth Century* consists of the main text of the work which was first published in 1939. Some 150 pages of additional material have been omitted from this popular reprint (this material included appendices on: Co. Kildare in 1683; John Dunton's Letters; Two Contemporary Views on Hedges and Fencing; Estate Work; Wild Birds and Animals; Trade Corporations or Guilds; Rules for the Common Brokers of the City of Limerick; Last Speeches of Condemned Rapparees; Agriculture and the Cattle Acts; Road Repairs; Funeral Entries; Inventories: Furniture, Livestock; Daily Fare in a Big House; A Commentary on the Legal System; A Post-Mortem; and The Dress of the People). As copies of the full work are available in nearly all main libraries in Ireland, Great Britain and the U.S.A. any reader wishing to go more fully into the subject will be able to consult the complete work in one of them.

I have received and taken a note of several suggestions as to aspects of life in the seventeenth century which might be dealt with more fully. However, at the age of 91, with much other work still on hand, I am unlikely to have time to undertake any further thorough research on the main subject of this book. I would like now to remind the reader that in the preface of the second and third editions I said, 'So far from claiming that the present volume is an exhaustive study of the subject I regard it merely as the first stage of an entertaining journey'.

January 1979   E. MacLysaght

CHAPTER I

Introductory

THE ordinary citizen, or average man, has until recently been somewhat neglected by historians, and particularly by those whose theme is Ireland. This book is an attempt to give an account of the affairs which concerned his everyday life in the second half of the seventeenth century, and especially in the years covered by the reign of Charles II—that is to say, the generation which enjoyed a time of comparative peace after the devastation and upheaval of the Cromwellian War and Settlement, until the accession of a Catholic king once more embroiled our unfortunate countrymen in a quarrel which was none of their own making.

This period is in many respects the most interesting in Irish history. Ireland, it is true, at the time counted for little in world affairs, even though the Boyne is considered to be one of the decisive battles of the world : her influence was negligible in Europe where a thousand years before she had been almost the last repository of culture and the mainspring of Christian effort, when she had merited in fact the title of " insula sanctorum et doctorum". That time, however, is so remote that it is difficult to reconstruct with any degree of certainty or of detail the social life of the people and almost impossible to appreciate the point of view of the man in the street, as we would call him now. At the other end of the scale the past hundred years, already the subject of innumerable political, economic and social studies, though intensely interesting, hardly seem to be history yet in a country where memories are centuries old. Again, the eighteenth century, so full of glamour in England, is for us a period of economic depression and national degradation, which lasted till John Keogh and Henry Grattan arose to put new life into the submerged majority. It is a century which has been depicted by autobiographers —by rogues like Dudley Bradstreet as well as by upright men like Richard Edgeworth ; in fiction his daughter Maria and other novelists have made us familiar with it ; diarists—Pococke, Young, and a score of others—have described its country-side, its agriculture, its customs and the character of its people ; and in the realm of pure history Lecky has left us a great work which needs little supplementing, except in one respect, that covered by Professor Corkery's *Hidden Ireland*.

The seventeenth century was, above all others, a period of transition. In Ireland, at any rate, it was still almost mediaeval at its opening, and long before its close the modern world was already in being ; and even in England, where in the previous century remarkable literary achievements and maritime activity had marked a great change from pre-Tudor times, under the Stuarts only two generations separate the Gunpowder Plot from the foundation of the Royal Society.

It is often said that the world has progressed more in the last forty years than in any century previously, and the immense changes which have occurred within the memory of any man who was more than a child at the outbreak of the first Great War give some colour to this, though on consideration they will, of course, be found to be the result merely of mechanical inventions, while little, if any, intellectual progress has been made. If we consider essential rather than superficial things we realize that the change which occurred in the short space of little over fifty years between the Flight of the Earls and the Restoration was even greater, because it was more fundamental. The world, and Ireland with it, finally shook itself free of the Middle Ages and became in its essentials the modern world which we know to-day, and even in superficial matters approximated to the modern world we knew yesterday. If the people who lived under the later Stuarts knew nothing of steam engines and electric light they thought much as we do now and acted from motives we have no difficulty in understanding. The actions of a Sarsfield, a Petty or a Dick Talbot, the view-point of David O'Bruadair or my own impoverished ancestor in County Clare, are as intelligible to us as those of John Mitchel, of William Dargan, of James Clarence Mangan, or of our own grandfathers, and indeed are far nearer akin to them than were those of their predecessors a couple of generations earlier, whose mediaeval outlook on life is revealed in the pages of such a work as *Pacata Hibernia*, or, let us say, as *Iomarbhaigh na bhFileadh*, for it must not be forgotten that native sources, hitherto shamefully neglected by historians ignorant of the Irish language, are of the utmost importance.

In the period we are going to consider, scientists had taken the place of soothsayers and poisoning and plotting had given way to politics. The modern idea of nationality, though not of nationalism, had so far developed that for the first time in Irish

history we find a war in which the Irish are on one
side and the British on the other, instead of as
heretofore the foreigner being assisted, through
jealousies and clan hostility, by almost as many
Irishmen as there were fighting against them. That
this actually resulted in the complete submergence
of the Irish race at home for nearly two centuries
does not affect the truth of the statement that it is
one of the clear signs that marked the beginning of
modern Ireland.

On the other hand, it was not until the last few
years of the century that the old order finally passed
away. In the reign of Charles II there were still
many landed proprietors who were Catholics ;
the old culture still survived, and Irish poets, even
as late as O'Carolan, were not necessarily peasants ;
the Irish language continued to be spoken, not only
by the mass of the people, for this it was till after the
Great Famine of 1847, but by people of standing,
many of whom used it habitually.[1] The structure of
Irish society was still essentially aristocratic, notwithstanding the preponderance of Cromwellian
nouveaux riches among the landowners ; and invectives against the purse-proud upstarts, whose
English ways excited the hatred and ridicule of the
Tadhgs and Diarmuids, are common in the Gaelic
poetry of the period. The old forests were no more,
but wolves were not yet extinct. Men and women
were no longer burned at the stake on account of
their religious beliefs—indeed there were very few
cases of this in Ireland in any century, but cases
of that form of death penalty for murder though not
for witchcraft are met with even in the eighteenth

[1] References to my authorities for this and any other statements made in
this introductory chapter which are dealt with subsequently will be found
in their appropriate place later on in the book.

century,[2] as are such sixteenth century survivals as the use of the ducking-stool[3] for village scolds, while excommunication[4] was still sometimes meted out, especially in the Protestant churches, for certain not uncommon offences.

Thus the times with which we are going to deal are made more interesting by the survival of some of the characteristics of an earlier age, when chiefs ruled with almost regal power, when clan warfare seldom ceased, when the Brehon Laws were in force almost everywhere outside the Pale, and when the profession of bard was the most honoured in the land : but, as I have said, they were only survivals in a world which was already modern in its essentials.

As I have suggested elsewhere,[5] I believe that if we can cast our minds back to the first decade of the present century and recall the life of rural Ireland then, we shall not find it very difficult to form a true picture of life 250 years ago. At the end of the last century, and indeed in the first decade of the twentieth, many people in the remote district of County Clare, where I spent the most impressionable part of my youth—admittedly an exceptionally inaccessible region—had never seen a motor car or even a railway train. There was, in fact, no really essential difference between the daily life which I remember there as a boy and that of the seventeenth century. On the farm we still used the swing-plough, and as often as not meadows were cut with the scythe and corn with the sickle, while the old-fashioned sawpit had not yet been discarded. We

---

[2] See p.57 infra.
[3] Frequent mention of this engine of punishment is to be found in seventeenth century documents. See for example J.R.S.A.I., Vol. VIII, p.293, where one is described and *ibid*. Vol. XXII, p.287 and Vol. XXXI, p.50.
[4] Dwyer, *Diocese of Killaloe, passim*.
[5] *Short Study of a Transplanted Family*. (Dublin, 1935).

thought nothing of riding or driving the 25 miles to Ennis and returning the same night. The same bogs, the same scrub and rough land, since largely reclaimed as a result of peasant proprietorship, offered unlimited sport to the fowler as they did in the seventeenth century when shotguns first came into use. We had no mechanical music or public entertainment and, if we did not go to bed as early as our ancestors, we had like them to depend on resources within ourselves for our evening amusement. Forty years ago customs and beliefs now condemned by the Church as superstitious, and preserved only in the pages of antiquarian journals, were as common as is the practice of raising the hat passing a Catholic church to-day. Even the wakes retained much of their old character and were often far from the quiet and respectable functions they now are.

In those days we had in the west hard-drinking squireens whose exact counterpart existed in the eighteenth century, if not so much in the seventeenth ; the Big House was there, with its retainers and hangers-on, with its traditional hospitality and its ever-increasing aloofness from the heart of the people. Even the rustic poets who celebrated local events in ill-scanned doggerel were successors, however unworthy, of the bards. And the Gaelic language was there : I never heard the fishermen speak English then, whether out in their curraghs* (themselves a pure survival of the seventeenth, and indeed of much earlier centuries) or at nights when they gathered in their favourite public-house in the village street.

* Detailed descriptions of the curraghs in use in different parts of the country will be found in Hornell *British Coracles and Irish Curraghs*, sections 3 to 5. See also Evans, *Irish Heritage*, pp.23 and 147 *et seq.*

Irish still survives as the vernacular in most of the western counties in spite of the National School system, which, though now, of course, it helps to foster the language, was in the Victorian era one of the principal instruments in bringing about its decay. Its decline affected the religious life of the people who gave up with it the practice of many traditional devotions, notably the general saying of the family Rosary at night. The eighteenth century, however, when the Penal Laws were most oppressive, and the nineteenth century, before the stimulating effects of persecution had begun to wear off, were the period of passionate faith, not the seventeenth, when the disabilities attaching to the old religion pressed less heavily on the laity than on the clergy. Nevertheless the most striking difference between the two periods I am comparing lies in the position of the Church : in the one case her buildings destroyed, her schools forbidden, and her priests in lay attire performing their duties surreptitiously ; and in the other a highly organized body gradually gaining complete control of the education of the youth of the country and exercising a remarkable discipline over the people as a whole.

In the seventeenth century pure religion, as well as its political repercussions, occupied men's minds continually, and after the Restoration only one question equalled it in importance as a matter of public interest and concern. This was the land question.

Like our ancestors who were affected by the Cromwellian confiscations and the Restoration Acts of Settlement and Explanation, the generation which won the Land Act of 1903 saw blood shed in the process of transferring the land from one set of owners to another ; but the actual physical appearance of the countryside, possession of which was lost and regained, was so different that in places where no striking feature, such as a lake or mountain, exists it would be unrecognizable now by one who was familiar with it in 1700. I do not mean on account of the disappearance of the woods, for these had already been devastated by industrialists like the first Earl of Cork or by the Cromwellian newcomers, uncertain of the duration of their ownership : the great difference is between the wide, unenclosed spaces of those days, intersected by a few scarcely passable tracks, and the innumerable fields of to-day, divided from each other and from the network of roads by hedges and walls and banks.

Next to the physical appearance of the countryside perhaps the most obvious point of dissimilarity lies in the clothes worn by the people. The change in this respect is, of course, very striking in the wealthier classes with whom English dress and manners became fashionable mainly through the social influence of the first Duke of Ormond who, essentially " West British " in his outlook, was the outstanding Anglo-Irish figure of the century, as Oliver Plunket and Owen Roe O'Neill were the outstanding Irishmen. Even those well-to-do Irish who remained unaffected by this anglicizing tendency retained only some of the distinctively Irish features of their costume, such, for example, as the linen head-dress worn by the women.[7]

[7] For peculiarities of Irish dress see *Cambrensis Eversus*, Chapters XII and XIII. Dr. Lynch's comments on the introduction of English fashions will be found on pp.193-195 of Vol. I of that work. There are a number of useful references to this subject in *Pairlement Chloinne Tomáis*. I have given several of these in Appendix Q. For Dunton's descriptions of Irish clothes see Index under " Dress." As no further reference will be made in the text to this matter except incidentally, mention should be made here of Walker's *Historical Essay on the Dress of the Ancient and Modern Irish*,

There was less change between 1700 and 1900 in the garb of the working classes, for though the famous Irish mantle was still fairly common even after 1641[8] it was already almost entirely discarded by the succeeding generation, and as for the " braccae," Dr. Lynch, in 1662, regrets their complete disappearance, and with them the renown of Irish runners for speed and stamina.[9] In the time of Charles II, and indeed almost up to our own day, the peasantry made their own clothes from the wool of their own sheep, brogues were the product of the hides of their own cattle, and probably the men in the fields were wearing two or three centuries ago something like the bawneen which the older generation of farmers in the west of Ireland have not yet given up. The rural community, in fact, was practically self-supporting. The average man, even among the gentry, had no assets except landed property and the stock it carried, and the value of land was low because of the sense of insecurity which accompanied its possession. The normal rate of interest for a mortgage on unencumbered land was as high as 10 per cent., and it was impossible to borrow money in Ireland on the very best of collective security at less than 8 per cent. at a time when Colbert got all he wanted at $5\frac{1}{2}$, and in Holland 4 per cent. was quite usual ; and this was but a

---

(Dublin, 1788) and particularly of a valuable study of historic Irish dress published since the first edition of this book appeared, viz. McClintock's *Old Irish and Highland Dress*, (Dundalk, 1943). I may add that, though containing no matter of special Irish interest, Racinet's *Le Costume Historique*, Vol. V (Paris, 1888) and Quennell's *History of Everyday Things in England* (1930 edn.) are useful for their excellent illustrations, as are several books written primarily for theatrical producers such as Barton's *Historic Costume for the Stage* (London, 1937), and Truman's *Historic Costuming* (London, 1936). Brereton's *Travels* contains (pp.155-160) descriptions of women's clothes in 1635.

[8] Works of Sir James Ware (1745 edn.), Vol. II, p.177.
[9] *Cambrensis Eversus*, Vol. II p.209.

reflection of the financial situation, which indeed was chaotic. The coinage was in a state of hopeless confusion. Money, however, does not play an important part in the life of a self-supporting rural community, and a countryman's purchases at that time were normally confined to salt, snuff and tobacco, the use of which had already become universal in Ireland, all classes, and even both sexes among the lower orders, being confirmed smokers.[10] Tea, which in our day has come to be regarded as one of the prime necessities of life, was only just beginning to be known, under the name of " china drink" or "china ale,"[11] to up-to-date city folk in Dublin.

There the beginnings of modern life were to be seen in abundance : indeed we might almost say that in Dublin the eighteenth century began before the seventeenth was ended. It was already a large city. It had its coffee-houses and its book-shops, its thriving theatre, and during the last decade of the century even its newspaper ; the Liffey was being quayed and spanned by bridges ; the Phoenix Park and St. Stephen's Green were laid out as pleasure-grounds for the citizens, and a harbour authority was established which was the nucleus of the present Port and Docks Board. Limerick and Cork, too, were rapidly losing their mediaeval character. In these places, as well as in Dublin, trade corporations of various callings, such as bakers, felt-makers and

[10] Women also smoked in England. Misson, writing in 1698, says that the practice was common in the West of England, though in other places, Middlesex for example, it was unusual. (*Memoirs and Observations*, English Translation, London, 1719, p.312). Celia Fiennes (the diarist quoted by Quennell, *Hist. of Everyday Things*, 1930 edn., pp.119-123) remarks that in Cornwall *circ.* 1695 women and even children smoked pipes. See also p.71 *infra*.

[11] It was of much later introduction as a popular beverage, and according to Arthur Young, was hardly known in places like Westmeath and Offaly a hundred years after the period we are considering.

goldsmiths, were being formed, and though these preserved to some extent the spirit of exclusiveness which marked the mediaeval guilds, one aspect of modern commercial life was in evidence then far more than in the succeeding century, for it was not considered derogatory for the aristocracy to partici-pate in business provided it was on a large scale[12] : the industrialists of the seventeenth century in-cluded not only men of the colonial millionaire type like the Earl of Cork, but aristocrats by birth, such as Lord Carlingford and Sir Henry O'Neill.

The gentry then, as now, were great sportsmen, and sport, too, had taken on a new complexion, so that—although a few still preferred hawking— horse-racing and hunting were becoming the usual re-creation of the well-to-do, while with the introduction of the " fowling piece," shooting became another recognized sport for gentlemen. The populace had no regular amusement except dancing, though hurling was played in some places and wrestling and bull-baiting often attracted crowds of sightseers.

The object of my researches into this period, of which I have given a very brief preliminary sketch, has been to obtain a picture of the everyday life of the ordinary citizen in Ireland, a field hitherto so little worked by the historian that Bagwell in the three volumes of his *Ireland under the Stuarts*, a standard work on that period, gives it but a dozen pages. The political history of the time is fully, if not always impartially, dealt with by such as he, and I shall have no need to refer to it except incidentally. It must always be remembered, however, that at that time, as there have been ever since, there were

[12] *Cal. of Orrery Papers*, p.232. Letter from T. Sheridan to Orrery, in which Lord Ibrickan's interest in trade is stressed, provides one of many contem-porary examples of this view-point.

two distinct nations in this country: the native Irish, with whom may be included the Normans and the "Old-English," a category embracing such eminent men as Geoffrey Keating, Father Luke Wadding, Dr. Thomas Arthur, Dr. John Lynch, Blessed Oliver Plunket and Patrick Sarsfield, on the one hand; and on the other the immigrants of later date, consisting of the more or less homogeneous product of the plantations of James I in Ulster, the Cromwellian landlords and farmers, who were scattered all over the country except in Clare and Connacht, and finally the English merchant element which formed the majority of the richer classes in the towns and completely controlled municipal government, though in a minority as regards their actual population.

These two very dissimilar sections of the people will often have to be considered separately, for they were not in the seventeenth century beginning to assimilate into one common and composite nation.[13] The Ireland championed by Swift and Molyneux was a Protestant Anglo-Ireland; these men were untouched by the patriotic ideals which were later to inspire Henry Grattan and Thomas Davis but have not yet been completely realized.

[13] The expressions "the Irish nation" and "the Irish people" when used in this book without qualification may be taken, as will no doubt be clear from the context, as referring to the first mentioned of these sections.

CHAPTER II

General Characteristics and Traits

WHILE I dissent from the view that the writing of history should be regarded as a pure science and not as a branch of literature at all, there is no doubt that the primary duty of the historian is to treat his subject scientifically. This necessitates the some-times rather tedious production and impartial weighing of evidence and so somewhat handicaps the social historian in his attempts to present a picture of the everyday life of the past. Indeed, if a man aims solely at doing this in a vivid and arresting manner he would be wiser to adopt the historical novel as his medium. No historian has surpassed Macaulay in narrative power and vivacity of style, or has enjoyed a greater popularity, yet his most picturesque descriptions never enabled the ordinary reader to visualize the men and women of the seventeenth century and their surroundings with the same verisimilitude that Scott and Dumas did. The novels of these men are, of course, full of inaccuracies ; but once a novelist begins to curb his imagination and applies to his work the restric-tions which bind the historian, he at once becomes, like G. P. R. James, dull and prosy.

So far, then, as it is possible within the limits of scientific historical treatment, my object in this book is to present a picture of everyday life in Ireland at a most interesting period in our history : to arrive at the truth and to tell it in a readable way ; and perhaps to provide the necessary raw materials for some future Irish Scott or Dumas.

The sources to which we have to go to obtain the

evidence required to build up our picture are
frequently unsympathetic, if not actually hostile,
in their attitude. Our own native authorities are
not so numerous as we might wish. There are,
however, quite a number of Irish manuscripts and
printed works to be consulted, as well as treatises
and commentaries by continental travellers, and
comparatively impartial English visitors and immigrants, to set in the balance against the evidence of
prejudiced witnesses.

We know from our own experience within the last
thirty years how biassed the categorical statements
of unprincipled propagandists and credulous tourists
can be, how misleading their generalities and half-
truths : the files of the old London *Morning Post*
will furnish ample examples of this. The Press, now
the most powerful factor in forming public opinion,
was practically non-existent in the seventeenth
century, but in the form of pamphlets and books the
written word did exercise a great influence on men's
views and feelings. Nothing published in the
seventeenth century had a greater and more lasting
effect than Sir John Temple's *History of the Irish
Rebellion*, which bore as its sub-title the words,
" Together with the Barbarous Cruelties and Bloody
Massacres that ensued thereupon." Even in the
nineteenth century it was treated as a reliable
authority by English historians of repute, and it was
not until Lecky exposed its gross exaggerations that
it ceased to be regularly referred to as if it were a
source of trustworthy information. Lecky described
it as " a party pamphlet by an exceedingly unscrupulous man, who had the strongest interest in
exaggerating to the utmost," and in refuting the
statements of Froude which were based upon it, he

points out that while Temple asserted that 300,000 Protestants " were cruelly murdered in cold blood, destroyed by some other way or expelled out of their habitations "—we may note the anti-climax—that figure is about ten times as great as the whole Protestant population of the country outside those towns where it is known that no massacre took place.

Even before this glaring example of prejudiced and lying propaganda was published in 1646 there was a marked tendency on the part of English writers to treat Ireland with contempt. The scathing protest of Geoffrey Keating, who died a year or two before Temple wrote his book, may be quoted to show how that eminent and patriotic man felt about this question. Having pointed out that historians from Geraldus Cambrensis to Campion and Camden, and political writers such as Spenser, Fynes Moryson and Davies had all sought to vilify the Irish people, he adds trenchantly : " Bé nós beagnach an priompalláin do-ghníd, ag sgríobhadh ar Éireannachaibh . . . acht bheith ar fuaidreadh go teagmhann bualtrach bó nó otrach capaill ris, go dtéid dá unfairt féin ionnta,"[1] and further on he remarks that these people make no reference to the undoubted courage, piety, generosity and hospitality of the Irish nobility and gentry, preferring to describe the uncouthness of the very lowest orders of the people and to generalize from the vices of the few.

Dr. Lynch, writing after the death of Cromwell, protests in the same strain, and the three volumes of his *Cambrensis Eversus*[2] are one long refutation of the calumniators of the old Irish nation.

---

[1] *Forus Feasa ar Éirinn* : Díonbhrollach.
[2] First published, in Latin, 1662.

Keating and Lynch, though themselves Anglo-Irish and not Gaelic in origin, wrote with all the traditional Irish respect for aristocracy. To us the manners and customs, the virtues and the vices of the peasantry, and even of the labourers at the bottom of the social scale, are of as much interest as those of the high-born and well-to-do ; and we shall not find that all the good qualities were confined to one section of the population and all the bad to another. In fact there were, and indeed are, many characteristics, both favourable and the reverse, common to all classes of Irishmen.

In the passage referred to above Keating mentions among other praiseworthy traits of the gentry of his own and his predecessors' time, hospitality, generosity and courage.

Ireland has always enjoyed the reputation of being a country second to none for hospitality, and this is not a matter to which any evidence to the contrary has, I think, ever been put forward, even by the most prejudiced witnesses.

The works of the Irish poets such as O'Bruadair (1625-1698), O'Rahilly (1670-1727) and O'Carolan (1670-1737) are full of appreciations of the open-handed hospitality of the " Big Houses " in Co. Limerick, Co. Kerry, Co. Roscommon, and elsewhere, while by way of contrast to their rather fulsome praise we may turn to Dunton's Letters[3] or to Moffet's *Irish Hudibras* where it is burlesqued in amusing doggerel verse and with true Restoration coarseness. It is worth noting here that there are two books entitled *The Irish Hudibras*: William Moffet's, published in 1728, but dealing with the life of the previous generation ; and the other a contem-

[3] See note 18 of this chapter.

porary work by James Farewell, issued in 1689. Both are satires intended to ridicule the semi-barbarous life of the native Irish, but both emphasize the lavish hospitality which was then universal in Ireland.

The same spirit existed in the poorer classes who, though they had less means and opportunity of providing entertainment, gave ungrudgingly of what they had. " The Irish," says a French traveller who often visited the houses of the peasantry, " are fond of strangers and it costs little to travel among them. When a traveller of good address enters their house with assurance he has but to draw a box of sinisine [snisín][4] and offer it to them, and then these people receive him with admiration and give him the best they have to eat." He adds that they love Spaniards, French, and other foreigners, but that the English and Scots are their " irreconcilable enemies,"[6] an attitude not unnatural on their part in 1644 when he made his tour.

Lady Fanshawe, who was in Ireland for a space of nine months some six years later, has also left on record her impression of the people in that war period.[7] She thought the native Irish " a very loving people to each other " though " constantly false to strangers, the Spaniards only excepted." Writing as she did in 1676, a quarter of a century after the close of the Cromwellian war, not for publication but for the private eye of her only surviving son, she may be regarded as tolerably free from propagandist motives, though as the wife of an English Royalist of considerable importance, her

[4] i.e. snuff.
[6] La Boullaye le Gouz, *Tour*, ed. T. Crofton Croker, 1837, p.43.
[7] *The Memoirs of Ann, Lady Fanshawe*, 1907 edn., pp.56-63.

view is naturally more circumscribed than that of le Gouz. While he penetrated alike into castles and cabins, her experience, except for an occasional night in a flea-infested lodging, was limited to the hospitality of the nobility ; and this she praises unstintedly. Her allusions to the " noble entertainment " she received at their hands are frequent, none being more noteworthy in this respect than Donagh MacCarthy (whom she calls Lord Clancarty, though he was styled Viscount Muskerry at the time) and Lord Inchiquin, better known in Irish history as Murrough O'Brien " of the Burnings."

" The inhabitants of this county," wrote Tadhg Rody, in his description of Co. Leitrim in 1683, " are very much addicted to hospitality, freely inviting and receiving all men into their houses and giving them the best fare they have."[8] And this may be regarded as true of all parts of the country, especially where the traditional Ireland of the past survived.

Dr. Lynch devotes two pages to the subject of Irish hospitality which, as he says, was traditional with the Irish people. Probably no other people have ever been more steeped in tradition than the Irish. The reverence for everything ancestral was an outstanding trait in seventeenth century Ireland, nor indeed did it pass away with much of the old order and even yet it is not quite dead. It was to this, perhaps, as much as to a love for the arts of poetry and music that the high position of the bards in the social scale of the Gaelic system can be ascribed. Nothing is commoner in Irish poetry than

[8] MS. T.C.D. I. 1. 2. For remarks on this important manuscript see pages 25 and 26 *infra*. Rody or O'Rody is described by Hardiman (*Irish Minstrelsy*, Vol. II.) as a man of great learning, both Gaelic and classical.

eulogies of the patrons of that art, whose descent is traced with loving care back to the dim ages of legend ; but, like so much that we read of in the period under review, "chroniclers" as well as poets had fallen on evil days.

There exists a valuable little work, published in 1674, which purports to record the observations of an Englishman who spent over two years in parts of Ireland off the beaten track. Considering the amount of useful information it contains on the everyday life of the people, it has not been quoted as much as might have been expected, and the one or two, like Dr. George O'Brien, who have used it, were apparently unaware of its author's identity. It was the work of Richard Head.[9] We can give more credence to his statements than to those of men like Fynes Moryson or Ludlow, who saw Ireland under conditions of war, or of Campion who only spent a short time in the country, and that in the Pale where, according to Mr. Waugh, his most recent biographer, he accepted without question everything he was told to the detriment of the Irish people. In spite of the efforts of Keating and Lynch to expose their shortcomings, the works of Fynes Moryson, Campion, Camden and Stanyhurst were accepted as the standard books on Ireland for nearly two hundred years, until they were eventually superseded in the second half of the eighteenth century by the school of which Arthur Young was the most notable exponent.

[9] For Richard Head's connexion with Ireland see *Dictionary of Nat. Biography.* The work referred to was published under the title of *The Western Wonder*, with a long sub-title. The references in these notes are to the original edition, a copy of which is in the Henry Bradshaw collection, Cambridge University Library. It was partly reprinted in the Journal of the Cork Historical and Archaeological Society (2nd series, Vol. X. No. 62, p.85), but the Editor did not know the author's name.

Head quite casually makes a remark which constitutes a rebuke to writers on Ireland, more applicable to a later time than his own : he considers two years an inadequate time in which to make thorough observations and to form reliable opinions on the country and its inhabitants. This is an attitude which is refreshing when we consider those journalistic writers who, like his nineteenth century namesake, Sir F. B. Head, with self-satisfied confidence, undertake to produce a comprehensive book on Ireland — or Hungary—after a few weeks' visit, and it cannot but increase our respect for the opinions he does express. I shall quote his estimate of the Irish character later on.

On the point of fact now under consideration he says : " The people in general are great admirers of their pedigrees, and have got their genealogy so exactly learnt that though it would be two hours work for them to repeat the names only from whence they are descended lineally, yet, will they not omit one word in half a dozen several repetitions.[10]

" Their greatest zeal is in keeping sacred some old sayings of their great grandsires, and preserving sacred some old relics of their grandmothers . . ."[11]

General summaries and estimates of national character are not really of very great value, for they depend too much on the political outlook of the estimator or, in the case of a stranger even if he be genuinely open-minded, on the particular people with whom he has chanced to come in contact

---

[10] *Western Wonder*, p.38. I have modernized the spelling in this, and in all quotations from seventeenth century writers, except in a few cases where for philological or other reasons it seems desirable to preserve the original spelling. I have also made some changes in their punctuation as many contemporary writers used stops in the most arbitrary manner, and some hardly employed them at all.

[11] For another aspect of genealogical study see p.23 *infra*.

during his stay in the country. Certain character-istics, of course, have become generally associated with certain countries: no doubt there was a foundation in fact for the popularly accepted picture of the dram-drinking, bawbee-saving Scotsman, of the Jew with his pound of flesh, of the Yankee with his cigar and big bow-wow, and of the easy-going, waltz-loving Viennese. Generalizations on national character tend towards exaggeration so that the Scottish traits which a friendly pen would portray as convivial bonhomie and praiseworthy thrift, become bibulousness and parsimony in the hands of the caricaturist.

Suppose some future historian were to try and estimate the national character of twentieth century England from the impressions left on record by Sir Edward Carson and Mr. de Valera, or better still, let us say by Miss Mary MacSwiney and Mr. Frank MacDermot, both Irish, and both, we may assume, perfectly honest in their opinions: there would not be much left if he only accepted what was common ground to these two.

However, observers with the gift of impartiality do and did exist. Richard Head was one of these, Arthur Young was another. A book appeared in 1746 describing a Tour in Ireland and purporting to be by two English gentlemen, in which the self-complacent, superior attitude usually evinced by tourists who describe their impressions of Ireland is not much in evidence, possibly because the author was not in reality a tourist at all. This relates, of course, to a time somewhat later than our special period, but national characteristics do not change very rapidly, and in considering such general questions greater latitude of date is permissible than when dealing with particular aspects of daily life such, for example, as dress, transport, commerce and so on. " From the inhabitants of this Kingdom that I have seen," says the author, " as far as I can judge, the following character may be given of them. They are rather tall than low, strong and active, and both sexes generally handsome, at least I think I have seen fewer people of a disagreeable countenance here than any part where I have been, England excepted, which is much on a par. They excel in most bodily exercises, endure fatigue of all kinds with great patience, and are satisfied with very sparing food. They are of a ready wit ; the ridiculous notion we have of their stupidity is the worst grounded in the world."[12]

Here is Rody's general summary of the characteristics of his own county : " The natives or Irish inhabitants are civil, hospitable and ingenious, very fond of their ancient chronicles and pedigrees and as much abhorring theft, they are great lovers of music and fond of news : they were not so bloody and cruel in the late rebellion as several in the adjoining countries, their women are handsome . . ."[13] We get a more particular reference to the " chroniclers " I alluded to, further on in the same manuscript : " There are in this country some Irish chroniclers, my neighbours, and one among the rest, the best of

---

[12] *Op. cit.* p.82. He then quotes Dr. Hoylen, whom he calls a very accurate English author, as follows : " They are prodigal of their lives, given to fleshy lusts, light of belief, kind and courteous to strangers, constant in love, impatient of abuse and injury, in enmity implacable, and in all affections most vehement and passionate."

[13] MS. T.C.D. I. 1. 2., p.137. I do not think that any useful purpose would be served by quoting from the numerous descriptions given by our authorities of the physical attributes of the people, as those vary in a remarkable degree. Some have it that the women were beautiful ; according to others they were little short of repulsive in appearance. Some describe the Irish men as fine specimens of humanity, others represent them as puny. A large number of quotations on this subject have been collected in Dr. Hogan's book, *The Irish People, their Health, Form and Strength*, Dublin, 1852.

them all, who if he pleased could answer the questions put to him, but would not, without being well paid, because he ' would have to go far ' to procure the necessary books." The writer in this case was one Joseph Keogh.

Genealogists of the traditional school such as those referred to by Head and Keogh still survived as part of the normal, though disappearing, life of the country. That the early generations of the traditional Gaelic pedigrees are fabrications is indisputable, as Professor T. F. O'Rahilly has shown,[14] but their authenticity was then, as in much more recent times, generally accepted. The accuracy with which, once established, they were handed down was remarkable ; but some of the better educated or more far-seeing of these genealogists, realizing no doubt that the ancient system of which they were the inheritors was rapidly breaking up, set themselves the task of committing to paper the pedigrees which had been handed down to them for the most part orally. So we have available to-day the genealogical work of the Four Masters and of men like Duald MacFirbis and Geoffrey Keating and such valuable products of the early eighteenth century as *An Leabhar Muimhneach* and O'Ferrall's *Linea Antiqua*. The seventeenth century, too, saw the rise of a new school of Anglo-Irish scholars who gave attention to genealogical as well as antiquarian study. Of these Sir James Ware was an outstanding example, and he formed a point of contact with the old school since he was wise enough to employ MacFirbis to help him in his researches. At the same time the Office of the Ulster King of Arms, which had been established

[14] *Early Irish History and Mythology* (Dublin, 1946), *passim.*

in the middle of the previous century, was doing useful work in keeping a series of records known as Funeral Entries, still preserved in the archives of that Office[15] in Dublin Castle. Their value in this respect may perhaps be fortuitous, since the information they recorded relates only to the immediate family of the deceased person and their primary object was heraldic rather than genealogical. At any rate it was not until the seventeenth century that anything in the nature of systematic records was kept by the Office of Arms, which by the end of the century had acquired to some extent a genealogical character, though its official function and principal activity was still to act as the heraldic authority for Ireland. In this connexion it may be observed that the use of armorial bearings was by no means confined to families of Norman or British extraction: the practice of heraldry was widespread throughout Europe and almost all the old Gaelic families used arms, though those who had resisted the process of anglicization did not, naturally enough, go through the formality of having them recorded in an office representing an authority to which they gave but a very reluctant allegiance.

Apart from Robert Boyle, the famous chemist, who was an Irishman by birth but not by ancestry, residence or inclination,[16] Ireland made little

[15] Now known as the Genealogical Office. There is no significance in the term " Ulster " as it was originally intended to create also a Leinster King of Arms and perhaps one for Munster as well. At the date of the establishment of the Office in Dublin (1552) Ulster was in fact the province least subject to English control and influence.

While the subject of heraldry is under discussion, it may be added that the fantastic method of blazoning the Harp of Ireland with a female head and bust, which persisted almost to our own times, was virtually an eighteenth century conception though occasional examples of it may be found in the last decade of the seventeenth.

[16] See his letters printed in *Cal. of Orrery Papers*, (ed. MacLysaght, Dublin. 1941).

original contribution to the scientific advance
which discovered the circulation of the blood and
invented the barometer. Nevertheless the last
three decades of the seventeenth century were a
period of great scientific activity, here as elsewhere,
and, no doubt, it was part of the movement which
resulted in the formation of the Dublin Philosophical
Society that in 1682 prompted Sir Wm. Petty's
idea of getting a chorographical survey of all the
counties of Ireland carried out. With this in view
something in the nature of a questionnaire was sent
out to selected resident gentlemen in all parts of the
country. Most of the resultant replies are contained
in two manuscript volumes now in the library of
Trinity College, Dublin.[17] Only two or three of
them have ever been printed in whole or in part.
Although Hardiman in his preface to O'Flaherty's
Description of Iar-Connacht expresses the opinion
that that is the only one of these surveys worth
printing, I do not agree with him, and I know of
few more illuminating sources of information about
everyday life in Ireland in the late seventeenth
century, than those contained in the manuscripts
in question, unless it be John Dunton's " Conversation in Ireland," published in 1699, and his hitherto
unpublished letters written in 1698.[18]

---

[17] MSS. Nos. I. 1. 2, and I. 1. 3.
[18] The original letters are among the Rawlinson manuscripts, preserved
in the Bodleian Library, Oxford. Mr. Charles McNeill's report on these is
printed in *Analecta Hibernica*, No. 2, p.50, *et seq.* These are printed in Appendix B, p.321, *et seq.* Two of Dunton's books, *The Dublin Scuffle* and *Life
and Errors*, contain the portion of his published work most useful for our
purpose, viz., his *Conversation in Ireland*. The edition of *Life and Errors*,
most easily accessible, that published in 1818, omits many of Dunton's
more outspoken comments. Cf. *Dublin Scuffle* (1699), p.340, and *Life and
Errors* (1818 edition), p.563, *re* Smock Alley, or p.399 and p.614, respectively
re punishment of " strolling courteous ladies of the town," for examples of
this. Dunton's value as a witness would be much greater if his fondness for
pornographic effect did not often lead him into making the most extravagant
statements, but his work, if read with discrimination, throws much light
on Irish life 250 years ago.

Though Petty was the prime mover in the project all the contributors to it were not Protestants : and the two of whom I have already quoted here, were, if we may judge from their names, of native Irish stock, though we may take it that they were, at least to some extent, of the " reformed " type in outlook, if not in religion.

These manuscripts are copies from the originals which are also in the Trinity College Library, and were transcribed about the year 1710. The second volume contains other matter besides the chorographical county surveys and includes an account of two journeys undertaken in 1709 by Dr., afterwards Sir Thomas, Molyneux, who was closely associated with Sir Wm. Petty in his scientific activities and was the younger brother of the better known William Molyneux. When I first wrote this chapter, after reading the manuscript, his identity was unknown to me, and I described him as a gentleman of tolerably liberal outlook and some gift of observation.[19] His notes on the roads and the means of travelling, though made a few years later than the time we are considering, will be of great value when we come to deal with the subject of travel and transport. The first journey he describes was to Connacht. In the course of this he paid a visit to " Old Flaherty," the well-known " chronicler," whom he found in a wretched abode some three hours west of Galway, and himself in a wretched condition, and even his valuable manuscripts almost all gone. In this district he tells us there was no sign of living creatures or houses, nothing but stones : " Yet here, I hear,

[19] The original, to be found among the Molyneux Papers (M.S. T.C.D. I. 4, 16 and 17), is stated by Hardiman to be in Molyneux's handwriting. MS. No. I. 4, 12, is another copy of this Journey to Connacht, and I. 4, 13 of his Journey to Kerry. The former was printed in the *Miscellany of the Irish Archaeological Society*, 1846.

lives multitudes of barbarous uncivilized Irish after
their old fashions who are here one and all in the
defence of any of their own or even other rogues that
fly to them . . . barbarous murders after shipwrecks
and all manner of rogueries protected that the
sheriffs of this county scarce dare appear on the
west side of Galway Bridge, which though Ireland is
now generally esteemed wholly civilized, may well
be called the end of the English Pale."[20] This was
written some eight or nine years after Dunton's
visit to the O'Flahertys. His description of this is
printed in full in Appendix B[21] and might well be
read at this point.[22]

It might be assumed from the observations of
Molyneux and Dunton, and from works such as the
two *Irish Hudibras*, that conditions, at any rate in the
more remote parts of the country, were quite
barbarous. We must beware, however, of accepting
too readily the travellers' tales on which these are
so dependent. The traveller home from the Indies
or the South Seas, sitting with pipe and glass and
spinning yarns for a circle of credulous stay-at-home
neighbours, is a familiar picture in all times, and
there are few of these who do not succumb to the
temptation to exaggerate for the sake of effect. Included in the manuscript to which I have referred
is a letter from Edward Lhwyd, in which he gives
an account of a tour in the Highlands of Scotland
in 1699. In this he refers to the English habit of
regarding as barbarous, all the non-English-speak-

[20] MS. *cit.* p.79.
[21] p.329 *et seq.*
[22] It will be observed that the barbarous practice of " ploughing by the
tail," so frequently censured by seventeenth century writers on Ireland, is
stated in Dunton's letter to have been given up by 1698, even in Iar-
Connacht, where manners and customs, long since abandoned in less
remote districts, were still part of the normal everyday life of the people.
See also Chapter VI., p.174 *re* discontinuance of that practice.

ing inhabitants of these Islands, be they Scots, Welsh or Irish, a mental attitude illustrated by Macaulay's well-known description of the Highlands in Chapter XIII of his History, and by his equally unflattering accounts, in Chapter XII and elsewhere, of what he calls the aboriginal Irish.

Dunton's opinions I am inclined to regard as of little value, but his descriptions ring too true to be dismissed as pure inventions, and I accept many of his statements of fact, while believing them to be often rather highly coloured. There is no doubt, however, that there was a predisposition to take it for granted that Irish and barbarous were practically synonymous terms. Thus the scholarly and sympathetic Dr. Crofton Croker falls into an almost ridiculous error in his notes on the *Tour* of la Boullaye le Gouz. Seeing the word *Irois* used by le Gouz, he alleges that in modern French the termination *ois* is used to denote uncivilized races, and quite gratuitously remarks that the author therefore regarded the Irish as barbarous, overlooking the fact that in the seventeenth century the words *Anglois*, *Francois*, etc., were the forms in general use.

Civilization as we know it was certainly still very backward in the remoter parts of the country. Nevertheless, we must not allow ourselves to regard the conditions in inaccessible districts as typical of the country as a whole. The numerous personal letters to be found among such collections as the MacGillycuddy and Orrery Papers, though they are usually Anglo-Irish, not Gaelic, in outlook, are a valuable source of information on the social life of the time ; and they bring home to the student of them how essentially similar to our own was the mentality of the men of 250 years ago. In fact if any one of us could by a miracle find himself in an Irish country house of the seventeenth century, there is no reason why he should feel unduly strange. Of course he would be lucky if he got even an occasional bath for practically everyone was dirty in those days, fashionable people in London as well as rustics in Ireland. Pepys, for instance, saw nothing very objectionable or remarkable in the fact that his head was at times full of lice, and the normal condition of Dr. Johnson's wig is notorious. If our visitor to the past were not one of those people who follow the modern tendency to identify civilization with hygiene, he would, I think, feel quite at home, provided he could ride a horse tolerably well, was not afraid of large meals, could at least make himself understood in the Irish language, and was prepared to drink and gamble at any hour of the day or night.

This propensity to gambling was a very striking feature of seventeenth century life in Ireland. References to it are so numerous that we may take one or two of them by way of illustration almost at random. We will begin with Fynes Moryson to show the prevalence of gambling at the beginning of the century. I am always a little reluctant to cite Moryson, because he can definitely be regarded as a prejudiced witness. He calls the Brehons, for instance, "altogether unlearned," a statement which obviously lessens his value as a reliable authority. However, there is always a distinct difference between the mere expression of an opinion and the description of something actually seen: and Fynes Moryson has the merit of seldom being dull.

"The Irish in general," he wrote, "more especially the mere Irish, being slothful and given to

nothing more than base idleness, they nourished a
third generation of vipers, vulgarly called carrows,
professing (forsooth) the noble science of playing
cards and dice, which so infected the public meetings
of the people and the private houses of lords, as
no adventure was too hard in shifting for means to
maintain these sports. And indeed the wild Irish do
madly affect them, so as they will not only play and
lose their money and moveable goods, but also
engage their lands—yea, their own persons, to be
held as prisoners—by the winner, till he be paid the
money for which they are engaged. It is a shame to
speak, but I heard by credible relation that some
were found so impudent as they suffered themselves
to be led as captives, tied by the parts of their body
which I will not name, till they had money to
redeem themselves."[23]

The bye-laws of the city of Kilkenny before
Cromwell's time contain orders designed to restrain
the gambling propensities of the citizens of that
town,[24] which I may mention is unanimously
described by all seventeenth century observers as
progressive and up-to-date and well in advance of
other Irish country towns in its architecture, its
gardens, and the civility of its inhabitants.

Gambling lost little or none of its hold on the
people as the century advanced : the success of
the many lotteries organized for more or less useful
purposes attests this. The Anglo-Irish aristocracy,
like the English and the French, were much addicted
to betting and even the most virtuous, like the Duke
of Ormond himself, counted reckless play no sin ;
it would appear too that few of the regular gamblers

[23] *The Commonwealth of Ireland.* (*Illustrations of Irish History*, p.248).
[24] Journal of R.S.A.I., Vol. II., p.329.

of the day were above cheating on occasion.
Gaming has not been the subject of as many statutes
in Ireland as in England but one passed in 1698[25]
imposed as the penalty for cheating at play or
horseracing the forfeiture of treble the sum won.
Here is a picture of the Irish-Ireland of 1683:
" The inhabitants of the county of Kerry, I mean
those of them that are downright Irish, are remarkable beyond the inhabitants of the other parts of
Ireland for their gaming, speaking of Latin and
inclination to philosophy and disputes therein. For
their gaming they are so exquisite that they generally make a prey of whatever stranger comes
amongst them, who will venture his stock or money
at cards or dice ; and even the very cowherds and
shepherds will be under a hedge with each other at
tables ; to which they are so devoted that a poor
cowboy shall make a pair of tables, set of men and
dice, with the stick he cuts from the hedge with his
twopenny knife ; when they can get no one to game
with them you shall often find them alone with a
book of Aristotle's or some of his commentators'
logic which they read very diligently till they are
able to pour out nonsensical words a whole day
about ; *universale a parte sei ens rationis* and such
like stuff, and this they do pretty fluently without
much hesitation, though all the while their Latin
is bald and barbarous and very often not gram-
matical." Further on we are told : " Those that
are loath to be called the inferior sort are generally
very litigious among one another and they will go
to law about the least trifle[26] : and this is the reason
(or perhaps the consequence) of this county's

<hr/>

[25] 10 William III, c.11.
[26] For a good story illustrating the disastrous consequences of this tendency, see Cork Histor. and Arch. Society's Journal, Vol. X., p.97.

abounding more than ordinary with men that are (as they term it) towards the law.''[27]

Several sixteenth century writers refer to the familiarity of the Irish people with Latin, and some-times even the Irish women were able to converse in that language.[28]   Mrs. Green, though often unreliable on account of her strong pro-Irish prejudices, does adduce sound evidence to prove that the general level of culture in Ireland was high in the sixteenth century before the Elizabethan wars destroyed the normal life of the country[29] and produced the appalling state of affairs which gave a colour of verisimilitude to the disparaging accounts of Fynes Moryson and other early seventeenth century observers.   In this connexion it may be observed that Dr. Thomas Arthur, who did not die till 1674[30], in his Commonplace Book[31] constantly uses Latin, for verse as well as prose, with ease and competence.

The passage in the Introduction to the *Clan-rickarde Memoirs* describing the bardic schools, with their long hours of study in darkened rooms, the generosity of the neighbours towards their up-keep and the students' visits to the houses of the gentry and farmers has been too often quoted to be given here. By the time of Charles II, however, the cultured conditions it describes were obsolete, and indeed the level of education had fallen very low. The anonymous editor[32] of these memoirs remarks that Keating " assumes the name of an Irish

[27] MS. T.C.D. I. i. 3, pp.13-14.
[28] See *Capt. Cuellar's Narrative*, ed. Crawford, London, 1897.
[29] See *The Making of Ireland and its Undoing, passim.*
[30] G.O. M.S. 224, p.163.
[31] B.M. Addl. MS. 31885. See note 86, p.220 *infra.*
[32] According to the Catalogue of the Bradshaw Collection, the editor of this work was Robert Lindsay.

antiquary . . . though I verily believ'd there was none of that sort remaining in the country, the study of the present generation reaching no further than to comprehend and write the common dialect of their language ; and not one in six thousand can pretend even to that." If he intends to convey that 5,999 out of every 6,000 people in Ireland in the middle of the seventeenth century were illiterate he unquestionably exaggerates.

There is a considerable divergence of opinion as to the standard of culture in Ireland in the second half of the seventeenth century. Reading some books and manuscripts the student might well conclude that it was relatively high ; others suggest a complete absence of it. Much depends, of course, upon the type of people with whom the writer happened to be most thrown. This is a case in which more weight should be attached to the views and statements of native writers than to outsiders who seldom had an opportunity of observing more than one aspect of the national life and who, be it remembered, were ignorant of the language in which, so far as literature is concerned, all the traditional culture of the nation had been handed down and was still preserved. Where all our authorities agree, be they Irish or English or Continental, friendly or hostile, we can obviously accept their evidence as conclusive. They are unanimous in telling us that the Irish people were, in the words of Good, written as far back as 1566, " mighty lovers of music." Poetry is, and was more particularly then, closely allied to music. Poetry was still really the only literary art form for, as Professor Corkery has pointed out, prose did not begin to be so regarded until the middle of the seventeenth century.[33] A country which produces poets and honours poets cannot be wholly uncultured. Illiteracy does not necessarily mean complete lack of culture. Many of the people, as a rule without school education and even unable to read and write, could recite whole volumes of traditional and contemporary Irish verse, while few if any did not eagerly listen to the reciters, a state of affairs not yet dead in the Gaeltacht of to-day.

This native Irish culture steadily waned with the displacement of the native aristocracy by the English and the abandonment of the Irish language, which was its medium of expression, by the upper classes.[34] Side by side with it we find the culture of the conqueror flourishing in the towns and in the country houses of men like Orrery and Temple. The vitality of the ancient culture which might have been expected to be as dead as that of ancient Persia after more than 200 years of submergence, is shown by the strength of its revival at the end of the last century. The conquest of Ireland by Cromwell, completed by William of Orange at the battle of the Boyne and by the last siege of Limerick, made Ireland into a British Colonial possession ; and the end of the seventeenth century, before the English settlers had been long enough in the country to lose any of their sense of being English colonists in a foreign land, was the period when this conception of Ireland's national status was at its height. English families in Ireland looked upon England as unquestionably

[33] *The Hidden Ireland*, p.70.
[34] The English language as spoken in Ireland to-day retains many usages and pronunciations which were normal in the seventeenth century but have since quite died out in England : the use, for example, of the words " presently " and " lawn " and the *ay* sound given to words like " tea " or the *eye* sound in " frieze." It would be out of place to pursue this interesting subject here.

their mother country, and Englishmen in Ireland regarded it as a place in which they could get a political job or make money in a commercial enterprise, as until recently they have looked upon South Africa or Jamaica. The idea of a distinctively Anglo-Irish culture had occurred to nobody. Swift was still only a boy and Goldsmith not yet born. Nevertheless, the English in Ireland were not mere bucolics and untutored merchants. As we shall see when we come to consider the daily life of Dublin between 1660 and 1700, the theatre there was on a level with that in London, booksellers were as numerous as they are to-day when the population of the city is eight times as large as it was in 1690, and the members of the Dublin Philosophical Society were only less active than those of the Royal Society in London.

The old Irish were traditionally fond of music and their successors in the transitional generation we are studying continued in this tradition.[35] Harping is one of the few things praised by Moffet with no element of sarcasm in his praise. It is said to have been an aristocratic pastime or accomplishment rather than a popular one, and le Gouz who wrote in 1644 tells us that nearly all the nobility were accustomed to play the harp as well as listen to it.[36] Nor was it confined to the Gaelic aristocracy for we find Sir Nicholas Armorer referring quite casually to the use of the harp in his own house at Duncannon.[37] But I have come across a presentment of the Grand Jury in Co. Cork, under date July, 1698, " that Tadhg Dash had a harper playing in his house

---

[35] Owen Roe O'Neill brought his own musician with him on his campaigns. MS. R.I.A., 12. K. 1. p.11.
[36] *Tour* (English Edn.), p.41 ; cf. p.111 *infra*, n. 70. See also *Duanaire Piarais Feiritéir* for interesting contemporary poem on the Irish harp (de Blacam, *Gaelic Literature Surveyed*, p.263).
[37] C.S.P.I., 1666-69, p.737.

contrary to the Act "[38] : and we may be sure that Tadhg Dash was no aristocrat, though perhaps he was descended from one. Hardiman says that the war of 1688, which completed the downfall of the ancient Irish families, also silenced their national instrument, which up to the middle of the century had been a work of art and treasured heirloom requiring several different tradesmen in its manufacture.[39] The people appear to have not only loved the rather sad music of the traditional Irish airs but to have been so fond of dancing that, if they did not go as far as their descendants in encouraging bad dance music, they at least tolerated good music badly rendered, if this scene depicted by Richard Head can be taken as typical. " Their Sunday is the most leisure day they have, on which they use all manner of sport[41] ; in every field a fiddle and the lasses footing it till they are all of a foam, and grow infinitely proud with the blear eye of affection her sweetheart casts on her feet as she dances to a tune, or no tune, played on an instrument that makes a worse noise than a key upon a gridiron."[42]

Dancing was the chief if not only relaxation of the poorer classes.

> " Even the very lame and blind
> If trump or bagpipe they do hear
> In dancing posture do appear."[43]

The same authority tells us that the old women were as much addicted to it as the young. I say " authority " even though the work in question is

---

[38] MS. T.C.D. N.3.20. The Act referred to is 7Wm. III, c.17 ; cf. also 1 C.I, c.1

[39] O Curry, *Manners and Customs*, Vol. III, p.258.

[41] See p. 159 *infra*.

[42] *The Western Wonder*, p.37.

[43] Moffet, *Irish Hudibras*.

frankly a satire or burlesque, because satires and burlesques to have any point must obviously have a foundation of truth, though themselves, of course, a distortion of it: if read with discrimination they throw light on details of everyday life not to be found in more serious works.

We have seen, then, that certain qualities were common to all classes: hospitality, respect for tradition and the aristocratic system, love of music, dancing and story-telling, and a great propensity to gambling. The hospitality which spelled extravagance on the part of the rich, and usually meant that the host's tenants bore the burden of it in the end, had its counterpart in the poorer classes in the improvidence with which they are so frequently charged by contemporary writers.

Bourchier describes the people of 1623, " especially the mere Irish," as " the sluggishest, nastiest, rudest, least painful and industrious of all civil countries,"[44] and as might be expected, Fynes Moryson uses somewhat similar words a few years earlier. In the reign of Charles I they are spoken of as " the most improvident people in the whole world," and about the same time the Earl of Cork expressed the opinion that idleness was the " very national disease of this island "[45] ; while in the next century Arthur Young remarks that the poorer classes, whom he found much more cheerful and lively than the English, hard drinkers, hospitable and quarrelsome, civil and obedient, but great liars and insatiably curious—in fact, very much what they were a hundred years earlier—were lazy at their work. Petty, who knew Ireland intimately

[44] *Advertisements for Ireland*, p.3. See Chapter III., note 11.
[45] C.S.P. Ire. Dec. 6, 1630, and May 18, 1631.

at the period with which we are specially dealing, considered that the Irish were not naturally lazy. Coming from one of the most distinguished Englishmen of the century, and one whose work in Ireland gave him splendid opportunities of forming a considered opinion, his words carry great weight. " Their lazing," he says, " seems to me to proceed rather from want of employment and encouragement to work, than from natural abundance of phlegm in their bowels and blood ; for what need they to work, who can content themselves with potatoes,[46] whereof the labour of one man can feed forty ; and with milk, whereof one cow will, in summer time, give meat and drink enough for three men ; when they can everywhere gather cockles, oysters, muscles, crabs, etc., with boats, nets, angles, or the art of fishing ; and can build a house in three days? And why should they desire to fare better, though with more labour, when they are taught that this way of living is more like the patriarchs of old, and the saints of later times, by whose prayers and merits they are to be relieved and whose examples they are therefore to follow? And why should they need more cattle, since 'tis penal to import them into England? Why should they raise more commodities, since there are not merchants sufficiently stocked to take them of them, nor provided with other more pleasing foreign commodities to give in exchange for them? And how should merchants have stock, since trade is prohibited and fettered by the statutes of England? And why should men endeavour to get estates, where the legislative power is not agreed upon ;

---

[46] It was only in Petty's lifetime that potatoes became the staple food of the people. See p.256, note 50.

and where tricks and words destroy natural rights and property?[47] They are accused also of much treachery and falseness and thievery; none of all which, I conceive, is natural to them."[48] The incentive to work, in short, was lacking, and I think we may discount a good deal of the adverse criticisms for that reason. The Irish labourer of to-day is often described as lazy, but without much justification, at least as far as rural workers are concerned, and no doubt the small farmers of the time of Charles II were not as bad as they were painted. This view is strongly supported by Vincent Gookin. " There are," he wrote in a pamphlet published in 1663, " few of the Irish commonalty but are skilful in husbandry and more exact than any English in the husbandry proper to that country." The women he describes as skilful in dressing hemp and flax and in making linen and woollen cloth. To every 100 men there were five or six carpenters and masons among the Irish: " these more handy and ready in building ordinary houses, and much more prudent in supplying the defects of instruments and materials, than English artificers."[49]

What is generally regarded as laziness and improvidence may be capable of another interpretation. When Camden said: " the people are strangely given to idleness, thinking it the greater wealth to want business and the greatest happiness to have liberty,"[50] he certainly had no intention of

[47] Col. Richard Lawrence in his *Interest of Ireland in its Trade and Wealth Stated* places the unsettled conditions of land tenure as the chief impediment to Irish prosperity and progress. For an interesing picture illustrative of this see the statement by Richard Pearce of Limerick (1679), printed *Analecta Hibernica*, No. 15, p.81 *et seq.*
[48] *Political Anatomy*, Ch. XII.
[49] *The Great Case of Transplantation Discussed*, p.17.
[50] *Britannia* (1772 edn.), p.379.

paying a compliment to the Irish nation, yet the idea of regarding freedom as of greater importance than material gain is one which would appeal to many people of philosophic and liberal outlook at the present day.

Richard Head's observations on such questions are usually worth considering. " It is," he says, " a thousand pities the people are so slothful being given to no manner of industry, husbandry or any other useful improvement . . . It may be conjectured their slothfulness may in part be occasioned by their ignorance : some of the indifferent sort being brought up to read, and by the pretence of gentility scorning a trade, never heed the further improvement of their fortunes, or understanding, till the father dies and the elder brother possesses the estate. They are a people generally envious especially of the rise of their neighbours ; naturally pragmatical and inquisitive after others' affairs and always babbling and telling tales ; and so litigious that they are ready to go to law if they see their neighbour's horse put his head over the hedge or his goose at their barn's door. The women are infected with the like quarrelsome humour."[51]

So he, too, gives the same general character to our people. We seem to come quite suddenly on something familiar when we read of envy at the success of neighbours, an unpleasing national trait which has often been the subject of a homily from the altar in our own days. Our author, however, definitely wishes to be fair. Having previously praised the gentry in general terms as " courteous to strangers and extraordinarily generous in their entertainments," he goes on : " insomuch that I have seen in a gentleman's house of indifferent estate, at a moderate treat, twenty dishes, many of them trebly jointed, to recompense the smallness of the meat. Their want of wine is supplied by most incomparable beer and ale, which seems as free as water on a visit: and if you do not drink as freely they think they have not made you welcome ; so that a man knows not how to take leave until he is unable to stir a foot. They are very courteous in their speech and noble in their carriage, firm (where they take) and constant in their resolutions, splendid in their public ceremonies . . ."[52] courageous, stout and great lovers of their prince and country, honourable in their inclinations and resolute in their enterprises. In short they are generally accomplished in most respects and greatly given to that they call hospitality."

Curiously enough, except in one passing reference on page 38 of his book, Head does not draw our attention to the superstitious beliefs and practices which were so prevalent among the people at that time. There is no doubt that the Irish people as a whole, the devout as well as the careless, were superstitious to a remarkable degree, as can well be believed by all but the quite young to-day, for it is only within the last thirty or forty years that many practices, which we would now count pagan and which the Church has at last succeeded in suppressing, have ceased to be commonplaces of daily life.

[52] Funerals, for example, were conducted with much pomp among the Anglo-Irish and the more anglicized of the Gaelic aristocracy. The horses were caparisoned with elaborate cloths and carried large black plumes. The cortège was marshalled with due regard to precedence and in the case of important personages was often arranged by Ulster King of Arms who duly recorded the proceedings and blazoned the armorial banners of the deceased. It was not unusual for the indoor and outdoor servants to be fitted out with mourning clothes at very considerable expense, as may be seen from contemporary account books.

The supernatural has always played an important part in the life of the people, especially in rural Ireland, and it would be safe to say that 250 years ago the implicit belief in fairies was universal here and almost as deeply seated as the belief in God.[53] On the other hand witchcraft—or perhaps we should rather say alleged witchcraft—was much less common in Ireland than in Great Britain and on the Continent.[54]

That the personal habits of the lower orders, and indeed of some of those calling themselves gentry in the more backward parts of the country, were rude in the extreme, can be seen from Dunton's letters as well as from such works as Dineley's *Observations* in the original MSS. before they were pruned by editors anxious not to shock the susceptibilities of modern readers.

Some idea of the character and traits of the Irish people is beginning already to emerge. We may take it that they were hospitable and generous, great gamblers, intensely conservative, credulous, superstitious, curious and eager for news, litigious, improvident and quarrelsome, fond of music and dancing, and not over strenuous at work.[55] Their hospitality and generosity tended to promote excessive drinking, a matter which we shall consider in the next chapter under the general head of morals.

[53] See Index for subsequent references to superstition.
[54] This question is discussed in Seymour's *Irish Witchcraft and Demonology*, Chapter I. Five of the nine chapters of that book deal with seventeenth century cases. At no time was there much persecution of witches in Ireland : while almost every indictable offence is the subject of letters, reports or orders printed in the Irish State Papers, witchcraft is very rarely mentioned in them.
[55] The character of the Irish people is fully discussed in a book entitled *Letters from an Armenian in Ireland to his Friends in Trebisond* (London, 1757). These show considerable insight, and the conclusions to be drawn from them tend to confirm the summary I have made and which I believe to be a fair one. No doubt the author was some Anglo-Irishman who wished to remain anonymous.

These qualities also connoted a natural courtesy, a trait which was very much in evidence in all classes of Irish life up till quite recent times.

If the Irish people were quarrelsome this defect was accompanied by the quality of physical courage, yet again a characteristic which has survived to our own times. Fynes Moryson describes the Irish as bold and warlike, Barnaby Rich tells how condemned men often jested on the way to the gallows,[56] and Sir John Morris in 1620 affirmed that there were no cowards among the Irish.[57] It is true that these men referred to Irishmen of an earlier generation than that in which we are specially interested, but there is plenty of evidence to support these statements in contemporary writings as we shall see later on. After the Battle of the Boyne the cowardice of the Irish became for a while a byword, at least among the frequenters of taverns and theatres in London, to whom Benburb and the Yellow Ford were not even vague names and who long remembered Londonderry and Enniskillen while conveniently forgetting Limerick and Clonmel. It is true that the infantry ran away at the Boyne. John Stevens's disparaging account of their behaviour is confirmed by other eyewitnesses. It is equally true, as Stevens makes quite clear in his journal,[58] that these troops were raw levies, untrained, undisciplined, unaccustomed to firearms and without even the advantage of being led by experienced officers. On the same day the conduct of the Irish cavalry under Sarsfield, on the other hand, was worthy of the best traditions of Irish

[56] *New Description*, p.76.
[57] *Advertisements for Ireland*, p.58.
[58] This valuable contemporary account will be frequently referred to.

military courage. Neither this, however, nor the heroic defence of Limerick three times within a space of forty years, sufficed to remove the stigma. It was not until Ireland had, in the fifty years following the Treaty of Limerick, given nearly half a million of her Wild Geese to the service of France that the good name of Irishmen was regained and their reputation as soldiers—officers as well as men —established as an accepted fact.

As well as being courageous our ancestors were hardy men and women[59] : " The Irish cradled in hardship are most agile and dexterous and swifter on foot than any other nation."[60]

Bourchier was enthusiastic about their ability to stand the rigours of war. In his view, " when once they break off-from sluggishness " no people in the world were " more hardy, able, active and painful." Twenty years earlier O'Donnell's troops on their way to Kinsale had accomplished by forced marches a feat of stamina and endurance which, having regard to the nature of the country they traversed, has seldom been equalled in the military history of the world.

Richard Edgeworth, the father of Maria Edge-worth, a good landlord of the type all too rare in Irish history, in a letter to Dr. Darwin says: " The people here are altogether far better than in England. The higher classes are far worse,[61] the middle classes far inferior to yours, very far indeed, but the peasants though cruel, are generally docile

[59] Cf. p.22 *supra*.

[60] Marco Antonio Correr, Venetian Ambassador, 1611, quoted by Rev. Reginald Walsh, O.P., in *Archivium Hibernicum* (Maynooth), Vol. V. See also p.156, *infra*.

[61] Maria Edgeworth states emphatically that her father was here referring to the political, not to the moral, character of the upper classes in Ireland. See *Memoirs of R. L. Edgeworth*, p.337.

and of the strongest power of both body and mind."

That, of course, was written in the eighteenth century, and it is true that the operation of the Penal Laws must by degrees have changed the Irish character, both native and Anglo-Irish, in some important respects. Nevertheless I am constantly being struck by the persistence of all its principal traits, and I think we may assume that by Edgeworth's time, some sixty or seventy years after our period, there were few fundamental changes in the national character. This indeed may be said, with some reservations, of Young, Luckombe and Campbell, who so fully described the Ireland of the seventeen-seventies, for as Barnaby Rich remarked in 1610, " custom is a metal amongst them that standeth whichsoever way it be bent."[62]

Having now considered the most noteworthy characteristics of the Irish people in a general way, before turning to their mode of life, we will deal in more detail with certain important aspects of the subject, and particularly with the moral standards prevailing in Ireland from the Restoration till the end of the century.

[62] I have discussed in this chapter and the next the value of many of the authorities which are our chief sources of information for this period.

CHAPTER III

Morals

MORALS, according to the definition of the Oxford Dictionary, are " habits of life in regard to right and wrong conduct ; also *spec*. sexual conduct." In modern parlance the word has come to be used almost exclusively in its restricted sense, but in heading this chapter " Morals " I do not wish to convey that it will deal exclusively with sexual morals, though, writing as I am of the second half of the seventeenth century, it is only to be expected that such evils as perjury, official corruption and even drunkenness will occupy less space than matters coming under the head of the Sixth Commandment.[1]

At that period in the upper classes family alliances were often concluded by the marriage of quite young children. After the ceremony the bride and bridegroom were forthwith taken back to their respective nurseries or schoolrooms to await an age more fitting to matrimony.[2] Marriage in its full sense was common at seventeen and eighteen, and sometimes the parties were brought together at a much earlier age than that. Thus Mr. Berry, in his article on the Jephson family of Mallow, states that the grandmother of William Jephson, who himself was married at twelve years old in 1686, was a bride at twelve and had her first child —his father—at fifteen.[3] This practice was common

---

[1] The Sixth Commandment in the Catholic Church is the Seventh in the Protestant.
[2] The marriage settlement sometimes contained a clause providing for the dissent of one or both of the parties on their attaining a certain age. *Vide*, e.g. *Orrery Papers*, p.196 (Marr. sett. of 1 Feb., 1678).
[3] Jnl. of Cork Hist, and Arch. Soc., 2nd Series, Vol. XII., p.3, *et seq*.

in England and on the Continent also ; it was
equally in vogue at the beginning of the century, as
is well illustrated by the matrimonial history of the
Boyle family,[4] and did not die out till after the time
of Queen Anne. In all classes, except the very poor,
marriages were usually arranged by the parents.[5]
In such a system, where love cannot enter into
marriage except occasionally by chance, and where
the most which can be hoped for is that common
interests and associations may in time engender
mutual respect and possibly affection, marital
infidelity might well be expected to be very usual,
not perhaps among unimaginative rustics of low
intelligence, but with a quick-witted and lively
people like the Irish. It is well known, of course,
that during the eighteenth and nineteenth centuries
Ireland was freer of sexual irregularity than any
other country in the world, though not necessarily
therefore an island of saints. In the seventeenth
century there was unquestionably a greater laxity
of morals in this respect, but at no time was the
excessive licence associated with the Restoration
period in England to be found in Ireland. The
upper classes who, it must be remembered, were
by this time predominately Protestant in religion
and more or less English in blood, if they regarded
mistresses almost as much as a matter of course as
wives, did not indulge in that promiscuity which is
the real test of depravity. The ordinary men and
women of the country, though they certainly had no
very high sense of morality, sexual or otherwise, were
on the whole a very decent sort of people, for in
weighing evidence on this point, even more than on

[4] See Townshend, *Life and Letters of the Great Earl of Cork*, *passim*.
[5] Cf. documents *re* marriage of Charles Carthy and Ellen MacGillycuddy
in 1672. *MacGillycuddy Papers*, folios 75 and 76.

other subjects, we shall have to take the statements
of all our witnesses, except the most reliable, with a
good many grains of salt. Obviously, we can give
less credence to those professional traducers of the
Irish people, whose bias and unreliability we have
discussed in the previous chapter, than, say to Dr.
John Brenan, Bishop of Waterford from 1671 to
1693, and during sixteen years of that period also
Archbishop of Cashel. He was, unlike most Catholic
Bishops of the time, continuously resident in his
diocese. Such a man had no propaganda purpose to
serve, and his confidential reports to the Vatican,
recently printed for the first time,[6] were not, of
course, intended for publication. It must be
remembered that Stanyhurst, Camden, Campion,
Moryson, Dymok and Carew wrote in war-time
and were observing the conditions produced by
warfare of a very terrible kind. As Dr. Lynch
observes in *Cambrensis Eversus*, " continuous wars
are generally the rankest hotbed of immorality."
Those men are all war-time witnesses. There is no
need to quote at length, or indeed at all, from them :
their sweeping indictment can be summarized in a
few lines. The charges were that adultery, incest
and promiscuous sexual intercourse were rife,
feminine modesty being a rarity, that polygamy was
common and divorce very easy, marriages often being
for a period of one year. Some of these charges are
positively confirmed by Strafford,[7] writing at a
time when the country had enjoyed over thirty
years of peace and had, with the recuperative
power for which Ireland has always been remark-

[6] *Irish Historical Documents*, No. 3. Edited by Canon P. Power, Litt.D., Cork
Univ. Press, 1932. (Subsequently referred to in my footnotes as " Brenan,
Letters ").
[7] See *The Earl of Strafford's Letters and Despatches* (ed. Wm. Knowles). London,
1739. Vol. I. p.188.

able, again become quite prosperous, if not contented. He lays special stress on polygamy ; and it is of importance to note that in 1634 it was actually found necessary to pass a law through the Irish Parliament to enforce monogamy : this was only carried after determined opposition in both Houses, which at the time were composed of Catholics as well as Protestants, and six years after the Bill became law the Lords made an unsuccessful attempt to get it repealed.[8]

Another peace-time writer, who being an Irishman by birth if not by tradition had a greater knowledge of the country than many of the usual authorities, must be consulted on the period preceding that with which this book specially deals : that is the author of the essay entitled " Advertisements for Ireland," who was in all probability Sir Henry Bourchier, as Professor George O'Brien has shown.[9] He wrote this very painstaking treatise in 1623, and before turning to other authorities quite contemporary with our period, we will see what he has to say on the subject. " They generally (be they never so poor) affect to marry timely or else keep one unmarried and cohabit with her as their reputed wife and they take much felicity and content in their procreations and issue " ; and again : " Many of the British inhabitants there and natives keep two wives at once in divers places, and the mere Irish ordinarily, after a private contract, or sometimes without any condition but like on both sides, cohabit with single women in public as their wives and never solemnize any other

---

[8] See House of Commons Journals, 1634 and 1640. Cf. frequent references to bigamy and polygamy in Vatican Books of Sentences and Abjurations up to 1651. MSS. T.C.D., 1233 and 1234.
[9] *Op. cit.* editor's preface.

marriage with them, and thereupon their issue, that by common report were held legitimate in their father's lifetime, after his death are found to be bastards, and that amongst the chief men of rank. And in this way they exceed most nations, which proceeds from the corruption of the clergy's officers that there wink at this upon private compositions."

The impression left on the mind after reading *Cambrensis Eversus*[10] is that the Irish people of the generation before the Restoration were much less given to loose living than is suggested by Bourchier, Strafford and others ; Keating is quite explicit on the point, saying of the people as a whole : " is follus gur dhaoine cráibhtheacha caonduthrach-tacha iad ó aimsir go h-aimsir" [11]; and the accounts of the successful efforts of those saintly and hard-working Jesuits[12] who laboured unceasingly at the end of the sixteenth century and on into the seventeenth to keep Ireland from becoming more or less pagan, give many examples of conduct on the part of the people quite incompatible with ignorance of the principles of Christianity.[13] Never-theless, I think it is true that up to the middle of the century there was some substance in these charges of loose sexual morality, and the best that can be said by way of extenuation is that Ireland did not perhaps differ very materially in this respect from most other European countries at the time, or from the England of a couple of generations earlier; and I may mention that in reading the depositions collected by Miss Hickson in her book on 1641, in all that great mass of charges, complaints and

[10] Especially Chapters XV., XXV. and XXVII.
[11] *Forus Feasa*, Díonbhrollach (I. Texts Edn.), p.22.
[12] See Chapter IX.
[13] See Dr. Hogan's *Distinguished Irishmen of the Sixteenth Century*.

allegations, comprising murder, diabolic cruelty and pillage, I have not come across a single case of rape. Having regard to the circumstances of the time, this must either mean that the Irish, who were represented throughout in the most unfavourable light possible, were singularly free from this crime ; or that cases were so common as not to be considered worth mentioning ; or again, that Miss Hickson was too delicate to transcribe them. In a Proclamation of 10th September, 1661, by the Lords Justices and Council,[14] a particularly disgusting case of rape is described, in what would seem to us unnecessary detail for a public document, but there is nothing in the Irish State Papers of the reign of Charles II to suggest that this crime was at all common.

The examples of it casually mentioned by Theophilus Lucas, if they can be taken seriously at all, merely indicate the low standard of morality of a certain type of unprincipled adventurer which flourished at that time.[15]

It is likely that some of the irregularities prevailing up to that time, especially bigamy, were confined to the richer classes, but there is no evidence to support the idea that the chastity, which was a striking feature of Irish peasant life in the nineteenth century, was a virtue much cultivated in rural Ireland before the Penal Code began to have any marked effect on the character of the people it persecuted.

[14] C.S.P.I. 1660/62, p.419.
[15] T. Lucas, *Memoirs of the Famous Gamesters in the Reigns of Charles II, etc.* London, 1714. (Repr. London, 1930). Five of the twenty-five rakes whose profligate careers he describes were Irishmen. Some rather revolting cases are mentioned in *Ireland from the Restoration to the Present Time* (London, 1716), e.g. on p.93 of that work, which, however, is notoriously biassed and unreliable.

After the Restoration there was a definite improvement in the moral standard of the people of Ireland, where Puritanism had never taken root, and so did not provoke the violent reaction which produced the licence associated with the England, more particularly with the aristocratic England, of Charles II's reign. When I say that there was an improvement in the moral standard I do not wish to convey that any sudden change took place : I might rather say, perhaps, that a moral standard of a sort took the place of what had been something like chaos.

Passing over the rather favourable comments of one of Rinuccini's entourage[16] on the modesty of the women of Ireland, on the grounds that a foreign ecclesiastic would not have the same opportunities of estimating the true character of the people as a resident Irishman, we will now turn to the period in which we are particularly interested, when there are stronger grounds for believing in the essential decency of the ordinary citizen, though not, of course, for suggesting that anything like the modern (or almost modern) point of view prevailed. I have already pointed out that anything which Archbishop Brenan had to say on this subject is worthy of particular attention. Writing in 1672, he reports some laxity of living and irregularity in marriages, but he adds : " However, the people, generally speaking, are very religious and pious, leading a Christian life without great faults or many scandals."[17]   There is some reason to believe that this was less true of certain other dioceses, particularly in Ulster, but his words represent very definite

[16] The Dean of Fermo. See Canon Begley's *The Diocese of Limerick in the 16th and 17th Centuries*, p.308.
[17] Brenan, *Letters*, p.34. See p.48 *supra*.

and trustworthy evidence in support of the general conclusions I have advanced.

Among contemporary observers Petty stands out as the first to bring a really scientific mind to bear on Irish affairs and his statements must therefore always be given due consideration. While he is not explicit on the matters in question he appears to suggest that some looseness was general at least as regards marriage.[18]

Richard Lawrence, writing about the same time[19] vigorously indicts Irish morals, particularly as regards gambling, whoring, drunkenness and perjury, but his tirade is directed really against the rich since he ascribes the failings of the less fortunate classes to the bad example of their social superiors.

Several writers have commented on the extremes of good and bad to be found among the Irish. Thus Camden : " The religious among them are very austere, watching, praying and fasting, but if they once give themselves to a vicious course they are the vilest creatures in the world."[20] Dr. George O'Brien draws attention to the fact that Sir Henry Bourchier obviously took his historical information from Camden, so that we may perhaps regard as coming from the same source his reference to "the common opinion that the Irish are ever in the extremes, either surpassing good or surpassing ill."

In the previous chapter I have already made considerable use of those hitherto unpublished manuscripts which contain a general survey of the country in the years 1683-4, comprising not only a description of its natural features but also of the

[18] *Petty Papers.* Vol. II. p.50.
[19] *The Interest of Ireland in its Trade and Wealth Stated*, pp.40-53.
[20] *Britannia*, 1772 edn. Vol. II, p.378.

manners and customs of its inhabitants, each county being separately dealt with by a specially selected resident. Sexual morality is unfortunately a subject on which these commentators seem reluctant to express an opinion, but one or two of them refer to it.

Speaking of the people in the Forth Barony in Co. Wexford, the writer, who in this case we know from internal evidence was a Catholic,[21] says : " they are not inclined to debauchery or excessively addicted to the use of any liquor."[22]

In the description of the people of Co. Kildare we are told : " they are not very lascivious, yet the ordinary sort of people take a sort of pride in prostituting their daughters or kinswomen to their landlords' sons or kinsmen . . . and if the young woman have a child or children, the parents are exceedingly fond of it and the grandfather divides his estate equally to such as to the legitimate : and further if they happen to nurse a gentleman's child whose parents fall into decay or want, they think themselves bound to provide for that nurse child as for their own . . ."

There is abundant evidence that illegitimacy was not only common but that it did not constitute a serious handicap in life. That it was not in the reign of Charles II regarded as carrying with it any social stigma is hardly to be wondered at, when we remember that the nobility of the time was largely recruited from the illegitimate sons of the King ; nor was this attitude confined to England and France : to take an example where the Ormond family

[21] Not to be confused with Col. Solomon Richards or with Robert Leigh, both of whom also dealt with the same part of the country. (Leigh's survey was printed in the Journal of the R. Soc. of Antiquaries, Ireland, 1858).
[22] MS. T.C.D. I. 2, p.50.

are concerned, Lord Ossory's father-in-law, Louis de Beverweert, was the natural son of Prince Maurice of Nassau. Under the Brehon code, which was, of course, practically extinct as a legal system by the time of Charles II, gavelkind had allowed equal rights to illegitimate and legitimate children, and several famous Irishmen of the sixteenth century, notably the father of the great Hugh O'Neill, are generally believed to have been illegitimate. When once English government had established itself as the undisputed authority in Ireland, and English institutions came into almost universal use here, the illegitimate son no longer held a position of legal equality and could only enjoy the rights, which his predecessors similarly situated would have regarded as naturally theirs, when specially provided for by his father.

Writing to Arlington (then Sir Henry Bennet) in 1663, Sir Maurice Eustace, the Lord Chancellor of Ireland, points out that he intends his natural son, Maurice Eustace, to succeed to his estate, and referring to the King's promise to bestow on him a peerage, he asks that he may be allowed to nominate young Maurice to succeed him in the title. This request appears to have been eventually granted.[24]

We may learn from the passage dealing with the people of Co. Kildare, quoted on page 54, that equally among people untouched by court influences illegitimate children were by no means unwanted or unfairly treated.

The Duke of Ormond was an exception, not indeed in regard to having illegitimate offspring, for even this paragon of virtue had one liaison, but in

[24] C.S.P. Ire., 1663/65, p.66, and 1625/70, Addenda, p.544. See, however, subsequent petitions of Maurice Eustace, reports thereon, etc., given at pp.113, 114 of *Analecta Hibernica* No. 1.

his desire to hide the result of it. In this he was successful for many years until an accidental circumstance revealed the secret.[25] For the most part the aristocracy of the time thought it no shame to keep a mistress openly. It was taken as a matter of course : thus in the " Information " of Hubert Bourk in 1678 he quite casually mentions a certain Mrs. Mortimer as the Earl of Tyrone's mistress.[26]

Such things, however, while going to prove that society then tolerated conduct not condoned to-day, do not necessarily point to any widespread depravity of morals, nor do I think it existed.

The ease with which divorces were obtained was one of the public scandals adversely commented on by writers in the sixteenth, and early seventeenth centuries, though stated by Keating in his *Dion-bhrollach* to be exaggerated. They were by now altogether less frequent but, if we are to believe the Protestant Archbishops of Armagh and Dublin, were still " decreed by Popish priests resident in Ireland."[27] Dr. Lynch admits the existence of some unnatural vices, the introduction of which into Ireland he attributes to the English soldiery,[28] saying that he himself was ignorant of their very names before he went abroad as a young man.[29] There is no reason to believe that they were at all general in Ireland in his time, any more than the vices retailed nowadays for the delectation of readers of the sensational Sunday press are really typical of the

[25] Burghclere. *Life of Ormonde*, Vol. I., p.42.
[26] See printed tracts on the " Popish Plot " in the National Library. For Tyrone, see Chapter V., note 74.
[27] C.S.P. Ireland, 1663/65, p.360.
[28] The increase in venereal disease at the time of the Cromwellian occupation, as evidenced by Dr. Arthur's Fee Book (see p.223 *infra*), may also be ascribed to the same cause ; but it should be observed that diagnosis was somewhat uncertain and many cases may have been diagnosed as venereal which were in fact something else.
[29] See *Cambrensis Eversus*, Chapters IX. and XII.

countries from which they emanate. Certain laws in force in England against some of these were among the Acts proposed for Ireland in 1611,[30] and in this connexion we may note, on the authority of the revised edition of Cowel's Law Dictionary,[31] that a well-known unnatural vice was, with perjury, an offence exempted from the general pardon at the Restoration. Writing in 1698, Henri Misson remarks: " The English say both the word and the thing came to them from Italy and are strangers to England. Indeed they love the fair sex too well to fall into such an abomination. In England as well as almost all other countries, it is a crime punishable with death."[32]

There was, of course, no sensational press, Sunday or periodical, in the seventeenth century, but the State Papers contain quite a number of examples of crimes which would have delighted the editors of the Yellow Press, notably one in which the chief actors finished by unsuccessfully attempting to poison their jailor and eventually paid the penalty, the man being hanged, drawn and quartered and the woman burned, presumably alive.[33] Burning alive was a punishment still inflicted, even a hundred years later: thus the notorious Darky Kelly, the proprietor of a Dublin brothel, was tried for murder in 1764 and publicly burnt in Stephen's Green.[34]

Under the Brehon Law incontinency was officially regarded as a misdemeanour. While not actually an offence against the State under English law in

[30] *Carew Papers*, Vol. VI., p.163.
[31] Published 1708. This crime (buggery) was the object of legislation in Ireland in the reign of Charles I. See House of Commons Journal.
[32] *Memoirs and Observations* (English edn., London, 1719), p.20.
[33] C.S.P. Ireland, 1666/69, p.356.
[34] Gilbert, *History of Dublin*, Vol. I., p.94.

Ireland, when free from any element of compulsion, illicit sexual intercourse was subject to penalties which could be imposed by the ecclesiastical authorities, and the courts of the Protestant churches have left many records of sentences involving either excommunications or public humiliation.[35] The latter usually consisted of standing for the greater part of a day in the public place of repentance, in some parishes this ordeal having to be undergone Sunday after Sunday for months, when the guilty person did not show proper signs of contrition.[36]

Prostitutes were to be found in the towns, as probably they have been in all countries and in most ages. Barnaby Rich, writing in 1610 after forty-seven years in Ireland, describing himself as an enemy to Popery but not to Ireland—" let them understand that I love Ireland "—noted that there were in Dublin a number of idle, lazy housewives called tavern keepers, most of them well-known harlots, and remarks that it is rare to find one of the innumerable taverns without a strumpet.[37] In 1644 le Gouz visited Limerick, and remarked : " In this city there are great numbers of profligate women, which I would not have believed on account of the climate." John Stevens, a Catholic like le Gouz, who also saw Ireland more or less under war conditions (1689), is very severe in his comments : " The women were so suitable to the times that they

[35] Dwyer, *History of the Diocese of Killaloe*, pp.350-366. For survival of public penance well into the eighteenth century, see *Alexander the Coppersmith*, p.96.

Though not, of course, a member of the Established Church, the famous Quaker, William Edmundson, was excommunicated in 1682 for his persistent refusal to pay tithes. This penalty was accompanied by a sentence of imprisonment. Wight, *Hist. of People Called Quakers in Ireland, 1653 to 1700.* 4th edn., 1811, p.135. See also Edmundson's *Journal*, Dublin, 1715. For Quakers see Chapter IX.

[36] See Session Book of Templepatrick Presbyterian Church, Co. Antrim, 1646. Printed Jnl. of R.S.A.I., Vol. LXXXI., pages 164, 165 : also Gilbert, *History of Dublin*, Vol. I., p.213 and p.255.

[37] *New Description of Ireland*. Introduction, and pp.70-71.

rather enticed men to lewdness than carried the least face of modesty, in so much that in every corner of the town might be said to be a public stew. In fine, Dublin seemed to be a seminary of vice, and an academy of luxury, or rather a sink of corruption and living emblem of Sodom."[38] By way of comment on this we may notice the opinion of Mr. Justice Clodpole in 1668, that Dublin was but the lesser Sodom but pure of Irish (i.e., it was not, in his opinion, an Irish town).[39] John Dunton, again, never tires of the subject of sexual looseness in Dublin, but this righteous hypocrite's obvious preference for a pornographic tit-bit to the dull truth detracts greatly from his value as a witness, notwithstanding his undoubtedly keen powers of observation. Nor were the institutions complained of, or enjoyed by our authorities according to their several characters and natures, entirely confined to the largest towns. In Bandon, for instance, one of the presentments of the Grand Jury of the County Cork in 1699 was against " Eliz. Dennis for being a whore and keeping a common bawdy house."[40]

In considering the general question of sexual morality we must keep in mind not only the difference which already existed between rural and urban life, and the difference between class and class, but also the fact that there were two fairly distinct races in Ireland, one constituting a powerful minority upheld by outside power, the other comprising the vast majority, but already descending towards that submergence which was completed a couple of generations later.

---

[38] *Journal* (ed. Murray), p. 93.
[39] *Carte Papers*, Vol. I., p.123. Quoted Prendergast, *Cromwellian Settlement*, p.297.
[40] MS. T.C.D. N.3. 20.

The two works known as *The Irish Hudibras* both purport to describe the native Irish in rural surroundings. Both were written by Englishmen, or at least by men of English blood : James Farewell is extremely coarse, but, beyond a reference to venereal disease, he has nothing to say against the morals of the ordinary people. His countrywoman is no doubt a rather revolting figure, but apparently virtuous enough, and it is only the " poor kitchen wench " who is ravished by tories, and unwillingly at that. William Moffet, writing later of the same time, is more explicit. The scurrilous abuse indulged in by his women during their dispute as to which of them belonged to the best family could hardly be equalled in Billingsgate : they accuse each other of indiscriminate relations with grooms and soldiers even after marriage, and one admits premarital indiscretions, but as she married the man afterwards she counts her wanton years no disgrace. " I was," she says, as a *coup-de-grâce* :

" I was 'tis true for debt in jail
But ne'er got living by my tail."

According to the same author it was their country way to " tumble together without screen from view." The fact that Moffet's book went into several editions is by no means a proof of the truth of the picture he paints, but it does indicate the existence of a market in those days as well as to-day, for both pornographic literature and anti-Irish propaganda.

There is nothing in the purely native authorities of the time to suggest that the moral standard of the people was particularly low. We have already glanced at the opinions of Keating and Lynch on the Irish people of the previous generation. In common

with the clergy, the poets dwell on drink more
freely as a theme than sexual looseness. O'Bruadair
constantly extols the virtues of the ladies of County
Limerick, though of course he was to some extent
a professional eulogist and so his testimony as regards the aristocracy may be regarded as not
impartial. With the lower orders, his bias was rather
the other way, but his satire is directed against their
roughness and uncouthness, never against their
morals. A specimen of this may not be out of place
here :

> " gurabé an bodach
> buanna an bhata
> bhuaileas dorrann
> ar a chaile
> faoi na maluinn "[42]

though he admits that he used to salute her with
kisses before they were married. *Pairlemint Chlainne
Tomáis*,[43] a satire on the boorishness of the labouring
classes written in the middle of the seventeenth
century, provides evidence of the laxity of sexual
morals in the lowest stratum of the community.

There is one poem by a well-known seventeenth
century Gaelic poet which throws some light on the
question under consideration, in relation to the
farming class. It is by Seafraidh Ó Donnchadha an
Ghleanna and takes the form of some very outspoken
advice to one Sheila Roche as to the various types
of suitors she should discourage.[44]

There is a Rabelaisian touch about that poem,
which, though quite common in similar works in
English, is absent as a rule from Irish verse. Most

[42] *Duanaire* (I. Texts). Part II., p.66.
[43] Printed in *Gadelica*, Vol. I. *Vide* e.g. ll.1377-1401, 1524-1527.
[44] Owing, no doubt, to the coarseness of the language used it was omitted
by Dr. Dinneen from his edition of O'Donoghue's poems and is accessible
only in manuscript : viz. R.I.A. 23. B. 37.

of the love poetry in Irish is so closely interwoven with allegory that it is hard to distinguish between a genuine love song and one where the allusions are really political. Take, for example, " Mo Róisín Dubh," where the lady is unquestionably Ireland and not a flesh and blood woman, yet what could be more intensely human than the emotion expressed in those two verses of it which are so often omitted from modern printed versions :

" A Róisín mhín mhodhamhail na mbán-chíoch
    gcruinn
  Is tú dh'fhág míle arraing i gceart-lár mo
    chroidhe
  Ealuig liom a chéad-shearc agus fág an tír
  'S dá bhféadfainn ná déanfainn bainrioghan
    díot, a Róisín dhubh.

" Dá mbeadh seisreach agam do threabhfainn i
    n-aghaidh na gcnoc
  'S dhéanfainn soisgéal i lár an Aifrinn dom
    Róisín dhubh,
  Bhéarfainn póg don chailín óg a bhéarfadh a
    h-óige dhom
  'S dhéanfainn cleas ar chúl an leasa lem' Róisín
    dhubh."

No girl has ever received a more intimate and beautiful love offering than these verses, and though the whole poem stirs the blood with its moving patriotism, it is hard to believe that its author was not inspired by an emotion more passionate than pure love of country when he wrote the lines I have quoted.[45]

[45] English translations of Irish poetry are invariably inadequate, but Mangan's " Dark Rosaleen " does to some extent catch the spirit of the original, though not the intricacy and beauty of the metre. This version is infinitely superior to Furlong's.
Cf. also " Mac an cheannuidhe," by Egan O'Rahilly.

" Bean lán de Stuaim " is another poem which some, jealous perhaps for the reputation of its supposed author for unworldliness, believe to be allegorical, but which I think should be taken at its face value. Though usually attributed to Keating, its authorship is not certain. In any case that worthy priest's conduct as described in the poem was quite unexceptionable. Indeed the priests of Ireland have always enjoyed a well-deserved reputation for chastity, as well in the days of general laxity as in more moral times.

Generally speaking, the relations between men and women were very much what they are and always have been. One has only to read the "Love Songs of Connacht," many of which were composed in the seventeenth century, to realize that. They fell in love with all the romance and ardour of their forefathers and of their descendants. Some people were fickle, some constant ; there were men without moral principles and women of easy virtue as there are to-day, and there were just as certainly men and women of high character. The differences lie rather in the circumstances and surroundings than in themselves. We can, in fact, feel reasonably sure that the average man and woman of the time were decent people, the same essentially as the average man and woman of to-day.

One is struck by the way in which le Gouz in 1644 accepted as a not very startling fact the exaggerated accounts of the massacre of vast numbers of Protestants in Ireland three years before : such an idea horrified men in the seventeenth century little more than the contemplation of statistics of road fatalities does in the twentieth. So, too, the accepted conception of what constituted decency was different at that time from our notions on the subject at the present day, just as the standards in this respect of two highly civilized nations may differ now. In France, for instance, a man may relieve himself or a woman suckle her baby unscreened without comment, whereas in England these things are regarded as outraging the proprieties. In Japan a professional prostitute may marry and become respectable ; in fact if we go outside the Christian countries, instances of such discrepancy could be multiplied *ad libitum*.

Though such fastidiousness seems hardly to accord with seventeenth century propensities it appears that a certain unpleasant habit was abominated[46]. The usual word for this is in some dictionaries, but it is stated to be " not in decent use," and there is no convenient polite synonym for it—such as ' eructate ' for ' belch.' Both Farewell and Moffet assume the reader's acceptance of this view, and I presume this is what Fynes Moryson had in view when he said : " I would name a great lord among them, who was credibly reported to have put away his wife of a good family and beautiful, only for a fault as light as wind (which the Irish in general abhor), but I dare not name it, lest I offend the perfumed senses of some whose censure I have incurred in that kind."[47]

[46] See Dunton's 3rd Letter, Appendix B, p.350. Dineley is even more explicit on the subject, he says that it " is so abominated by an Irishman that he either quarrels, or flies from you and crosseth himself " : page 262 of original MS. (in National Library, Dublin). This passage and others which throw much light on the personal habits of the people, were considered unprintable and omitted from the published edition of his *Observations*.

[47] Fynes Moryson, *The Commonwealth of Ireland* (Falkiner), p.284. The word in question is used in a letter written by no less a person than the 2nd Earl of Orrery to his mother the formidable Dowager Countess. He says that Rev. Mr. Vowell remarked to him that in certain circumstances "he would not care one farte for me (I pray pardon for that worde for it was his owne expression)". *Orrery Papers*, folio 414, not quoted in printed edition.

An English traveller in 1635 was rather shocked when he saw in Waterford " women in a most impudent manner treading clothes with their feet ; these were naked to their middle almost, for so high were their clothes tucked about them "[48] ; and Fynes Moryson described as remarkable a somewhat similar scene he witnessed, which from our modern point of view would have seemed considerably more indecorous.[49] Barnaby Rich, too, noted something of the kind, but like John Dunton in Iar Connacht at the end of the century, he was more offended by the proximity of food to the woman's bare thighs tnan by her nakedness.[51] Gédéon Bonnivert, a Huguenot follower of William of Orange, who wrote a short diary of his stay in Ireland in 1690, takes a more modern view. Describing his first impression on landing at Carrickfergus he notes the large numbers of poor people and adds : " The women are not very shy of exposing to men's eyes those parts which are usual for the sex to hide."[52]

To the Irish of the seventeenth century, however, mere nakedness—in its proper place—did not seem any more indecent than the exiguous bathing costumes of to-day do to us.[53] The habit of sleeping naked dates from early times. It was quite general in Ireland in the seventeenth century ; but it was not peculiarly Irish. Wright's *Domestic Manners of the Middle Ages* gives many woodcuts illustrating this custom, several of them belonging to the

[48] Brereton's *Travels*, p.160.
[49] *Description of Ireland* (Falkiner), p. 226.
[51] *New Description of Ireland*, p.40.
[52] Proc. R.I.A. Vol. XXX., Sect. C, No. 13, p.337.
[53] See *Dublin Scuffle*, p.401.

seventeenth century, from which we may see that
ladies of quality in England slept naked,[54] just as
the lower orders of society did ; and, of course, it is
well known that the practice persisted even among
quite respectable people well into the nineteenth
century.

The sleeping accommodation, where small houses
and large families were concerned, has been the
subject of frequent comment by travellers and
others. " Beds for the most part of the common
people," says Dineley, " are of mere straw and that
scarce clean, some have ticking stuffed with straw,
without sheets, nay they pull off their very shirts
so as not to wear them out. These cabins abound
with children which, with the man, maid and wife,
sometimes a travelling stranger, or pack-carrier,
or pedlar or two ; aye nine or ten of them together,
naked heads and points."[55] A description of the
same custom written in 1841 is so much to the point
that I venture to quote it in full : " The floor is
thickly strewn with fresh rushes, and stripping
themselves entirely naked, the whole family lie
down at once together, covering themselves with
blankets if they have them, and, if not, with their
day clothing ; but they lie down decently and in
order, the eldest daughter next the wall, furthest
from the door, then all the sisters according to their
ages. Next the mother, father, and sons in success-
ion, and then the strangers, whether the travelling
pedlar, tailor or beggar. Thus, the strangers are
kept aloof from the female part of the family ; and
if there is an apparent community, there is great
propriety of conduct. This was the first time my

[54] See woodcut on p.411, *op. cit.*
[55] *Observations*, p.21.

friend had seen the primitive but not promiscuous mode of sleeping [A.D. 1799]. He has, however, often seen it since."[56] Wright states that the taste for domestic privacy grew up in England in the sixteenth century among the upper classes, with a consequent alteration in the accommodation provided in their houses,[57] but such changes occur gradually, and as a rule came to Ireland later than to England.

Referring to the question of nakedness and morals, the remarks of Philip Luckombe, author of a "Tour" in 1779, are of interest. The *Tour* is one of the best of its kind, though not, of course, as important as Arthur Young's or entirely free from the customary condescension of such writers. "From the promiscuous way these people lie together," he writes, "a suspicion naturally arises in a stranger's mind, that incest is unavoidable amongst them. Yet upon the strictest enquiry, I find the fact to be otherwise. They are bred up in such an abhorrence of the turpitude of this crime, that I am inclined to think it is as infrequent here, as among more civilized nations. The better sort of people seem rather surprised that I should entertain such an opinion ; which only shews, that what we see practised in our infancy, though ever so unnatural, makes no impression. A little reflection, however, will remove even the ground of suspicion. Bred up from childhood together, their wonted and innocent familiarity is carried on step by step, without impure emotions being excited.

[56] Rev. Caesar Otway, *Sketches in Erris and Tyrawley*, p.32.
Otway's descriptions of housing and other domestic conditions in 1798, as well as sleeping accommodation—see pp.28 and 29 of his *Sketches*—are remarkably similar to those of Dunton exactly 100 years earlier.
[57] *Domestic Manners*, p.442.

One of these poor souls is no more influenced by the nude bosom of a sister, than in a more affluent state he would be at seeing it covered with gauze. There is no indecency in mere nakedness."[58] This was equally true of an earlier generation.

These eighteenth century tours, which are quite numerous, are of less value in assisting us to form an opinion on the morals of the people than on their manners and customs. The latter do not change rapidly. In fact, as I have already pointed out in my preliminary chapter, in many respects the lapse of 200 years, from 1680 to 1880, effected no material change in rural Ireland. Morals, as distinct from national characteristics, are, on the other hand, subject to much more rapid change.

While the habits and daily life of the people, at least in rural Ireland, were much the same in 1680 as they were in 1630, we have seen that the standard of morals, using the word in its limited sense, had very definitely improved. In no respect are more striking changes possible in a comparatively short space of time, than in the extent to which drunkenness is prevalent. A Father Mathew can, temporarily, if not permanently, completely reform a whole country in a crusade of a few years. Foreign observers, of course, record what they see at the time of their visits. Few native writers thought it worth while to describe, deliberately, the normal life surrounding them, until the advent of the novelist. There, too, we have not been fortunate: we have had a Charles Lever, where Scotland has a Walter Scott.

[58] *A Tour through Ireland, interspersed with Observations on Manners, Customs, etc.*, Dublin, 1780, pp.164, 165. It would appear that several pages of this book, including the passages here quoted, were taken almost verbatim from Thos. Campbell's *Philosophical Survey of the South of Ireland.* (1777, p.149).

Drunkenness seems to have been a national weakness at most times. Allusion is made to it by almost all authorities I have consulted on morals, manners, customs and the like, native and Gaelic as well as Anglo-Irish or English and Continental, though the angle of approach is different. Father Hollywood, S.J., in 1605, ascribed the introduction of the " foul habit of drinking " to the English soldiery.[59] Compare O'Bruadair's tolerant reference to a " Súmaire múnloch 'na leidhce fhliuch,"[60] with Fynes Moryson's categorical statement : " the mere Irish are excessively given to drunkenness," or Bourchier's equally sweeping : " the Irish, and chiefly the mere Irish, give themselves unreasonably to both kinds, especially the latter liquor."[61] In his satire on a barmaid,[62] interesting sidelight in itself on our period, O'Bruadair's vituperative powers are so trenchant that the reverend editor omits altogether the line in which he delivers his *coup-de-grâce* ; but the invective is directed not against the sin of drunkenness but against the woman who refused to serve him on credit. The well-known song, " 'Sí mo chreach," which has been translated under the title of " Ode to Drunkenness," enthusiastically extols the joys of that form of excess,[63] and while Seaghan Ó Neachtain in his " Magaidh Láidir " is rather more restrained in his praise of drinking, the popularity of these productions of the second half of the seventeenth century goes to show that public opinion was lenient towards the drunkard.

[59] Hogan, *Distinguished Irishmen*, p.419.
[60] See Irish Texts Edition, Part I., p.74 and *passim*.
[61] i.e. Aqua-vitae, uisge beatha or whiskey. *Advertisements for Ireland*, p.16.
[62] *Seirbhíseach Seirgthe, op. cit.* Part II., p.220
[63] Hardiman describes it as " an ingenious satire on our extra jovial propensities." *Irish Minstrelsy*, Vol. I., p. 137.

Dr. Hugh O'Grady, in his painstaking but rather chaotic work on Strafford, has amassed a great deal of evidence to show the prevalence of excessive drinking in Ireland before '41. In this matter, however, as in sexual morals, public morality showed an improvement as the century advanced. Professor George O'Brien summarizes the state of affairs in what he calls the period of Reconstruction (1660-1689) in the following paragraph : " Complaints of drunkenness are not very common during this period. The sale of drink was subject to many regulations requiring licences to be taken out and otherwise ; and although Petty complains that too many people were employed in the manufacture and distribution of ale, he does not infer that too much was drunk. On the contrary, the reform which he advocated was the establishment of an arrangement by which the same amount of drink could be sold in a less wasteful manner. Richard Lawrence [as has already been noted[64]] complains of the prevalence of drunkenness, but too much reliance should not be placed on what he says on the subject, on which he was obviously a fanatic. On the other hand, in a pamphlet of the period of the most scurrilous anti-Irish views, it was asserted that drinking was not a national vice of the Irish."[65]

The pamphlet Professor O'Brien refers to is *A Brief Description of Ireland.*[66] He might well have coupled with it another somewhat similar publication. In 1699 a pamphlet appeared entitled *A Trip to Ireland.*[67] Whether it was printed in Dublin or London is not known, but its authorship is attributed

[64] p.39, *supra.*
[65] O'Brien, *Economic History of Ireland in the Seventeenth Century*, p.126.
[66] London, 1692.
[67] Sub-title : " Being a description of the Country, People and Manners, as also some select Observations on Dublin."

to the celebrated or notorious Tom Brown.[68] For
sheer scurrilous abuse this booklet outdoes anything
else of the kind I have seen. Dunton could be
outrageous enough in his descriptions of the country
and its inhabitants, but if his favourable comments
were mostly reserved for people whom he regarded
at least as his social equals, he does not leave the
reader with a perpetual bad taste in the mouth as
does the author of *A Trip to Ireland*. This man, who
frequently, after the manner of the period, uses
without acknowledgment whole passages of the
most pornographic parts of Dunton's recently
published *Conversation in Ireland*, has nothing good
to say of anybody or anything, except the nobility
of English origin, for like all his kind he was a
toady; he attributes to the Irish "the cruelty of a
Spanish inquisitor, the lechery of an Italian, the
levity of a Frenchman, the cowardice of a Savoyard,
the perfidiousness of a Scotchman, the ignorance of
a Muscovite, and the rebellious temper of a Dutchman." Yet surprisingly we find him offering
evidence for the defence in the matter of drunkenness. "Drinking," he says, "is not so much their
vice as some of their neighbouring nations, unless
their so excessive smoking be reckoned in, to which
both the men and women are so generally addicted,
yea, the very children, too, that an infant of their
breeding shall take more delight in handling a
tobacco pipe than a rattle, and will sooner learn to
make use of it, than another shall of its sucking
bottle." A work so contemptible as this is of value
to us less for any light it throws on the question of
drunkenness than as an example of the semi-
humorous and wholly obscene sort of scribbling

[68] See Bradshaw Collection, Hib. 4. 699. 2.

which had a considerable public at the end of the seventeenth century. Referring to a companion volume in which he had made a Dutchman the butt of his vituperation, he remarks in his preface : " If Teigue can but please as well as Myn-heer the bookseller has gained his aim, the author his and the reader more than he could expect since in drawing the picture of a Dutchman he might have thought nature had been exhausted of all her deformities."

Corroboration of the comparative sobriety of the people at this period is to be found in the contemporary authority already quoted on page 54, and the number of these county surveys which make no reference at all to the question suggests that in the years they were made (1682-1684) drunkenness was not a particularly remarkable feature of Irish life ; though a few years later, Dunton, if we can believe him, deplores the fact that drunkenness " is now become a feminine vice."[69] Allusions to drinking are, of course, frequent enough in the correspondence of the time : but when we read in a semi-official letter from Dublin that " this being St. Andrew's Day the Scothmen (*sic*) about the town here are as drunk as beggars," we need not take that as any more typical than the exuberance shown by Irishmen in London after a victory at Twickenham. The simile in this case—as drunk as beggars—is worth noting.

It cannot be doubted, however, that the clergy were somewhat given to this failing. Not only was this true of the Catholic priests who had fallen away from Rome and of the Protestant clergy, most of whom—especially in rural districts—were little ornament to the Church, though no doubt hardly

[69] *Dublin Scuffle*, p.222.

meriting R. P. Mahaffy's description of their predecessors of a generation or two earlier as " a set of very profane and drunken fellows " [70] ; it was true also of the otherwise exemplary priests who were under the control of the Bishops. Speaking generally, Cardinal Moran expresses the opinion that, considering the circumstances of the time, abuses were few. Drunkenness must have been deeply rooted in some districts, for Archbishop Plunket became an abstainer as an example to his clergy : " Give me an Irish priest without this vice," said Blessed Oliver, " and he is assuredly a saint." [71]

No doubt there was a tendency on the part of all sorts of Irishmen to be fond of a drop, but at no time do they appear to have been very self-indulgent in the matter of food. Barnaby Rich states that in his day the eating of meat on Wednesdays, Fridays or Saturdays was regarded as a more deadly sin than drunkenness or lechery, [72] and in this connexion it is interesting to note that the inhabitants of the Forth Barony in Co. Wexford, who are described as very devout and staunch Catholics, always abstained from meat on Fridays and Saturdays, few using even eggs, butter or milk on Fridays, and that they also observed Wednesdays as fast days, until about 1670 " they were dispensed withall, or rather commanded to the contrary." [73] Jouvin, too, a Frenchman who toured Ireland in 1666, notes that Irish Catholics did not eat flesh or eggs on Wednesdays, Fridays or Saturdays. [74]

[70] C.S.P. Ireland, 1625/33, Introduction, p. xxxv.
[71] Moran, *Memoirs of the Most Rev. Dr. Plunket*, p.78.
[72] *New Description*, p.40.
[73] MS. T.C.D. I. 1. 2, p.46.
[74] A Jouvin, *Description of England and Ireland* (printed in Falkiner's *Illustrations of Irish History*), p. 418.

These faults we have so far been considering, in fact, if not condonable, were at least to some extent set off by the compensating virtues of generosity and parental affection. We now come to a sin and a crime in extenuation of which it would be hard to find anything to say : perjury.

While perjury appears to have been too common in Ireland, I think there are little grounds for believing that it amounted to a serious blot on the good name of the country, especially in the second half of the seventeenth century. It is true that Bourchier says : " Perjury is so usual in the realm, especially amongst the common sort of peasants, as against any great man of the natives no right can prevail on a stranger's side ; or if one that is but weakly befriended in the country where his matter is tried if the proof there rest upon their oaths. And yet I never heard any to have suffered any rigorous punishment for this so usual and capital a crime which in the old law was chastised with death."[75] Barnaby Rich remarks that in forty-seven years in Ireland, " though the multitude of the ruder sort of Irish are regardless of their oaths," he had never known anyone punished for perjury.[76] Payne, on the other hand, says that the Irish kept their promises faithfully.[77] His estimate of Irishmen is much higher than that of most of the Englishmen who have left their opinions on record. While giving due regard to their statements of fact I am not inclined to attribute great importance to their opinions, good or bad, and moreover, the date at which Payne wrote (1589) is too early to be of

[75] *Advertisements for Ireland*, p.42.
[76] One of the punishments prescribed by an Act of 28 Eliz., still in force a century later, was having the ears nailed to the pillory ; one or both ears might be cut off for forgery.
[77] *A Brief Description of Ireland*, p.3.

more than passing interest to us, but as resident manager of some 10,000 acres of land[78] he must have spoken with first-hand knowledge of the people of his adopted country. Camden, in his catalogue of Irish iniquities, does not give perjury a prominent place ; in fact, he tells us that perjury, where the oath was one regarded generally as solemn and binding, brought public infamy on the man who committed it.[79] It would seem that 100 years later it was sometimes not so much fear of public opinion which deterred perjurers as a superstitious fear of physical ill-effects. Thus, in 1683, Sir Henry Piers mentions what he calls a fabulous story implicitly believed by the Catholics of Co. Westmeath, a belief in the power of a certain relic so great that none of them dared swear falsely on it for fear of deformity or death following.[80] Joseph Keogh, speaking of Connacht, gives an instance of the fate of one who swore falsely by the crozier and staff of St. Barry, the relics of which were kept " buttoned about in green cloth, and a fee of one groat paid to the keeper for each occasion it was used." This person's face is stated to have turned permanently " awry " as a result of his false oath.[81] There is a suggestion of a belief in the supernatural punishment of perjurers in Father White's account of the trial of Doctor Pierce Creagh in Cork in 1705, when the floor of the court collapsed and all the people were precipitated into the cellar. One of the " false witnesses was crushed to death in the ruins " and the other fled ; " and none escaped falling down with the floor except the Judge whose

[78] *Ibid.* Introduction.
[79] *Britannia*, 1772 edn. Vol. II., p.379.
[80] M.S. T.C.D. I.1.2, p.329.
[81] *Ibid.*, p.163.

seat was supported by an iron bar and our Prelate whose chair happened to be placed on a beam which did not give way, and he continued sitting as it were in the air. The Judge cried out that Heaven itself acquitted him, and he thereupon dismissed him with a great deal of honours."[82]

Unscrupulous men of the criminal class are always to be found, of course, and Carte says that Petty boasted of having available " witnesses who would swear through a three-inch board."[83] Perjury was rife, of course, at the time of the " Popish Plot," but no general charge can be brought against the Irish people of 1678, because a number of worthless renegades perjured themselves for gain. The Duke of Ormond's opinion of them is well known : " those [witnesses for the Popish Plot] that went out of Ireland with bad English and worse clothes are returned well bred gentlemen, well coronated, periwigged and clothed. Brogues and leather straps are converted to fashionable shoes and glittering buckles : which next to the zeal Tories, Thieves and Friars have for the Protestant religion, is a main inducement to bring in a shoal of informers."[84] In this connexion the comments of Carte, who is our authority for Ormond's words just quoted, are of interest. " It is still more strange," he says, " that such notorious perjurers as plainly appeared in this affair of the Popish Plot, no law should yet pass in England for the severe punishment of persons guilty of that crime, where the lives of others are taken away, their estates forfeited, their blood tainted." At the same time, perjury as an offence against the State rather than the individual was, as we have

[82] MS. R.I.A. 24. D. 21. fo. 219.
[83] Carte, *Life of Ormond*, 1815 edn., Vol. IV., p.386.
[84] *Ibidem.*, Vol. V., p.164.

already noticed, officially regarded as serious enough to be included among the few crimes reserved from the general pardon at the Restoration ; but if anything can be argued from that, would it not be its rarity rather than its frequency?

Lying under oath is really only a stage worse than lying and dishonesty in ordinary commercial transactions. In a communication from an important official in Dublin, dated 25th November, 1667, the two are regarded as complementary : " Some of the merchants here are very glad that orders are coming from England to appoint a commission to enquire into embezzlement in connexion with the great Genova prize,[85] which abuses, together with that thing called perjury is so common with some people here that a friend of mine did this very day desire me to send into England the account in the enclosed paper to be added to the first Gazett there as a thing worthy taking notice of. Please do it, for I believe it is a true story." The memorandum is worth quoting in full : " From Ireland perjuries and forgeries are grown so common here that this last week upon a trial in the court of Common Pleas, there was no less than 29 men took their oaths that one Mr. Blackwell, who is a sheriff of a county here, had signed a deed whereby he should convey five towns and several thousand acres of land to one Major Mihill and his heirs for ever for little or no consideration. But, upon trial of the deed there was proof so unexpectedly come in of Mr. Blackwell's

[85] Public Lotteries were controlled by the government in so far as the right of conducting them was restricted to certain duly licensed persons. (See, for example, the licence dated 10 March, 1676, printed in *Analecta Hibernica*, No. 6, p.390). Sometimes the profits were allocated for a specific purpose. In 1665, for example, a monopoly was granted to certain prominent Englishmen which covered both England and Ireland. The money in this case was required to raise stock for the Royal Fishing Company. C.S.P. Dom., June 21, 1665.

side, which was so certain and convincing that [it] manifested the immediate hand of God in discovering those men guilty of 'pergerry and forgerry.' The chief conspirators were Major Mihill, John Clarke and one Capt. Hewlet, who was condemned to be hanged for murdering the late King."[86]

Generally speaking, however, though Lawrence mentions the badness of credit due to defaulting gentry as one of the great impediments to trade,[87] complaints of crooked dealing and dishonesty in trade are sufficiently rare to satisfy us that these shortcomings were not unduly prevalent in the commercial life of the time. Thieving, no doubt, especially petty thieving, was common. Dineley, who like all other tourists seldom shows a sense of humour, did perhaps smile as he completed this very lengthy sentence : " They have certain concomitants, nastiness and laziness, wherefore having enough beforehand to furnish them with potatoes, milk, and tobacco, which they toss from one to another in a short pipe with this word, shaugh, sitting upon their hams, like greyhounds in the sun, near their cabin, they'll work not one jot, but steal, which is such an inseparable vice to them, that a gentleman in the county of Clare complain'd to me that they stole his box of pills because gilded."[88] Dunton was much annoyed by the theft of various small belongings of his, during his travels through the country. " The thieves of Drogheda are saints

[86] R. Leigh to T. Williamson, C.S.P. Ire. 1666/69, p. 487. Cf. *London Gazette*, 23 Nov., 1667. This and subsequent references to the *London Gazette* are taken from a MS. book of extracts relating to Ireland compiled from the *Gazette* by Mr. Patrick O'Connor of the National Library of Ireland, who kindly lent it to me. Cf. also Ormond's interesting despatch to Arlington on forgery and "gross and foul" offences of the like nature. C.S.P. Ireland. 1670. p.172/3.
[87] *The Interest of Ireland*, p.10. The Revenue Abstracts 1689–1700 (MS. Nat. Lib. not yet catalogued, ref. *pro tem.* UL) indicate the extent of the defaulting which occurred as a result of the next war.
[88] *Observations*, p.17-18.

compared to the pickpockets of Kilkenny," he exclaimed, after a particularly exasperating experience at that place.[89]

There was, of course, much organized pilferage by tories and the like, but their delinquencies, in this respect at least, may be ascribed to the historical causes of their existence rather than to a defect in the national character.[90] In fact, having regard to the absence of any organized system of order comparable to the modern police system, even allowing for the scarcity of valuables in most dwelling houses, the remarkable thing is not the prevalence of what we would now call burglars but their comparative rarity.

In one respect public morals were unquestionably lax : bribery and corruption were part and parcel of the seventeenth century system. Here again we are dealing with an abuse which is not unknown in other centuries and in other countries. The Brehons were supposed to have been susceptible to influence by gifts of cows ; whether they were or not hardly concerns us here. Coming nearer to our period we find Bourchier devoting much space to the exposure of official corruption and we can see how the seeds of coming trouble were sown, as much by this weakness in the body politic as in any other way. It permeated the whole government service down to the menial customs officers who would pass gentlemen's trunks unopened when bribed to do so.[91]

In 1661 Petty drew attention to "the difficulty of executing justice, so many of those in power being themselves protected by officers and protecting others."[92]

[89] *Dublin Scuffle*, p.400
[90] See Chapter VIII.
[91] *Advertisements for Ireland*, p.23.
[92] See O'Brien, *Economic History of Ireland in the Seventeenth Century*, p.133.

Political influences sometimes resulted in the exposure of corruption. Perhaps the most remarkable case of this kind was that of Thomas Sheridan, who was Chief Commissioner of Revenue and, according to Bagwell[93], was forced upon Tyrconnell as his secretary by James II. The whole career of this man, and indeed that of his son too, makes an interesting commentary on the vicissitudes of political life in the reigns of Charles II and James II. The charges of corruption brought against him were for the most part upheld by a commission of five judges set up specially to adjudicate in this case[94]; but it should be added, having regard to the moral standards of the time, that there appears to be something to be said in his defence.

In fact a perusal of the Irish State Papers for the reign of Charles II will leave no doubt in the mind of the reader that almost everyone from the highest to the humblest official, had his price, and examples from the notorious scandal of Arlington's acquisition of the O'Dempsey (Portarlington) estate to the pettifogging charlatanry of obscure nonentities, whose names are not worth recalling, could be multiplied without difficulty. It is only just, however, to except that most unpopular Lord Lieutenant, Lord Robartes, from this indictment; and also to give some credit for integrity to the Duke of Ormond. The least reputable actions of this great man—for great he was, however much we may deplore his shortcomings as an Irishman—were straightforward and honourable compared with those of his predecessors in Elizabethan and early Stuart times.

[93] *Ireland Under the Stuarts*, Vol.III, p.167
[94] *Analecta Hibernica*, No.1. p.46 *et seq.*

CHAPTER IV

The Gentry and their Dependants

In the last chapter I referred to the constant vilification of everything Irish by certain English writers. One of the most prominent of these popular authors, William Camden, expressed the opinion that " the greatest corruptions and debaucheries of Ireland are to be imputed to no other cause than this method of nursing."[1] Arguing that the tie of fosterage was closer than that of blood—in which contention he is supported by most writers who deal with this subject—he informs us that the Irish thought it a disgrace to nurse their own children, " but man and wife will abstain from each other for the sake of the foster child ; they think it a good cause to be lewd to have the suckling of an infant."

Fosterage is an example of a custom universal in the sixteenth century which was to pass away with the coming of the modern world. It certainly survived after the end of the seventeenth century, but by that time there is little evidence to show that it was practised as more than a convenience[2] : foster-mothers, once an integral part of the social system, had sunk to the level of little more than wet-nurses. When the practice was in its heyday, it was customary for children to be reared by foster-parents of a station somewhat similar to that of their natural parents. In its degenerate form, however, it involved an intimate contact between people of different classes, which was something like—and

[1] *Britannia,* 1772 edn. Vol. II., p.378.
[2] Cf. *Alexander the Coppersmith,* p.119.

indeed more intimate than—the relationship which often exists between an old family nurse and the sons and daughters of the house whom, one after the other, she has passed through her hands.

We know from *Cambrensis Eversus* that it was considered as an honour in Dr. Lynch's time, and the passage quoted on page 54 shows that the obligations attached to fosterage were still regarded as binding in 1683, ten years after Dr. Lynch's death.

Dineley makes two short references to the custom. " To be foster brothers is such an obligation of love, that there is no greater, according to the manner of this Kingdom," and again : " Irish nurses are very tender and good to the children of others of higher degree, and most commonly their love is more to them than their own, this begets a relation and kindred without end, and they become followers to their foster brothers and sisters." We cannot depend too much on Dineley, except when he obviously describes things from his own observation, but the persistence of fosterage up to the last decade of the century is attested by John Stevens's comments on the want of discipline in the Irish Army of King James : " the commissioned officer could not punish his sergeant or corporal because he was his cousin or foster brother."[3]

---

[3] *Journal* (ed. Murray), p.64. Cf. Narrative of Adrian Adornes : Bodleian MS. Rawl. C. 439, fo.241 : " ' Tis a matter of fact that all these cousins and gossips, fosterers and followers of all sorts have hindered them [the Irish] of doing justice, and for want of justice all went topsy-turvy : for fosterers and followers were as good as their masters, a cousin and a gossip as high in their coat of arms as a Lord, a soldier as brave a joy and as deserving a man as his Captain, a Captain not inferior to his Colonel, a Lieutenant-Colonel and a Major as deserving as a Brigadier of the army and as skilful in military affairs . . . Some Irish officers have confessed to me after the Battle of the Boyne that they were afraid the Kingdom would be lost because there was neither order nor justice nor obedience nor any regular military discipline among them, every one thinking himself capable and worthy of a great employment."

In a letter written in 1756 by an Irish exile, Daniel O'Huonyn, who had become an admiral in the Spanish navy, to his grandnephew, Andrew Lysaght,[4] of Killaspuglenane, Co. Clare, a passage occurs which indicates the survival of the custom and obligations of fosterage well into the eighteenth century. The admiral had remitted a certain sum of money to his relatives at home, " towards the repair of the Mass-house " and for other purposes, having detailed which, he goes on : " £3 to my foster-brother William Corcoran whose poverty you express moves me to pity him, and I beg of you and all my nephews to protect and render him and his brothers [all] the service you can without prejudice to yourselves ; this I recommend in gratitude of their submission to my will when young and the rare love their good mother (whose memory is dear to me) had for me preferable to those she bore, which is the extent of filial love I had not reflexion then to comprehend."[5] Capt. Dudley Bradstreet, on the other hand, attributes the wild and immoral course of his life to the bad influence of the foster-father with whom he was left at the age of seven. He was born in 1711 in Co. Tipperary.[6]

Allusions to fosterage are rare in the Gaelic poetry of the later seventeenth century ; nor have I found the least reference to it, however indirect, in the abstracts of Chancery and Exchequer Bills which I have examined, though perhaps this is to be expected since foster-relationship was not one recognized by English law.   Similarly Richard

---

[4] Uncle of " Pleasant Ned."
[5] *Journal of the Limerick Field Club*, Vol. III., p.246, where Mr. G. U. Macnamara appends a note to the effect that fosterage in a modified form lasted well into the nineteenth century.
[6] *Life and Uncommon Adventures of Capt. Dudley Bradstreet*. Dublin, 1755, Chapter I.

Head, who appears to have been very thorough in recording his observations, is silent on the subject. Writing in 1670, one of the secretaries of the Court in Dublin describes the bravery of a Tory called MacQuade, evidently a remarkably fine figure of a man, who " might have escaped if he would, but resolved to fetch off his foster-brother, which he did. He kept a pass against thirty-seven men all alone, and hurt two of them."[7] Ten years later Redmond O'Hanlon was shot for the sake of a money reward by one Art O'Hanlon, " a fosterer of his, out in rebellion with him,"[8] an act of treachery rare among foster kindred.

That the custom of fosterage survived to some extent may be assumed from the passages I have quoted, and we must infer from the remarks of John Stevens and Admiral O'Huonyn that it still constituted a bond between the two main divisions of society, the gentry and their tenantry, though not the actual labouring class. It is not my intention in this book to go into any detail on the subject of land tenure, though, as I have already mentioned, the agrarian and religious questions were those uppermost in the minds of all sections of the population at this period. The general relationship of landlord and tenant, however, comes within the scope of my present essay.

There is good reason to believe that the old landlord class habitually oppressed their tenantry, and the various exactions, such as cuttings, cosher-

[7] Frowde to Williamson. C.S.P. Ire. 1669/70, p.197. See also *London Gazette*, 18 July, 1670.
[8] An account of this murder is given in a pamphlet published in Dublin in 1681, a copy of which is in the Royal Irish Academy, Box 94, Tract 11. References to the capture of Tories for reward are too numerous to be given. That in *Analecta Hibernica*, No. 15, p.286 may be mentioned here because it deals with the apprehension by a Major Cavanagh of a man named Cavanagh, though their relationship is not specified.

ing, coyne and livery, customary under the Brehon system, would have been as burdensome as the rack-renting practised by their successors, whose system Professor Curtis describes as " English landlordism without its better features,"⁹ had it not been for the human element in their relationship.¹⁰ This was absent later, though even then, of course, there were notable exceptions. The pitiless exposure by Arthur Young in his *Tour* of the irresponsible and selfish drones of the eighteenth century, or by Dutton in his *Survey of Co. Clare* a few years later, can be set off to some extent by the humane conduct and just dealing of landlords like Richard Edgeworth.

There was ample and ever-increasing justification for the Irish peasantry hating their social superiors, and that many did so can be seen from the bitter satires of the eighteenth century Irish poets, of which none is more justly famous than that of Seán Clárach mac Domhnaill on the death of Col. Dawson of Aherlow.¹¹

The feelings expressed in that poem can be paralleled, though less bitingly and less trenchantly uttered,¹² in the seventeenth century too. The poems of David O'Bruadair are full of invectives against the purse-proud upstarts who were in possession of the finest estates in the country ; but always there is the suggestion expressed or

⁹ Curtis, *History of Ireland*, p.264.
¹⁰ Dr. H. R. McAdoo, in an unpublished essay on *Pairlemint Chloinne Tomáis* which I have been privileged to read, stresses the distinction between the small tenants and the purely menial labouring class who felt no loyalty to the Gaelic aristocracy and even looked upon Cromwell as a deliverer.
¹¹ *Amhráin Sheagháin Chláraigh mhic Dhomhnaill*, ed. Dinneen, Dublin, 1902, p. 51.
¹² This qualification cannot be applied to Egan O'Rahilly who, born in 1670, may be regarded as a product of the 17th century, though his bitterest outburst, that written on the death of Turlough Griffin, was composed about 1725. His most scurrilous effort, written about 1699, hardly equals in abusive power the lampoon of Domhnall na Tuile which occasioned it.

implied, that it is not the social system with its
class distinctions which is inveighed against, but
the intrusion of the foreigner with his unaristo-
cratic, un-Irish ways : the underlying sentiment
throughout is praise and regret for the good old
aristocratic days as much as dislike of the new order ;
and we may remark that the traditional devotion
of the tenants to the gentry was to some extent
transferred to the new landlords, at any rate when
they were inclined to adopt a more or less Irish
outlook on life, as a certain number of them did.

Several of Carolan's poems are in praise of
Protestant newcomers with names like Peyton,
Jones and Cooper ; though it is only right to add
that in such cases there is a somewhat perfunctory
air about his eulogies, and they sound hollow
compared with those which were obviously inspired
by something deeper than self-interest.   Egan
O'Rahilly, on the other hand, was quite whole-
hearted in his praise of one Warner :

" Ceannasach séimh glan sughach,

Do bhí san mbaile gheal aosta chlúmhail,

Flaith nár bh'fhann roimh dheoruidhe,"

and there is no hint of saire in his description of the
" hospitable mansion of the Munster Protestant,"
John Blennerhassett.[13]

The actual relationship between the " Big House"
and its surrounding tenantry retained for a long
time, at least on the part of the tenants, and
particularly of the servants and retainers,[14] something of the warmth which had characterized it in
old times, and which was still very much in evidence

[13] *Dánta Aodhagáin uí Rathaille* (Irish Texts), pp.40 and 205.
[14] For an interesting account of the numerous officials and retainers in the
household of a sixteenth century Irish Chief, see *Dublin University Magazine*,
Vol. 53, p.463, *et seq.*

in the period we are specially considering. There is abundant evidence of the affection and loyalty of the people at that time to the families which should have been their natural leaders and coun-sellors. O'Bruadair lived to see the great but gradual change which took place in the character of the Irish aristocracy, as step by step it ceased to be either Irish or Old-English (as the contemporary phrase has it), and became, what it has remained until recently, something alien and superimposed, regarding the native population as " native " in the modern colonial sense.

In the period of transition, while many of the old families still existed side by side with those newcomers who eventually almost entirely sup-planted them, we are not surprised to come across such observations as this : " the Gentry (for the most part) are extracted from very ancient families, who are adored by the commonalty ; and to give them their due are good natur'd gentlemen, exceed-ing free, and courteous to strangers and extra-ordinary generous in their entertainments " ; and again in the same book : " The commonalty are extremely awed by their superiors, in such sort, a tenant fears as much to speak against a lord of the manor, or their next powerful neighbour, as wise men would dread to speak treason against a prince under whose allegiance he lives and hath sworn to.[15] And I have heard say that some of them will swear and forswear anything that may tend to the benefit of that landlord from whom he hath any dependence and think it no great crime."[16] These passages were written in 1674.

[15] Cf. Rich. *A Short Survey of Ireland*, p.3, and Lawrence, *Interest of England in the Irish Transplantation*, p.23.
[16] *The Western Wonder*, pp.24 and 33.

I think it is hardly necessary to labour this point by further quotations from contemporary sources. No doubt the attitude of mind indicated was at least partly responsible for the ease with which peasant girls allowed themselves to be seduced by men of the landlord class. In this connexion I would refer the reader to the passage already quoted in the previous chapter.[17]

The description of Co. Kildare in 1683, from which it is taken, is given in Appendix A. That valuable document refers to a variety of interesting aspects of country life, and its author imparts to it a human touch usually absent from such reports. The methods of farming at the time were rudimentary : Irish live stock as a whole was inferior to English, very little hay was made,[18] and permanent fences and enclosures were few ; superstitious customs in connexion with dairies and cattle were observed everywhere ; but the farmers were not as inefficient as is often suggested.[19] Backward though they were in many respects, they were able to supply practically all the requirements of the home market and in normal years to have also some surplus available for export. There was no lack of energy and resourcefulness in the way in which the staggering blow dealt to Irish agriculture by the British Cattle Acts was met and, after a short time, even turned to the advantage of the producer. While hardly coming within the scope of a purely social history, these Acts did affect the daily avocations of large numbers of people in

[17] p.54.
[18] See Rawdon to Conway, C.S.P. I. 1663/65, pp.458, 533, 537 ; Bagwell III., p.78, etc.
[19] See p. 38 *supra*.

Ireland.[20] A very clear exposition of their nature and the effects they had will be found in Appendix J, a perusal of which will also throw some light on the system of farming in vogue at the time.[21]

Another interesting reference in the manuscript under consideration is to the division and sub-division of properties. This practice later became an abuse and produced the most uneconomic congestion in one class and poverty and debt in the other. The tenants known to this writer were evidently industrious and intelligent, if lacking in technical agricultural knowledge. Yet tenants were punctual in the payment of their rents. Indeed, it has always been noted by historians that the Irish were readier to pay high rents than English tenants, and so were able, in spite of regulations to the contrary, to procure the occupation of the greater part of the land for themselves ; and no doubt, in the circumstances, they were always anxious not to fall into arrears in order to ensure as far as possible the security, or at least the continuance, of their tenure. I do not, however, want to pursue this subject which would lead me into a field already covered by historians and economists.

The Irish gentry, we are told, were hospitable, courteous and generous, and it is not surprising to find these qualities accompanied by a corresponding weakness : they shared with all other sections of the people, except the merchants of the towns, the reputation of being very improvident. I mentioned

---

[20] Large numbers of Irish people were employed in the woollen industry, but its discouragement, or rather its deliberate ruin, which had such far-reaching and disastrous results belongs rather to the eighteenth than to the seventeenth century, even though the first steps to that end were taken some years before its close and in due course were implemented in the Prohibition Act of 1698.

[21] See also Chapter VI.

Chancery Bills and Exchequer Bills earlier in this chapter. Those that have come specially under my own notice provide the most striking example of the improvidence and litigiousness of the ordinary country gentleman ; and in going through them I had the interesting experience of unfolding the gradual reduction of a typical Catholic country gentleman, one William MacLysaght, my own direct ancestor in County Clare, who having been possessed of a considerable estate in 1672, was " brought to penury " in 1698. His improvidence, or rather that of his son in this case, was carried to such lengths that in 1709, while his impoverished old father was still alive, he sold his right of reversion in all the Clare property for £20 in cash, £10 payable on 1st May, 1710, 50/- a year " and a nag."[22] His folly on this occasion, which was perhaps understandable in view of the fact that the estate had already been overburdened by the old man with mortgages and encumbrances, was more than equalled by that of another young Irish, or in this case Anglo-Irish gentleman, John Edgeworth, who, when short of cash one day, " actually sold the ground plot of a house in Dublin to purchase a high-crowned hat and feathers, which was then the mode."[23] This incident occurred in 1665 and may be regarded as quite typical of the almost comic improvidence of the Irish gentry at the time.

The generally accepted picture of the hospitable, feckless, hard-drinking, fearless, fox-hunting, fire-eating Irish landlord, which is probably no caricature, belongs properly to the eighteenth century, but

[22] Exchequer Bill (Ans.), 5th Nov., 1709, and Reg. of Deeds Office, Vol. III., p.269, No. 913.
[23] *Memoirs of R. L. Edgeworth*, p.6.

the type was already by no means uncommon in the reign of Charles II. Arthur Young tells us that the country squireen of his day was the only survival of the traditional swashbuckling Irishman,[24] which seems to suggest that the original must have been in existence at least a hundred years before ; though, incidentally, I do not know how he could overlook bucks of the Hell Fire Club type, who were certainly not squireens and unquestionably were swash-bucklers. The duels, which were an everyday occurrence in their lives, were common enough, too, in Restoration Ireland, and the results were often fatal : frequent reference is to be found to them in the State Papers of that reign and the consequences were such that before long it was considered necessary to issue orders that officers engaging in duels should be cashiered.[25] While it can hardly be termed a duel, since the weapon of one participant was a " great unwieldy cane," and of the other a pocket knife, an incident is described in one of the earliest newspapers ever published in Ireland which illustrates the undisciplined life of the upper classes. One Nicholas Fitzgerald repudiates the charge of " Sir Toby Butler," as he calls Mr. Theobald Butler, Counsellor at Law, who had accused him of attempting to assassinate him. He says that Butler was the " aggressor and hot-headed after a whole night's debauch at the London Tavern in Waterford." This announcement appeared in the form of an advertisement inserted by Fitzgerald, and it is worth noting that the printer got into trouble for publishing it.[26] From the names of the persons

---

[24] *Tour* (ed. Hutton), Vol. II., p.153.
[25] C.S.P. Dom. 1702/03, p.651.
[26] *Dublin Intelligence*, No. 128, April 13, 1693, and *ibid.*, No. 130.

concerned, they seem to have belonged to the Irish nation, or at least not to the new English whose unpolished manners so much incensed O'Bruadair.

Bad manners, indeed, were no part of the make-up of the Irish gentry. On the contrary, Ireland has ever been famed for the courtesy of her people, an attribute by no means confined to the educated, or supposedly educated, classes, and the civility of the peasantry, as well as the courtesy of the gentry, is frequently noticed by travellers.[27]

In noting their courtesy to strangers, the writer from whom I quoted on page 87 was referring particularly to the gentry of ancient Irish families. The " Big House " was in the latter half of the seventeenth century a feature not only of the landscape but also of the social system. The Big House, however, might be either Irish or alien in character according to its location or the race and inclinations of its owner. Thus practically all those in the six northern counties,[28] the greater part of which was so successfully planted by James I, were alien. They were in fact less Irish than similar houses are to-day, for they were occupied either by quite recent settlers or by families whose tendency to become assimilated with the Irish, if such ever existed, was extinguished by the events of 1641 ; nowadays, the Big House in the north, if not Irish in the southern conception of the meaning of the word, is certainly not English, except where it is occupied only at intervals by a family whose headquarters are across the Irish Sea. In Connacht, on the other hand, and in most of

[27] For a very striking but no doubt exaggerated example of rustic good manners, see anecdote quoted by Rev. James Graves in Dineley's *Observations*, p. 56, note.
[28] These, of course, were not the same as what are now usually termed " The Six Counties," as they included Counties Donegal (Tyrconnell) and Cavan.

Clare, excluding the one-mile belt,[29] the alien Big House would have been an exception.

Since the " Big House " is under consideration at the moment, it would be well perhaps, before we proceed to study the character and occupations of its inmates more in detail, to devote some pages to a brief description of those houses themselves and of those which sheltered the poorer sections of the population.

It is on this subject that the *Observations* of Thomas Dineley are particularly valuable to us, writing as he did in 1681 ; for, while his comments on the manners and customs of the people are often perfunctory and sometimes evidently not the result of personal experience, his numerous descriptions of inhabited dwellings are enhanced by his habit of illustrating them with quite excellent drawings. It is true that these are illustrations of castles and gentle-men's country seats, but their value in helping us to visualize the houses of the period is not confined to " Big Houses " alone because adjacent rural cottages or village streets are often included incidentally. Unfortunately Dineley's tour, in which he covered a great part of the South of Ireland during his twelve months' sojourn in the country, did not bring him to the house of any native Irish gentleman of the old school. All his hosts were Protestants and nearly all of English blood. Some, however, particularly in County Clare, the most remote part of the country visited by Dineley, were obviously places taken

[29] The Cromwellian Settlement, under which certain Catholic landowners were transplanted to Clare and Connacht, provided that a belt of four miles along the coast line should be left for Protestant settlers. This provision was, of course, a dead letter so far as the wild Atlantic coast was concerned, but it did operate along the shore of the Shannon estuary west of Limerick. Even there, however, the area of this reserved land was much reduced by making it one mile wide instead of four.

over by planters from old Irish owners: as, for example, Ballycar Castle and Ballyluddane, renamed about that time Mount Ivers, and still so called.

There is little difficulty in picturing that type of gentleman's country house which consisted of little more than one of the old square keeps whose ruins are still to be seen throughout Ireland, especially in Munster. One of these, Lohort Castle, built at the beginning of the thirteenth century, was in occupation as a gentleman's house up till our own times.[30] I remember calling there once as a boy and taking particular note of the way in which the accommodation was laid out. The ground floor consisted of a huge kitchen, which comprised larder, scullery and pantry, and was the only place available for the servants, whether on or off duty. The winding staircase led up to the dining-room on the first floor. All the furniture, except quite small pieces, in this and other upstairs apartments had to be made inside the rooms themselves, the narrow stairway and narrower windows making it impossible to bring in from outside anything like a table or press. In modern times an additional building near the castle, but not communicating with it, provided sleeping accommodation for most of the occupants, so that the second floor was not required for this purpose and was divided into two sitting-rooms, leaving only the top-storey for bedrooms.

This arrangement was quite common in Dineley's time: in some the additional accommodation was built on to the original castle as in the case of Ross

[30] Monanimy, too, a square keep near Castletownroche, Co. Cork, is to this day used as a dwelling-house, the present owner being Miss Barry. (Burned out since this note was written and no longer inhabited).

Derryhivenny Castle, Co. Galway.

D: O'M ME· FIERI: FECIT 1643

(*Reproduced from "Irish Castles" by courtesy of the author,*
Mr. Harold G. Leask, M.R.I.A., and of the publishers, M. W. Tempest, Dundalk.)

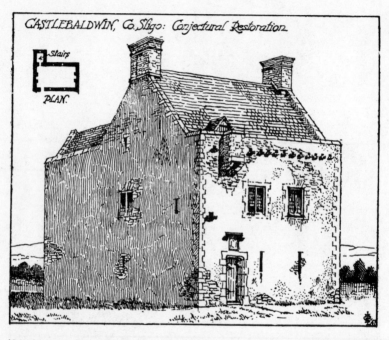

CASTLEBALDWIN, Co. Sligo: Conjectural Restoration.

STAIRS
PLAN.

(My thanks are due to Mr. Harold G. Leask. M.R.I.A., for the drawing reproduced above.)

Castle which was finished in 1688[31] and, though rendered uninhabitable soon after as a result of military occupation its shell is still to be seen by visitors to Killarney—as a rule there was internal communication with it, as in the case of Clonroad and Ballyclogh Castles in County Clare, and Ballingarde in County Limerick ; in others, as at Ralahine (County Clare), they were detached from the old building. These additions varied from an imposing structure, with three storeys and a modern hall-door, incorporating the old castle as part of what amounted to almost a new house—such was the case at Ballyclogh—to a mere couple of rooms as at Ralahine. It is worth noting that the accommodation for the horses (and perhaps the grooms) at Ralahine, " now in the hands of Giles Vandaleur, Esq., who hath built unto it the fairest stable of the county," was much more of an architectural achievement than that provided for the surplus occupants of the castle itself.[32]

Another type of house was that where the original castle, though perhaps part of it still remained intact, was no longer distinguishable, the new building which superseded it being of a consistent style throughout. Ballykitt, near Kilrush, was a good example of this. Dineley says : " it was anciently a castle but reduced to what it is by Henry Hickman, Esq." His sketch of the building so " reduced " shows a most substantial country house, having a central door, on each side of which are three large windows, and on the first storey

[31] *Kenmare MSS.*, p.404.
[32] The use and adaptation of castles as dwelling-houses in the changed conditions of the seventeenth century is fully dealt with by H. G. Leask in his *Irish Castles* published since the first edition of this book was written. He describes the second half of the century as, architecturally speaking, a featureless gap. *Op. cit.*, p.150.

seven of similar size, while the rather high-pitched roof is broken by a number of dormer windows and the whole is topped by three nicely proportioned chimneys. This house may therefore have contained as many as sixteen good rooms as well as anything up to fourteen attic bedrooms. At the time, of course, it would have been regarded as a modern country house and was quite unlike the mansions of the native Irish gentry, among whom we may include nearly all the old Norman-Irish families, and indeed some of those who came over in Elizabethan times and became hibernicized.

Though well-known men like William Robinson, who is said to have designed the magnificent Royal Hospital at Kilmainham,[33] were doing fine work at the time there were few professional architects and the country gentleman who employed one was a rare exception.[34] The landlords of the seventeenth century were their own architects and with the help of their agents and intelligent tradesmen they built what they wanted with every few plans or drawings. Whenever building was of sufficient importance to be done in stone it was solid and unhurried. Dr. Arthur's house in Limerick took three years to complete and the additions and alterations, for which a special limekiln was set up on the site, occupied workmen from June 1645 to September 1649.[35]

[33] J. R. S. A. I. Vol. LIII., p.101. According to Childers and Stuart, *Royal Hospital*, p.13, it was designed by Sir Christopher Wren, being begun in 1684 and finished, except the steeple, in 1684, at a cost of £24,000. Robinson was the architect who carried out the work.

[34] Prof. Maxwell ascribes Beaulieu, Co. Louth, to Sir Christopher Wren (*Country and Town in Ireland under the Georges*, p.32). Carnelly, Co. Clare, and Eyrecourt, Co. Galway, are cited (*ibidem* p.73) as fine examples of seventeenth century houses still standing and inhabited but there is no mention of an architect's name. Carnelly, however, was probably built early in the eighteenth century.

[35] Arthur MS. (B.M. Addl. 31885) fo. 239-241.

Even the most modern houses at that time, though often expensively and elaborately furnished,[36] and comparatively clean and comfortable, possessed few of the conveniences now regarded as essentials, and modern methods of sanitation were of course undreamt of. Indeed even to-day there are country houses of some standing which are without a bath-room ; and I know one " Big House " where the water supply is obtained to-day, as it was 300 years ago, by the diversion of a small stream which runs in a cascade through a wide sink in the kitchen, where a continuous flow of fresh water is thus provided.

Personal cleanliness, as is well known, was not considered essential even amongst people of refine-ment who were otherwise particular in their habits. There is little direct evidence on the point in regard to Ireland. Dunton makes some contemptuous references to the filthy condition of the lower orders, but the inhabitants of crowded cabins can hardly be regarded as particularly barbarous on account of their lousiness in an age when an Englishman of standing like Samuel Pepys was not ashamed to own that he often found lice in his wig. As for baths, many prominent people in the best society thought nothing of going a couple of months without taking

[36] The pages of Mrs. Freke's Diary (see Chap. VIII., note 14) contain many interesting details regarding furniture and household matters. Various contemporary inventories, such as those printed in Hickson's *Ireland in the Seventeenth Century* (Vol. II., p.97) in *Orrery Papers*, p.108 *et seq.*, in H.M.C. Ormonde MSS, N.S. VII pp. 497-527,
give a good idea of the richness of the beds, carpets, hangings, etc., in upper-class Anglo-Irish houses, while the poems of O'Bruadair and O'Rahilly testify that those of the Irish aristocracy were not devoid of a certain magni-ficence. Dr. Thomas Arthur's Journal contains many entries which show that the well-to-do professional classes were no less given to spending money on household effects. In the list of the goods which he left in the custody of his wife in Limerick, specially noteworthy are numerous utensils for home brewing and distilling, including a brass " kettle " weighing four cwt. able to contain a hogshead of liquor, and a huge brass pan in which a whole quarter of beef could be boiled. (Arthur MS., fo. 250).

one. In the detailed inventory of household goods at Castlemartyr made in 1677 the only bath mentioned is a " bathing tub " stowed away in a back room with broken furniture and boxes of papers.[37] Even in France, where the Court of Louis XIV set an example of refinement to the world, the habit of bathing the whole body in the modern way did not become customary until the last decade of the seventeenth century, though the general fondness for outdoor bathing and swimming to a certain extent compensated for this, at least in the summer months. In winter, at any rate, the liberal use of perfumes did not succeed in overcoming the stronger scent of unwashed bodies.[38] In Mazarin's time fashionable people did not always wash even their faces every day. The gallants of the period are advised in a contemporary booklet, *Lois de la Galanterie*, " d'aller quelquefois chez les baigneurs pour avoir le corps net ; de prendre la peine de se laver les mains tous les jours et le visage presque aussi souvent."[39]

It is a matter for regret that we can glean so few architectural details from O'Bruadair's frequent eulogies of the mansions of his patrons, who it is hardly necessary to say were not of the planter class (and even less from those of O'Rahilly), but only a general impression of a kind of rough magnificence—

" Sinistreach seomrach sómplach seanta

brothallach bruidhneach bíomach beannach,"[40]

palatial luxury, spacious rooms, beams, turrets :

[37] *Orrery Papers*, p.174.

[38] G. F. Bradby, *The Great Days of Versailles* (London, 1906) p.60. Among the unpleasant features of seventeenth century life described in this book the prevalence of bugs in summer, even in the beds of people in high society, may be mentioned.

[39] Quoted by Racinet, *Le Costume Historique*, Vol. V., Section D.U. (This work is not paged).

[40] *Dúanaire.*, Part I., p.166.

how often he stimulates our imaginations with his vivid pictures of Cahirmoyle, Gortnatubred and other Big Houses, but always when we bring the prosaic faculties of the architectural engineer to bear on his words we are left vague and unsatisfied.[41]

Evidently these spacious and palatial places cannot have been mere square keeps even with additional wings such as I have already described. Probably the interior of one of the exceptionally large structures of that type, such as Bunratty Castle, would have been spacious enough to justify O'Bruadair and his bardic predecessors in their grandiloquence. Dineley made a drawing of this castle which shows it as more extensive than one would expect from looking at the present remains. Here, too, were additional buildings of considerable size.

Among Dineley's illustrations we find a very modern-looking house at O'Brien's Bridge, one of the residences of the Earl of Inchiquin. It somewhat resembles Ballykitt, though more picturesque and less gaunt in outline. In fact, the study of Dineley's drawings must convince the student that, if housing in general was not what we would call up-to-date in the twentieth century, there were a great many more decent, comfortable, well-constructed country houses in Ireland in the last quarter of the seventeenth century than is generally imagined. Clarendon remarked about this time that " within little more than two years . . . were many buildings raised for beauty as well as use, orderly and regular plantations of trees, and fences and enclosures

---

[41] Prof. O'Brien states that up to the middle of the seventeenth century timber was the usual material employed in building Irish houses. *Economic History of Ire. in XVII Century*, p.44.

raised throughout the Kingdom ".[42] Not only does Dineley show many of the Big Houses as I have described, but the inns, and often even the cottages, are well-built and as a rule have chimneys. The village of Staplestown, in County Carlow, is very spick and span, and quite unlike our present idea of an Irish village, much less one 250 years ago. However, in this case, the names of the landlord of the Crown Inn, with its hanging sign, and of the tenants of all the comfortable houses occupied by the various tradesmen—carpenter, " shoomaker," farrier, etc., even of the man who was both " taylor and victualler "—are English without exception ; and Dineley tells us they were all Protestants, so we can imagine them as the specially favoured dependants of Sir Wm. Temple, who, though no longer resident in Ireland when Dineley visited Staplestown, was a good example of a landlord of the " ascendancy " type.

In the County Wexford about the same time the mansion houses of most gentlemen in the Barony of Forth were " fortified with castles of quadrangle form, some sixty feet high with walls five feet thick," and we are told that not many of these were ruinous.

The same contemporary authority tells us that their houses were built with stone walls, having spacious halls, in the centre of which, according to the ancient mode, were open fire hearths. He adds that these were now antiquated, all more recently built houses having chimneys.[43]

It would be a mistake to assume that the dwellings of the poorer people at this time were usually without chimneys, at any rate in the less remote parts of

[42] Quoted by Macaulay in his Essay on Temple.
[43] MS. T.C.D., I.1.2, p.52.

the country. When Thomas Phillips made his very
elaborate Military Survey he embellished it with
water-colour illustrations which are attractive in
themselves and are at the same time executed with
the meticulous care of a professional engineer. These
represent not only ground plans of harbours, towns
and fortifications, but also take the form of pictures
of towns, some of them little more than villages. In
these, clustered beside the newer stone buildings of
distinctively urban type, are many thatched cottages
which appear to differ in no respect from the
ordinary single storey whitewashed thatched house
still common throughout rural Ireland ; and in all
his illustrations hardly one of these is to be seen
without a chimney. This Survey, which has never
been published, was made in 1685.[44]

The mediæval castles, of course, were provided
with chimneys,[44a] as can be seen from the ruins still
existing, or from Dineley's illustrations, which show
them even on such bleak and formidable fortresses as
Mount Ivers and Knockananeen (how fine sounding
a word compared with its modern equivalent, Bird-
hill) ; indeed, the much criticized system of allowing
the smoke to escape through an aperture in the roof
would only be practicable in a one-storey dwelling.

By way of contrast to some of Dineley's neat and
almost villa-like dwelling-houses, here is a description of the country house of an influential " native",
taken from Moffet's burlesque, which may be
compared with those of John Dunton, given in
Appendix B :

> A house well built, and with much strength,
> Almost two hundred foot in length,
> A house with mountains fortify'd,
> Which in the clouds their heads did hide.

[44] MS. Nat. Lib. No. 660.
[44a] The architectural details are shewn in Leask's *Irish Castles, passim.*

At one of th' ends he kept his cows,
At th' other end he kept his spouse
On bed of straw without least grumble.

. . . . .

And when occasion did require,
In midst of house a mighty fire
Of black dried earth and swinging blocks
Was made, enough to roast an ox ;
From whence arose such clouds of smoke,
As either me or you would choke :
But Gillo and his train inur'd
To smoke, the same with ease endur'd ;
For sitting low on rushes spread,
The smoke still hovered over head ;
And did more good than real harm,
Because it kept the long house warm,
And never made their heads to ache ;
Therefore no chimney he wou'd make.

. . . . .

And thus for smoke, altho' 'twas dear,
He paid four shillings every vear ;[45]
And tho' his wife no muslin wore,
Nor silk, she was all spotted o'er
With new-made ermin, which did fall
From roof of house, and side of wall,
Which was with cow-dung plaister'd round,
With which the house did still abound ;
Yet not so close but that the smoke,
Being long confin'd, thro' crannies broke.

. . . . .

But if perhaps you do admire,
That this great house did ne'er take fire,
Where sparks, as thick as stars in sky,
About the house did often fly,
And reach'd the sapless wither'd thatch,
Which like dry sponge the fire would catch,
And where no chimneys was erected,
Where sparks and flames may be directed ;
St. Bridget's Cross hung over door,
Which did the house from fire secure.

. . . . .

Directly under Bridget's Cross
Was firmly nail'd the shoe of horse
On threshold, that the house might be
From witches, thieves, and devils free . . .[46]

[45] An allusion, of course, to the tax known as hearth-money.
[46] *The Irish Hudibras* (1755 edn.), pp.5-7.

After describing the fare[47] served up at the gargantuan meal provided for the inmates of the house and their guests, Moffet goes on :

> Of rushes there was benches made,
> On which the meat was partly laid :
> But all the mutton that was sing'd,
> Was laid on doors that were unhing'd ;
> So that we may truly say,
> Gillo kept open house that day.
> The rest was placed in stately sort
> On planks which firkins did support :
> As for the guests, when grace was said,
> And all in Latin tongue had pray'd,
> Some ran to this, some ran to that,
> And what they catch'd they thereon sat ;
> Some sat on stones, some sat on blocks,
> Some sat on churns . . .
>
> .   .   .   .   .
>
> The brisk young sparks, with their kind wenches
> Did place themselves on rushy benches.

The use of rushes to cover the floors, and even in place of beds,[48] was very common and was not confined to that great majority of the Irish people who, according to Petty, lived " in a brutish, nasty condition as in cabins with neither chimney, door, stairs nor windows."[49] Fynes Moryson's description of lousy feather beds and the want of any beds at all is too well known to bear repetition, but another less frequently quoted traveller, practically a contemporary of Moryson's, the Spaniard, Capt. Cuellar, says : " they sleep upon the ground on rushes, newly cut and full of water and ice."[50] This, however, was in war-time, when it was the custom of the chiefs " to withdraw themselves to the mountains with their women and cattle." Let us advance half a century and come nearer to our own special

---

[47] It would not be out of place to deal here with such matters as diet, hours of meals, and so on, but to do so would make this chapter entirely too long and the subject must be postponed till later. (See Chapter VIII).

[48] See page 66 *et seq. supra*, on sleeping accommodation.

[49] *Political Anatomy*, p.30.

[50] Capt. Cuellar's *Narrative* (Translated by Robert Crawford), p.62.

period. Le Gouz's description of the houses of the
nobility might well fit any of these square keeps
whose ruins are one of the most striking features of
the Irish countryside.   Having emphasized the
darkness of the interiors, due to the narrow windows which in his time were still sometimes needed
for the better defence of the castle, he goes on to tell
us that they contained little furniture, presumably for
the reason already noticed in my remarks on Lohort
Castle : " They cover their rooms with rushes of
which they make beds in summer," but in winter
straw was used for this purpose. The rushes were
often a foot deep on the floors and on the window
sills.   The ceilings, he tells us, were frequently
ornamented with branches. Describing " houses in
the country " other than those of the nobility and
gentry, he writes : " Two stakes are fixed in the
ground across which is a transverse pole to support
two rows of rafters on the two sides, which are
covered with leaves and straw. The cabins are of
another fashion. There are four walls the height of a
man, supporting rafters over which they thatch
with straw and leaves. They are without chimneys
and make the fire in the middle of the hut, which
greatly incommodes those who are not fond of
smoke." I take the former to have been the temporary summer dwelling of people who did not
belong to the poorest class. Rudimentary though
such places appear to have been, they were not, as
Le Gouz makes clear,[51] the cabins alluded to by
Petty.

Three of the authorities from whom I have
frequently quoted in this book, Richard Head, John

[51] *Tour*, pp.40 and 42. Le Gouz mentions that the towns were built in the
English fashion.   I omit all reference to towns here, as I shall be dealing
with urban life in a separate chapter.

Dunton and John Stevens, have left very vivid pictures of those cabins[52] and, though these passages have been several times printed in full or in part, I think it would be more interesting to give them here verbatim than to summarize them in my own words :
" The cots are generally built on the side of a hill, not to be discerned till you just come upon them. The cottage is usually raised three feet from the eaves to the ground on the one side, and the other side hath a rock for a wall to save charges, in regard carriage is dear and money but scarce especially to such who never see it but once in seven years . . . . The hearth is placed in the middle of the house and their fuel is made of earth and cow-dung dried in the sun,[53] The smoke goes through no particular place, but breaks through every part between the rods and the wattles[54] of which they make their doors, sides, and roof of the house, which commonly is no bigger than an overgrown pigstye, to which they have two doors, one always shut, on that side where the wind blows ; from whence I believe it is that they brag they have the quickest architects in the world,[55] because they can build a house in a day."[56] Here is what John Stevens said on the subject in his *Journal* fifteen years later : " In the

[52] For other descriptions of the same kind see Gernon, *Discourse* (p.355 in Falkiner's *Illustrations*) ; Lithgow, *Travels*, p.429 : Campbell, *Philosophical Survey*, p.146, etc.
[53] Turf, however, was in general use by this time. Cf. Petty, *Political Anatomy*, p.82 : " Their fuel is turf in most places ; and of late, even where wood is most plentiful, and to be had for nothing the cutting and carriage of the turf being more easy than that of wood." Evans (*Irish Heritage*, p.42), says with truth that furze was much used for fuel as well as for fodder.
[54] According to Campbell (*Philosophical Survey of the South of Ireland*, p.146) they sometimes had a hole in the roof to let out the smoke. Cf. remarks on p.68, note 58 ; the passage here referred to is also given by Philip Luckombe on page 163 of his book.
[55] In a County Tipperary lease of 1695 permission is given to the tenant " to carry the dwelling house he now lives in " to his new holding provided it be done within nine weeks of the date of the deed. Bowen Papers. *Analecta Hibernica* No. 15, p.13.
[56] *The Western Wonder*, p.29.

better sort of cabins there is commonly one flock bed, seldom more, feathers being too costly ; this serves the man and his wife, the rest all lie on straw, some with one sheet and blanket, others only their clothes and blanket to cover them. The cabins seldom have any floor but the earth, or rarely so much as a loft, some have windows, others none. They say it is of late years that chimneys are used, yet the house is never free from smoke."[57] Dunton describes the accommodation and method of construction in detail in one of his letters.

The cow, the sheep and the hens were brought into the cabin at nights, not so much for shelter, but rather for safety. Cattle and live stock generally were liable to be carried off by thieves or attacked by dogs, or even wolves,[59] while foxes were numerous and a danger to poultry.[60] Add to this the fact that well-fenced fields were rare and animals not under the eye of their owner might stray away of their own accord, even if not interfered with by ill-disposed persons.

This practice among the poor had its counterpart in the custom of driving in all the live stock at nights into the bawn which usually surrounded castles and the old-fashioned country houses of the gentry.[61] Even in Dineley's illustrations of quite modern dwelling-houses an enclosure surrounded by a strong stone wall is nearly always shown around or beside them, but there is nothing to indicate whether these represented the up-to-date counterpart of the old

[57] *Op. cit.*, p.139.

[59] It is stated in the " terrier " attached to the Down Survey Map of Ballybay (Offaly) that few sheep were kept in that barony on account of the prevalence of wolves there. *Analecta Hibernica* No. 8, p.423.

[60] See Chapter V., p.135.

[61] For an interesting and scholarly article on bawns, see Journal of the Ulster Archaeological Society, Vol. VI., p.125.

bawn or merely a space devoted to gardening of some kind. Dineley himself is silent on the point. Molyneux noted some fine pleasure grounds in his travels, particularly in Co. Kilkenny and the adjacent counties.[62] Gardens, however, were at this time not considered an essential adjunct to a country house of importance, and were the luxury of the leisured few—such as Sir Wm. Temple and Lord Lanesborough—rather as green-houses and conservatories might be regarded nowadays.[63] Orchards appear to have been fairly common, the neighbourhood of Kilkenny again being the most up-to-date in this respect.[64] Archbishop Oliver Plunket's house had an orchard attached to it, and when Dr. James Stritch was appointed parish priest of Rathkeale, in Co. Limerick, about 1679, he found that a well-kept garden went with it.[65] Regular kitchen gardens were more usual with houses situated in towns, not only in a single street

[62] MS. T.C.D. I. 1. 3, pp.72-129.

[63] The cultivation of named varieties of fruit trees was practised as early as the seventeenth century and a few of these, in spite of the improvements effected by modern scientific crossing, have survived to the present day. e.g., the May Duke cherry and the Bellegarde peach. The family papers which I examined during my three years as inspector for the Irish Manuscripts Commission contain a fair number dealing with horticulture. The following taken from a collection examined subsequent to the publication of my reports in *Analecta Hibernica, The Kenmare MSS.*, etc., is a typical example.

Lane Papers (briefly referred to in *Analecta Hib.* No. 15) under date 1687. " Directions how to rayse ye caine aple by seeds otherwis called the Irish strawberry tree or arbutus. Take ye berrys w^h they are ripe and put y^m in a box close covered for fear of mice & w^h they have lain til ye beginning of March y^u wash y^m & take all & drye y^m at ye sun, winnowe them that ye light stuf be cleansed, then pick ye little bowls that y^u will find & in y^m lyes ye seeds wch y^u must save in ye fattest earth y^u can gett, put ye earth in a case or box & keep it in a shady place & ye seeds will com up."

[64] References to the prevalence of orchards around Kilkenny are to be found frequently earlier in the century, e.g., in Luke Gernon's *Discourse* and in Brereton's *Travels* (printed in Falkiner's *Illustrations*, pp.369, 371, 384). Rawdon, always a pioneer in rural development, often mentions the planting of apple trees in his letters. In the 17th century, as in the 20th, Holland was famous for her nurseries, and we read of fruit trees being imported into Ireland from that country. (C.S.P. I. 1666/69, p.693 ; Journal of Rev. R. Davies, 1689, p.33 ; etc. See also *Analecta Hibernica*, No. 15, p.157.)

[65] Fitzgerald's *Narrative of the Popish Plot*, quoted Begley, *Diocese of Limerick*, Vol. II., p.489.

such as Rathkeale, but even in a large city like Dublin. Out in the country people rarely attempted more than a small plot of cabbages, cultivated in the acre or half acre devoted to tillage on the ordinary tenant's holding.

As the century drew to a close landowners and their agents began to give some attention to the art of forestry which, while the natural woods of the country were still plentiful,[66] had not concerned them. The Government, too, realized its importance and as early as 1654 a regular forestry service was established in the Counties of Wexford and Wicklow where a head wood-reeve was appointed with four assistants and a clerk, this being subsequently extended to Cos. Carlow and Kildare,[67] and supplemented by a Royal Order in 1661 regulating the felling and use of timber in the woods of Shillelagh.[68] Later in the century the principle of compulsory planting of trees in certain cases was introduced.[69]

The squalid congestion of the cabin and the comparatively clean discomfort of the castle can be easily imagined. In the seventeenth century men lived much out of doors ; hunting, shooting, the supervision of the work going on on their estates and the long time occupied in travelling over bad roads when going to visit friends, or to the nearest town,

[66] The old forests still provided much timber for commerical purposes. Details of the large quantities of staves, hoops, rafters, laths, plough-timber, etc., as well as bark for tanning taken from 1697 to 1699 from the old woods of Barlone, in the barony of Bantry, Co. Cork, are given in *Kenmare MSS.*, p.390. Petty states that the uses of timber in Ireland were : 1, for fuel for iron-works ; 2, for fences ; 3, for shelter ; 4, for timber for housing and shipping ; 5, for hoops and casks ; 6, for ornament. He estimated that the woods of Ireland might, with the help of Norwegian imports, last some 50 years from that date (1673). *Petty Papers*, Vol. II., p.126.
[67] J.R.S.A.I., Vol. XXIII., p.274.
[68] C.S.P.I., 1660 /62, p.429.
[69] 18 Wm., III., c.i.   Section 4 of this Act is printed in Falkiner *Illustrations of Irish History*, p.158.

filled up most of their days, and few hours were spent indoors, except during meals or in wet weather perhaps, when there would be guns and rods to be attended to or handy jobs to be done by men who were more at home when using their hands than their intellects. The ordinary country gentleman did not read much, and indeed the lack of artificial light, which was the normal condition after dark, did not encourage even those of them who were at all studiously inclined. There was little to do but sit around the fire, drinking whiskey and talking. The harpers, who were part and parcel of every Big House in earlier times,[70] were almost extinct, and it is little wonder that Carolan was always sure of an audience when he visited the house of one of his patrons, and that O'Bruadair could generally expect a welcome, though he brought nothing with him but some verses of his own composition : not always, however, for he complains that poets are no longer esteemed as they had been—" D'imthigh an éigse i bhfanntais bhrigh "—and that, hanging around the house where formerly he was a welcome guest, he cannot even get a naggin of ale.

While there was a certain amount of intercourse between the gentry of the old stock and those who had acquired their estates as a result of the Cromwellian confiscations, the distinction between them was ever present in the minds of the people. We may regard O'Bruadair's bitter satires on the purse-proud boorish upstarts who usurped the places of their betters as accurately expressing the feelings

---

[70] " You shall find but very few of their gentry, either man or woman, but can play on the harp ; also you shall not find a house of any account without one or two of those instruments and they always keep a harper to play for them at their meals " (circ. 1610). MS. R.I.A. 24 G. 15, p.21.

of the tenantry in general.[71]   Any of them might
well have exclaimed with him :

"   Gach árdmhac uabhair uasamh agus poimp
     Do dháil i mbuaibh's i n-uanaibh geala a
        ghnaoi
     Geadh lánfhada uaidhsean luascadh a dhearc
        dom dhruim
     Ar sráid dá thuar is luath mo hata dhíom."

He himself, of course, was hardly what is called a
peasant poet, as Eoghan Ruadh Ó Súileabháin and
Seán Ó Tuama were in the following century.   As
early as 1674 O'Bruadair found himself reduced by
the circumstances of the time to working for his
living with his hands, but he calls the labourers, with
whom he had to consort, rude, illiterate boors,[72] so
we may assume that they did not appreciate his
literary efforts, though judging from Professor
Corkery's *Hidden Ireland*, there must have been
many of the class who would have done so fifty
years later :   perhaps because by that time so many
of the better sort had descended in the social scale.
Professor O'Brien points out that " there was always
in Ireland a low class of agricultural labourers
who were the menials of the owners of the land,
whether the clan system or the English system
prevailed, and who formed what Dr. Sigerson has
aptly called ' the settled substratum of Irish
society,' " and in 1674 no doubt this class had not
been widely recruited from the ranks of those above
it :   the dispossessed gentry had not yet accepted
the alternative of exile or servitude and, still hoping
for restoration to their former status, preferred to

[71] Cf. even in 1641 : satire on Col. Jones by Turlough O'Connor. MS.
T.C.D. H. I. 17.
[72] See p.85 *supra*, note 10.

become tories or, pathetically preserving their now
useless title-deeds, to live on the charity of those
who had once been their tenants.

Nowhere can we see the change which came over
the countryside as a result of the Cromwellian
settlement better than in the poems of O'Bruadair,
who regrets the passing of so much that was
common in his younger days. Cautiousness or mere
ostentation have displaced hospitality, harp-strings
are untouched and pipes unplayed, the poor are
oppressed and learning is dispersed, the planters
are materialistic in outlook, godless upstarts dese-
crate the shrines of the saints with their gaudy
tombs, old customs are gone, joy and mirth are
fled, dancing is no more and on May-day maidens
no longer muster proudly, a spirit of disunion
infuses the laity and in the churches the chant of
choirs is silenced. Thus we may summarize his
plaint.[73]

This contempt for " upstart " gentry was felt
by Bourchier, who has little in common with
O'Bruadair, twenty years before Cromwell came
to Ireland. That it was not confined to the peasantry
later on, but was shared by men of old family who
still retained their position in society,[74] is aptly
illustrated by the well-known anecdote related by
Boswell. " The few Irish gentlemen yet remaining,
have the highest pride of family ; Mr. Sandford,
a friend of the Doctor's, whose mother was Irish,
told him, that O'Hara, who was true Irish both by
father and mother, and he, and Mr. Ponsonby,
son to the Earl of Besborough, the greatest man of

[73] Egan O'Rahilly witnessed the next step in the disintegration after the
Williamite war, but the burden of his message is very much the same as
O'Bruadair's.
[74] See also p.121 *infra*.

the three, but of an English family, went to see one of these ancient Irish, and that he distinguished them thus, O'Hara you are welcome ! Mr. Sandford, your mother's son is welcome ! Mr. Ponsonby, you may sit down."[75]

Men of influence and position, however, most of whom were of English origin, or had close connexions with England, no doubt regarded gentlemen like that unnamed Gaelic aristocrat as quaint or impossible, according to their outlook on life, mere back-numbers in fact, as we would now regard some old-fashioned relic of the past who considers it demeaning to have any connexion with business or trade.

The old Irish gentry were fast sinking into the position to which they finally fell after the breaking of the Treaty of Limerick, and becoming like the O'Sullivan Beare who is described in 1699 as living at Berehaven " in a cabin at the foot of the hill."[76] I wonder did he, in spite of his reduced circumstances, strive to keep up the traditions of his forbears, as some of his kind did many years after his time. Here is an interesting account of one of them who died not so very much more than 100 years ago and was proud of being one of the last remaining representatives of old families who kept up the traditional hospitality of his class. " He was known only by the name of O'Leary. He lived in a small house, the lower part consisting of little more than parlour and kitchen, the former of which,

[75] *Tour to the Hebrides with Dr. Johnson*, Sept. 28, 1773.
[76] MS. T.C.D. N. 3.20. This MS. contains, as well as the Co. Cork juries' presentments which I have had occasion to cite from time to time, Bishop Downes's account of his diocesan visitation, 1699/1702, and that part of it has been printed in the Journal of the Cork Historical and Archaeological Society for 1908-9. I took the words quoted above from the original manuscript, and was surprised, on comparing the printed version with it, to find that this reference to O'Sullivan Beare is apparently omitted there.

THE FLIGHT OF KING JAMES

(*Reproduced from a well-known contemporary Print*)

THE BOYNE

(This well-known contemporary print of the battle is included here on account of its interest as an illustration of various aspects of Irish life and landscape unconnected with war)

properly supplied with every article of good cheer, was open to every guest, and at every season ; and, what will more surprise, this profusion was accompanied with perfect cleanliness and decorum. His cellar, well stocked with good liquors, never knew the protection of a lock and key ; for, as he said himself, nobody had any occasion to steal what anyone might have for asking. It derived security, however, from other causes ; from deference to his sway and respect for his person, both of which were universally felt within the circle of his influence. He was also a justice of peace for the county. He possessed, indeed, some admirable requisites for a maintainer of the peace ; for he was a very athletic man and always carried a long pole, of which the unruly knew him to be no churl. To these good qualities, O'Leary added an inexhaustible fund of original humour and goodnatured cheerfulness ; and being fond of the bottle himself, it was impossible to be long in his company sad or sober."[77] This will serve as a good picture of a country gentleman of the old school.

Another amusing and well-known anecdote is worth repeating, not only because it is typical of the ready wit of the Irish gentry, but also because it shows that they were not all too proud to turn their hands to trade when dispossessed of their estates. Daniel Byrne, known in Dublin as " Daniel the tailor," was the son of a dispossessed landowner, and taking to business he made a fortune by supplying clothes to the army which he reckoned was the most likely to pay his account. His son, Gregory, was made a baronet at the Restoration. A short time

[77] Townsend, *Statistical Survey of the Co. of Cork*, quoted Hardiman, Vol. I., p.175.

after this, father and son were walking together in Dublin—" Father," said Sir Gregory, " you ought to walk on the left of me, I being a Knight and you but a private individual." " No, you puppy," replied Daniel, " I have the precedency in three ways : first, I am your senior ; secondly, I am your father ; and thirdly, I am the son of a gentleman and you are but the son of a poor lousy tailor."[78]

It is perhaps worth noting in this connexion that a Dublin barber, who dined with Dunton on one occasion, counted himself a gentleman. Dunton himself, though in trade as a bookseller, was the son of a clergyman of respectable family and was related by marriage to many of the English aristocracy. Barbers, of course, were surgeons as well as being hairdressers, and were members of the guild or corporation of barber-chirurgeons.[79]

Hardiman states that it was not unusual for Irish gentlemen of fallen fortune to inculcate maxims of moderation and humility to their families. Of Denis O'Connor, of Balanagare, he says : " This venerable descendant of Irish Kings himself handled the plough [on the farm to which he had been obliged to move from his ancient property] ; observing that although he was the son of a gentleman, they were to consider themselves but as the children of a ploughman."[80] While interesting in itself, I do not think we can regard this as very typical of the mentality of the venerable and dispossessed aristocrats of the period.

We have seen that the attitude of the Irish gentry towards the English newcomers was generally

[78] A full account of this Daniel Byrne is given in Gilbert's *History of Dublin*, Vol. I., pp.157 to 159.
[79] See Chapter VII., note 103.
[80] *Irish Minstrelsy*, Vol. I., p.xliv.

one of contempt, but the influences which in subsequent centuries gradually undermined their national allegiance, and made most of the survivors of their class almost indistinguishable except in name from their supplanters, were already making themselves felt. O'Bruadair complains that men of Gaelic tradition not only aped English ways but even pretended to English origin,[81] and an example of this snobbishness, as we should now call it, is to be found in the very family of whom the anecdote quoted on the previous page is related, for Sir Gregory Byrne's descendants in due course adopted the surname Leicester. Up to 1693 the incentive was little more than mere snobbery, but after that date to remain Gaelic and Catholic was almost tantamount to courting complete ruin.

As I have said there was some intercourse between the old gentry and the new; and in a place like County Clare transplanted Catholic families of standing were no doubt on visiting terms with their Protestant neighbours of the fertile strip beside the Shannon,[82] just as we find in the previous generation Lord Muskerry a frequent guest of the ultra-Protestant Earl of Cork at Youghal and Lismore. But as yet there was little real fusion. Later we find the influences of social position and self-interest gradually weaning the old Catholic families away from their traditional allegiance, so that in my youth the principal props of Protestantism in County Clare were actually men of the old Irish stock : O'Briens, Macnamaras, Crowes, Moloneys, O'Callaghans and Bradys, in whose establishments something of the old tradition of the Big House still lingered.

[81] *Dúanaire* (I. Texts edn.) Part I., p.30.
[82] The " One mile belt " reserved to Protestants under the Cromwellian Settlement. See p.93 *supra*.

The name Crowe does not at first sight suggest a Gaelic origin. During the seventeenth century, however, Irish surnames underwent great changes, particularly in the first half of it. The change over from Irish to English as the language of authority, and especially of the Law[83] was, I think, the main cause of this. The Brehon system was in operation over the greater part of the country until near the end of the sixteenth century. The process began when it became necessary for non-Irish speakers, usually unfamiliar with even the names, to say nothing of the language of the country, to record in legal documents the names of Irish people and places.[84]

My own name is a very good example of the metamorphosis which took place. Thus in sixteenth century and some later documents it appears as McGilleseaghtie, McGillysaghta, McGillysaghtee, to mention only three of many variants, all approximating quite closely to the original Gaelic form. At the beginning of the seventeenth century we see the process of abbreviation and simplification taking place and we find the forms McGillisacht, McLisaght, Gillisaght, and so on, while not infrequently in the transition period alternatives are given, as Lisagh *alias* McGillisagh.[85]   Probably

<hr/>

[83] Though the use of Latin in legal documents was temporarily discontinued under the Cromwellian regime it was not abolished till 1738.

[84] An Act (17/18 Ch. II., c.2) provided that new names of places " liker English " be inserted in grants by patent with an Irish alias, such names thereafter to be the only ones used officially.

[85] Roll of Criminal Cases at Clare Assizes, 24 Jan., 1587, Miscellaneous, Plea Roll, No. 63 ; *ibid.*, 17 Feb., 1592 ; Chancery Bill, 15 May, 1620, etc. ; Fiant No. 568. Elizabeth, 12 Oct., 1563 ; Roll of Criminal Cases at Clare Assizes, 10 Aug., 1601 ; Summonister Roll, No. 17. Clare Quarter Session, 6 Oct., 1625 : (Six weeks earlier, his name then spelt without the final *t*, the same man was fined 40/- " for acquitting a prisoner ") ; *ibid.*, Roll No. 35, Clare Assizes. 15 March, 1637/8 ; and Patent Roll, 3 June, 1610.

few Gaelic names presented more difficulty to English ears.[86]

Orthography in the Irish language has always been fairly exact, but prior to the eighteenth century people were notoriously indifferent to the spelling of English, not only of ordinary words, but even of their own names ; so that a Mr. Fowlue, *alias* Foley, sometimes signed himself Fowler. Leigh might be synonymous with Lye[87] and even Bromley with Brownlow[88]. In the records and documents in English which I have examined over a number of years,[89] I have come across no less than thirty-eight variants of the name McLysaght. While most of these are due to the unfamiliarity of law-clerks and copyists with Irish names, some are simply the result of carelessness, as for example when it appears spelt in three different ways in the same document,[90] or to take another case, when Keating is so far distorted as to be written " Kerther."[91] Thus, too, the good old Clare name of McEnchroe became Crowe and lost in its anglicized guise almost all trace of its original form. In the case of Crowe the essentially Irish prefix *Mac* was permanently discarded, and the same thing occurred with another well-known Clare name which was in the course of the seventeenth century abbreviated to

[86] My reason for using this name as an illustration rather than any other is that to obtain equally fully documented particulars about another surname would have involved a great deal of laborious research far less interesting to myself and of no greater historical value than what I had done in respect of the name McLysaght.

[87] According to H. F. Hore, Leigh or Lye is a corruption of an ancient Gaelic name, also often written Lee. J.R.S.A.I., Vol. IX., p.18.

[88] Hickson, *Ireland in the Seventeenth Century*, Vol. II., p.173n.

[89] Certified abstracts of those lost in the tragic destruction of 1922 have fortunately been preserved and are now in the archives of the Public Record Office, Dublin.

[90] Chancery Bill, 1 July, 1639.

[91] Frost, *History of Clare*, p.342.

Clancy. In the same way it became the custom
seldom if ever to use the *O* with Quin, Gleeson or
Mulcahy, to mention a few examples at random.
With most Irish surnames, however, especially the
common ones such as McCarthy, McSweeney,
O'Sullivan, O'Callaghan, etc., the *Mac* and *O* were
retained or dropped to suit the individual taste.[92]
On the other hand, a few rarely appear without the
prefix, e.g. O'Brien, McDermott, McGillicuddy,
O'Neill.[93]

All those names retained at least some vestige of
their original form even where, as in the case of
Crowe, Lee and Gleeson, that in which they were
finally standardized has a distinctly English flavour.
We come now to an entirely different kind of name
change, and one which, though it was taking place
even up to the end of the seventeenth century, dates
back long before it. In the fourteenth century an
attempt was made by the Statute of Kilkenny to
force Irishmen to assume English names, but while
no doubt many Gaels did as a result take as
patronymics English words signifying places or
trades, or call themselves by colours such as Brown
and Black, most of them probably reverted in due
course as English authority weakened, and in any
case they were counterbalanced by the steady
hibernicization of the early settlers who adopted,
with Irish dress, customs and language, names of an

[92] Nowadays if a man with an O name wishes to find it in a list or an index
he turns without question to that letter of the alphabet. He would not have
done so in the seventeenth and early eighteenth centuries, if the list were one
of Irish names. Thus, for example, in the list of subscribers printed in Hugh
MacCurtin's *Brief Discourse of Ireland* (Dublin, 1717), O'Donoghues and
MacDermotts are given under *D*, Macnamaras and O'Neills under *N*, and
so on. Cf. lists in Civil Survey, 1659.
[93] As the eighteenth century with its de-Gaelicizing influences advanced,
the prefixes were dropped by the great majority of the people except in the
case of these and a few other surnames.

Irish type.[94] The work which the Statute of Kilkenny failed more than temporarily to do by compulsion was effected to some extent in the seventeenth century by more insidious means. Thus Sir Henry Piers states in 1683 that in County Westmeath the inhabitants, who were " formerly barbarous," are now accepting English ideas and " becoming civilized".[95] As an example of this he cites the adoption by them of English surnames, instancing the substitution of Smith for McGowan, Cock for McKelly, and Spencer for McSpillane.[96] We may note, incidentally, that he does not mention any O name.

Sir Henry Piers comments on the pride of the old Irish gentry, their interest in genealogy, and the contempt in which they held the English families around them. " One great evil of this vanity of our Irish gentry," he says, " is that you shall hardly find any of them that he will scorn to take to any trade or calling whereby to get an honest livelihood " ; and he adds that though the ancient landlords were great oppressors of their tenants they could be relied on to protect them in all cases of disputes with outsiders.[97]

[94] A certain number of names of the sobriquet type originated from an entirely different cause having little or nothing to do with English influence. When not due to some special circumstance these usually arose from the prevalence of a particular surname common to many families in a district, causing the adoption of a descriptive epithet by one or more of them which in due course superseded the original name. The Irish language was almost invariably used in such cases : Bane, Duff, Lauder, Maghery, Creagh, Deasy and Lynagh are examples. It is worthy of note that principals and witnesses to seventeenth century deeds sometimes used no fixed surnames when subscribing their signatures : thus for instance in 1633 the son of one Dermod (Hurley) signs as Daniel MacDermod and a little earlier in the same collection of deeds (family papers of O'Grady of Kilballyowen) there is a similar case where no clue survives as to the real surname of the parties.
[95] Cf. Sir R. Cox's *Description of Co. Cork*, printed in Journal Cork Hist. and Arch. Society, Vol. VIII., 2nd series.
[96] MS. Nat. Lib. No. 412, p.100. Cf. Bradshaw Collection Hib. O. 7192, *Tryall of James Johnson alias MacShane*.
[97] MS. Nat. Lib. No. 412, p.113. Cf. Lawrence *Interest of Ireland*, p.8.

After 1641, and particularly after the Restoration, the fusion which had begun to take place between the two distinct elements constituting the Irish upper class was checked ; religious differences were much more marked and formed a bar to intermarriage. At the same time we must remember that the term Catholic gentry includes very many of the " old English," who were by 1680 almost merged with the residue of the aristocracy of the " mere " or pure Irish. Carew as far back as 1614 notes a change in the attitude of the Old English of the Pale towards the " mere Irish " and ascribes it to three causes : first, that intermarriage, formerly rare, was now frequent ; second, that the mere Irish had become civilized by travel abroad ; and third, that there was a natural tendency towards combination against the new settlers.[98] That the assimilation eventually proceeded along different lines we have already seen.

In a different class of life intermarriage between Irish and English started a process of assimilation which might have been the foundation of a permanent settlement if the war of James and William, with its disastrous consequences, had not intervened. The Cromwellian soldiers, as distinct from those who were granted large areas of land and became great landlords, were designed to form a strong yeoman class loyal to England in the districts in which they were settled. In many places one or two individuals, usually officers, bought up cheaply from the other soldiers the farms allotted to them and by this means acquired extensive estates[99] ;

[98] *Desiderata Curiosa*, Vol. I., p.430.
[99] See D. Gleeson, *The Last Lords of Ormond, passim.* A good example of this is to be found in the transactions of Capt. John Nichols of Kilbolan, Co. Cork, recorded in *Analecta Hibernica*, No. 15, pp.5-9.

but there remained a considerable number of Cromwellians who were satisfied to make a permanent home in Ireland on a comparatively humble scale. While they were still under military control every effort was made to prevent them from falling victims to the charms of the Irish girls, but in spite of army proclamations and ordinances many of them continued, even before the war was over, to marry them, a practice which in Elizabethan times was regarded as so dangerous that an English poet did not scruple to describe it in words more complimentary to the strength of character than to the feminine attractions of Irish womanhood :

> " We know from good experience
> It is a dangerous thing
> For one into his naked bed
> A poisoning toad to bring ;
> Or else a deadly crocodile,
> When as he goeth to rest
> To lie with him ; and as his mate
> To place next to his breast."[100]

It has always been the policy of English statesmen, excepting those who went so far as to advocate the total extirpation of the Irish, to keep the two races separate : the English as masters, the Irish as hewers of wood and drawers of water. Assimilation was not favoured because their experience was that assimilation meant hibernicization not anglicization. Among the gentry we have seen that assimilation did gradually take place (where extirpation had not already occurred) and the resultant type approximated much more nearly to the English than to the Irish. In the class below them the reverse was the case. The descendants of

[100] Derrick, *Image of Ireland*, quoted Prendergast, *Cromwellian Settlement*, p.261.

the Cromwellian settlers in County Tipperary, for example, were among the most stalwart fighters in the Land League struggle, and perhaps the " palatines " of County Limerick are the only instance to the contrary, excepting, of course, those parts of Ulster where the natives were, after the plantations, greatly outnumbered.

Even in northern Ulster, however, one class of the native Irish, if not undisturbed, remained at least in large numbers. The labouring class, that permanent " substratum of society " to which I referred above, had to remain because there was no one else to do the menial work and, being always in a state of poverty and depression, suffered no vicissitudes comparable to those experienced by other classes of Irishmen. This must be kept constantly in mind, and with it the fact that the cottiers and small-holders constituted about seventy-five per cent. of the total population of the country. These people, of course, remained Irish, their blood unadulterated by intermarriage with another race. Their condition was wretched in the extreme. I have already referred to the miserable cabins in which they lived, mere huts which could be thrown up in a day or two. They enjoyed little or no recreation beyond dancing, and such amusements as they had will be noticed in the next chapter. Very few of them ever travelled more than a few miles from their homes, if homes they could be called : their long hours of work did not allow them time to do so ; even had they desired it, and been possessed of the necessary means of transport, they had little inducement, for they had no money to spend in towns, and, being practically self-supporting, had no needs which the itinerant pedlars could not supply. In this class of life the pedlar had been important since the beginning of the century[101] and was recognized as such by the authorities, as may be seen from the State Papers of 1664 and 1665, one of which is quoted in full at the foot of this page.[102]

The pedlar supplied the poorer people with salt, tobacco and snuff, and those of them who had a few acres of land to till sometimes required a piece of iron for a ploughshare or a spade. He usually lodged where he happened to be at nightfall—we have noticed the pedlar included in the descriptions of the sleeping accommodation in cottages which I quoted in the last chapter,[103] and it was probably he who brought the latest news, or more often the last rumour, of happenings in the distant world of towns and politics. Weekly newspapers, quite a

---

[101] See Moody, *The Londonderry Plantation*, p.347.
[102] Whitehall, 20 Sept., 1644.

*The King to the Lord Lieutenant and Lord Deputy for
Mr. Hamilton and Captain Roche.*

An Act was passed in 39 Elizabeth against rogues and vagabonds, wherein, amongst others, " pedlars and petty chapmen were so deemed and adjudged." In 1617, on the petition of many honest pedlars and petty chapmen who showed that their trade was very useful to those who lived remote from towns, and that if they were encouraged they would greatly increase the manufacture of the nation, " To the end the honest and industrious petty chapmen might be encouraged, and the idle dissolute rogues and vagabonds, who travel and wander in the habit of pedlars and petty chapmen, might be suppressed and called in according to the statute aforesaid," King James erected an office for licensing pedlars and granted to Sir Abraham Williams and others the right to license such petty chapmen as should produce a certificate under the hands of two Justices of the Peace to testify to their honesty and faithfulness to the Government, and likewise give £40 bond and security for their good behaviour. This patent is expired and the officers deceased " and the former abuses and misdemeanours grow greater, partly through neglect and partly through the depredations of the late ill times." We have therefore thought fit to revive the said office and grant the management thereof to Colonel Edward Gray, Thomas Killigrew and others, under our Great Seal. We intend to erect a like office in Ireland and desire you to grant it to George Hamilton and Captain James Roche at a rent of twenty marks a year. (C.S.P. Ire. 1663/65, p.437).

The office was granted to Hamilton and Roche for a period of 31 years. They were ordered not to grant licences except to persons who brought certificates, signed by two Justices of the Peace, for their honesty and their faithfulness to the Government. (*ibid.*, p.569). For Rawdon's views on this affair see C.S.P.I. 1666/69, p.5.

[103] p.66 *supra*.

novelty at the time,[104] had very little circulation outside Dublin, and indeed were but poor purveyors of news. In England manuscript news-letters prepared by some individual who combined the functions of reporter, gossip-writer, editor, producer and distributor, to some extent supplied the place of the modern newspaper, and found their way into the coffee-houses of provincial towns and the homes of the country gentry. This species of journalism was very little practised in Ireland, and letters from friends in Dublin, London and Paris were the chief source of news for the gentry, which no doubt in turn percolated through the servants' hall to the surrounding countryside.

A visit to Dublin on the part of an Irish country gentleman was an event of comparatively rare occurrence except when he happened to live within twenty or thirty miles of the city ; unless he was, like Orrery[105] and Ormond, involved in the political world and only regarded his country home as the family headquarters, or like Rawdon, required to go to the capital from time to time in connexion with the affairs of the absentee for whom he was agent. The journey from such a place as Ennis or Dungarvan to Dublin was then an undertaking as long as from Dublin to Warsaw to-day or rather yesterday before the advent of air-travel, and far more arduous.[106] The larger towns, such as Cork, Limerick, Waterford, Galway and Kilkenny were

[104] According to Gilbert, *History of Dublin*, Vol. I., p.178, the first newspaper published in Dublin was issued by Robert Thornton, a bookseller, of Skinner's Row, in 1685. See Chapter VII., note 68. In a letter dated 14 Nov., 1670, Robert Leigh remarks that there is so little news to " stuff " the Gazettes in Dublin that their publication has ceased. C.S.P.I. 1669/70, p.303.

[105] Young Lord Broghill did the Grand Tour on the Continent in 1686 (see *Orrery Papers*, p.313 et seq.) but travelling of that kind was confined to the richest of the Anglo-Irish aristocracy.

[106] See Chapter VIII.

therefore of more importance socially than they became when transport facilities improved in more recent times.

Life in the towns, while having a certain amount in common with the country life we have been considering in this chapter, presents many differences from it, which fully justify the devotion of a separate chapter to that subject. Meanwhile we will return to the consideration of the occupations normally engaging the various classes of society which made up the majority of the people of Ireland in the years which elapsed between the time of Cromwell and Queen Anne.

CHAPTER V

Sports and Recreations

MORE than one writer has quoted Macaulay's dictum: " Ireland was probably then a more agreeable residence for the higher classes, as compared with England, than it has ever been before or since." He was speaking of the period after peace was established in 1651. Macaulay's works, especially his History, are not without value to the student of the Ireland of James and William, but the wide reading and research which mark his treatment of English affairs did not extend to Ireland: he relied too much on authorities like Archbishop King, Walker and Story, and was unaware of the existence of many sources now available to us. This particularly applies to social questions. Nevertheless his conclusion, quoted above, can be accepted in a general way of the generation which succeeded Cromwell, at least as far as the Protestant ascendancy was concerned.

A state of affairs where warfare of some kind may break out at any minute does not make for " agreeable residence ", except perhaps for one who loves fighting for its own sake. The period referred to was definitely one of peace. Ireland had hardly ever enjoyed thirty years of complete freedom from warfare before, except from 1601 to 1641, during which generation the upheaval of the Ulster plantation, followed by the predatory policy of Strafford, created a universal feeling of insecurity. Immediately after the Restoration, of course, the uncertainty and confusion of ownership was greater

than ever, but this was removed by the Acts of
Settlement and Explanation which, however unjust
they were to the individuals who found themselves
deprived of the properties they believed were rightly
theirs, at least seemed to have some air of finality
about them.

Any responsible man who studied the situation
could not but realize the impossibility of satisfying
anything like all those whose claims could be justi-
fied, either on the grounds of legal or honourable
obligation ; nor were there wanting in Government
circles officials who pointed this out, none more
clearly than Sir William Domville, whose masterly
summary of the agrarian position in 1664 took the
form of a memorandum to the Lord Lieutenant.[1]
Ormond himself well understood the problem,
declaring that if all engagements were to be satisfied
a new Ireland would have to be discovered.[2] No
doubt any man of good-will, who wished to see
devised as fair a solution of a practically insoluble
problem as possible, must have given up his well-
meaning efforts in disgust in the face of the success
of such unblushing corruption and injustice as
surrounded the disreputable acquisition by Arlington of the O'Dempsey estate, or the selfish indifference of the Duke of York to the rights of his
future all too faithful subjects, who, even if, as
Professor Curtis says, he did what he " considered
all that was possible under the circumstances "
to obtain toleration for his co-religionists in
Ireland, was not ashamed to accept a very large
grant of Irish land to the exclusion of deserving
claimants.

[1] C.S.P., 1663/65, p.415, *et seq.*
[2] Carte, *Life of Ormond* (1851 edn.), Vol. IV., p.81

Sir William Temple found Ireland an agreeable place of residence, though he left the country a few years after the Restoration. While living at Staplestown he adopted the role of country gentleman and became a landlord of the improving type. His benevolence appears to have been somewhat exclusive, and his attitude rather one of the upholder of the British[3] and Protestant interest among the natives ; for we may believe that it was he, and not his successor whom Dineley found in possession, who created the conditions described in the last chapter. No doubt he found those natives pleasanter people than the fiendish savages depicted in 1646 by his father, who lived to regret the unscrupulous calumnies he had published.[4] In my introductory chapter I pointed out that the essentials of modern life (other than those associated with mere mechanical progress) were present in the second half of the seventeenth century, and these unverified charges against an enemy, of indulgence in vices and barbarities of the most revolting description, are but the forerunners of the war propaganda of our own day, which invented German atrocities like the reduction of human fats in the " cadaver factory " and the use of living priests as bell-clappers in the church towers of Cologne.[5]

There were hundreds of men like Temple who, if they had not the same record of hostility to the people, regarded themselves as " England's faithful garrison," the standpoint which persists in the

[3] The use of the word ' British ' began to come into favour towards the end of the seventeenth century, though it was a long time before it was extensively adopted. For an early example see quotation on p.49 *supra.* The modern expression "for King and Country" can also be traced to this period. Cf. *Cal. Orrery Papers,* folio 118, (not quoted in the printed work).
[4] See Lecky, *History of Ireland,* Vol. I., p.76, n.
[5] See Leyton Richards, *The Christian's Alternative to War,* 5th edn. (London, 1935), pp.74, 75.

mentality of so many of their successors to this very day. I think, however, that the majority of the gentry of Ireland, once they felt that they would be allowed to remain undisturbed in possession of their estates, however acquired, gave little thought to politics. The landed gentry, of course, constituted the great majority of the members of the Irish Parliament, but no parliament sat between 1666 and 1689 and politics were more concerned with intriguing in Government circles in Dublin than with legislation. They enjoyed life each in the way which best suited his own inclinations : some lived for sport ; some devoted themselves to agricultural improvements and building ; others, emulating in a small way the first Earl of Cork, established rural industries ; while the old-fashioned survivors of the bygone order attempted to keep up a pale shadow of the traditional past, with its harpers, its hospitality and its bands of irresponsible retainers.

It is a feature of modern life in Ireland that sport in all its branches is as much the province of the poor as of the rich. The best packs of hounds are followed by anyone who can beg or borrow a horse and stay on over a fence ; the country is ranged by professional fowlers and bank-clerks with guns every Sunday in the season, and for that matter before it opens at all ; labourers eke out a scanty living by hunting rabbits ; nearly every village in some counties has its hurling or football team, and even greater crowds flock from all the four provinces to Croke Park than to Lansdowne Road. All this is a healthy development of democracy undreamt of in the seventeenth century. Sport, and games as far as they were played at all, were, except hurling to a limited extent, a matter for the gentry as much as organized covert-shooting with keepers and beaters is in England to-day. Legislation favoured this state of things and, apart from that, no other class had the money, nor as a rule the time, to indulge in sporting occupations. Guns were scarce and expensive, and no poor man had the opportunity, even if he had the inclination, to go shooting among the bogs and unreclaimed scrub-lands, which were full of duck, snipe, woodcock and even pheasants ; fishing alone of all sports was within his compass, but there is little evidence that it had many devotees in Ireland, though Isaak Walton was flourishing in England at the time of which I am speaking. Many references are to be found in our authorities to fishing, but rather as a source of food supply than as a sport.[6] In his unpublished letters John Dunton twice describes unorthodox methods of fishing which, though designed with a view to supplying food, must have had a considerable element of sport in them too. In his first letter he mentions that on a lake near Mullingar he saw geese with baited hooks attached to them used for fishing, how is not clear, and incidentally that pike were caught there on an ordinary hook and line, requiring play to land them. In his fifth letter he is more explicit : on the occasion of his trip to Malahide he describes the way in which cormorants were used to catch fish for their owners very much in the same way as is done in the Far East at the present day.

[6] Fynes Moryson in his *Itinerary* mentions that Mountjoy enjoyed " fishing and fishponds." The following papers by Dr. A. E. J. Went deal very thoroughly with the Irish fishing industry in the seventeenth century :

" The Galway Fishery," Proc. R.I.A., 48, C, 5, 1942 ; " The Galway Fishery," Proc. R.I.A., 49, C, 5, 1944 ; " Fishing Weirs of the River Erne," J.R.S.A.I., 75, 213-223, 1945 ; " Irish Fishing Weirs—I," J.R.S.A.I. 76, 176-194, 1946 ; " The Irish Hake Fishery 1504-1824," J. Cork H.A.S., 51, 41-51, 1946 ; " Pilchards in the South of Ireland," J. Cork H.A.S., 137-157, 1946 ; " Sir William Hull's Losses in 1641," J. Cork H.A.S., 1947 ; " The Irish Pilchard Fishery," Proc. R.I.A., 51, B, 5, 1947.

Bourchier complains that in his time fish as well as fowl were destroyed at all seasons of the year. A proclamation of November, 1662, orders that for the preservation of game for the benefit of the Lord Lieutenant and officers of state all persons were forbidden " to take any pheasants, grouse, hares, or any prohibited game whatever by hawks, nets, guns, setting dogs, greyhounds or any other engine whatsoever."[7] The worst offenders against this prerogative of the upper classes were the soldiers who, under the normal slack discipline of the army of Charles II,[8] had ample opportunites for poaching, and could indeed plead long arrears of pay as their justification._ They probably came under the last phrase of the proclamation I have quoted—" any other engine whatsoever." Colonel Edward Cooke, the manager of the newly-established Phoenix Park, in a letter to Ormond written in November, 1668, mentions the poaching propensities of the private : " there is scarcely a partridge left in these parts . . . trammels[9] are carried out every night under red coats."

This proclamation gives us an idea of the methods adopted by unauthorized persons to capture game.

[7] Some 35 years later a Game Law was passed which not only prescribed penalties for deer poachers but also contained clauses regulating the activities of the numerous officers and private soldiers who indulged in shooting and coursing.
[8] There was no Mutiny Act in force in Ireland in the seventeenth century and army discipline, as we understand it, was unknown in the time of Charles II. In peace-time the soldier was treated as an ordinary subject. He could fall asleep on sentry duty without incurring any penalty more serious than dismissal. Insubordination was not a legal misdemeanour unless accompanied by a blow or other physical act, which could only be treated as if it were an ordinary case of assault. Officers therefore had to rely on the prestige attaching to their class to maintain any degree of discipline at all. And, of course, in addition to all that, there was the fact that the pay of the army was always very much in arrears and the troops were often obliged to maraud and poach in order to get enough to eat. Cf. C.S.P.I., 1662, p.597, *et seq.*
[9] i.e. traps. This letter from Carte MSS. is quoted Burghclere, *Ormonde*, Vol. II., p.57.

Hawks are mentioned, but as a legitimate sport hawking, once the most popular of aristocratic recreations, was by now becoming old-fashioned. " A hawk, a hobby and a Limerick mantle are all the commodities for a Gentleman's pleasure in these parts," wrote Archbishop Alen to Thomas Cromwell,[10] and constant allusions in the State Papers in the first half of the seventeenth century attest the continued popularity of hawking, until it was gradually superseded by shooting with the forerunner of the modern sporting gun. Ormond himself, who was in most ways a leader of fashion, was, like his master, King Charles II, very fond of hawking[11] and even preferred it to racing, though he frequently went to the Curragh attended by the nobility of Dublin, where not only racing and hawking but hunting, too, were indulged in.

We are not told what form the hunting took beyond the fact that there was a pack of hounds. Foxhunting was then an innovation, and the sport enjoyed was much below the standard of later times. Dineley informs us that " a run seldom goes two miles outright." As the fox was presumably as swift and clever as he is now, we may assume that the hounds, to the scientific breeding of which little attention had yet been paid, were at fault, though we must remember that not only in the Curragh but throughout the country there were few fences to assist the fox and check the speed of the huntsman. The idea that the fox was an animal which might have to be preserved had occurred to nobody. At the end of the sixteenth century they were simply classed with the " badgers " as " such like vermin ";

[10] J.R.S.A.I., Vol. VI., p.76.
[11] H.M.C. Ormonde MSS. N.S. 4, p.164 and *passim*.

by 1683 they are occasionally mentioned as too
numerous. However, even at that time a certain
glamour already surrounded the fox-hunter and
his quarry. A manuscript of 1679, which gives the
notes to be sounded on the horn for some dozen
incidents of the chase, includes the call appropriate
to the death of the fox[12]; nor did the poets ignore him.

> " an sionnach ruadh ar an gcarraig
> Míle liu ag marcaigh
> A's bean go dubhach san mbealach
> ag áireamh a cuid gé ' "[13]

and again :

> " Óir atá an sionnach ag fás agus ag forbairt
> tré bás Mhuiris, óir ba h-é sás a bhfadach agus
> a ndíothchur é, agus leis sin bíd na cearca dá
> síorchaoineadh tré éirleach an t-sionnaigh-
> theora."[14]

Both of these vivid pictures bring to our minds not
only " the red fox rockward speeding and horsemen
all hallooing," but also " the woman in the roadway
lamenting her lost fowl." The reference, too, in
Seán Ó Duibhir a' Ghleanna to " lámhach gunnaí
tréan " in connexion with the long-billed woodcock
is a reminder of the extent of which shooting had
become a recognized sport[15] in place of hawking,
which is not mentioned in the poem.

[12] This page of MS. is reproduced in J.R.S.A.I., Vol. XXII., opposite
p.157. Its application to Ireland may be assumed from the partial use of
the Irish language by its compiler.
[13] *Seán Ó Duibhir an Ghleanna.*
[14] O Bruadair : " D'éig an fheile " (prose passage following stanza lxx.).
I. Texts edn. Vol. II., p.292.
[15] It has been stated (J. K. Millner *The Irish Setter, its History and Training*,
London, 1924, p.24), that it was not until the middle of the eighteenth
century that the practice of shooting birds on the wing came in, pot shots
being the fowlers' method in the preceding century. This may be true to
some extent but it is hard to believe that at any period it was possible,
except very occasionally, to shoot a sitting woodcock! Trevelyan (*English
Social History*, p.280), says that in Charles II.'s reign, it was not unusual
to " shoot flying".

Dr. Lynch tells us that partridges and pheasants " abound here perhaps more than in any other country. Ireland is well stocked with all the fowl that usually graces the costly banquet and her inhabitants are expert fowlers." To the fowler, indeed, even though his muzzle-loading single-barrelled gun was a slow and cumbrous weapon compared with its modern equivalent, Ireland was a paradise. Occasionally we meet complaints that game was scarce near Dublin, especially partridges, whose rarity is also noticed by Fynes Moryson ; but the references to the abundance of pheasants, wood-cock, wild duck, etc., all over the country are too numerous to specify.[16]

Another of the new landed proprietors in the north who was particularly interested in silviculture was Lord Massareene (Clotworthy). His letters contain frequent references to his experiments with different kinds of pines and other conifers : in one of them, addressed to Sir Richard Newdigate, he remarks that his " greatest entertainment is planting."

I may specially mention, however, the letters of Sir George Rawdon, which contain a great deal of exceedingly interesting information about sport, as well as the everyday life and management of a large estate in the north of Ireland, covering as they do, apart from political and family topics, a range wide enough to include bees, fruit-growing, cattle and horse-breeding, forestry, building and leases. All sorts of local industries had to be initiated and over-seen by an estate agent like Rawdon. Here is an extract from a typical letter of his : " It seems your Lordship is resolved and concluded for setting up a

[16] Jouvin (*circ.* 1666) says that waterfowl were frequently obtained in such quantities as to take away the pleasure of the sport. *Description of England and Ireland* (ed. Falkiner), p.419.

glass work, which I heartily wish may prove according to your expectation ; but I doubt it, having been so burnt in the hand with projecting and setting up manufactures here and particularly the stocking trade of late."[17]

His frequent references to sport include a description of a four hours' run with deerhounds, the making of a " cockglade " and, in particular detail, an elaborate duck decoy.[19] It is clear from Rawdon's letters that hawking was still a recognized sport. On the other hand, I think he does not make anywhere any allusion to fox-hunting or foxes.

War conditions, of course, had been favourable to the continued existence of the wolf. Although much reduced by the deforestation of the country, at the end of the Cromwellian campaigns, these animals were so numerous, up to the very outskirts of Dublin, that a public wolf-hunt was organized in December, 1652, in the barony of Castleknock. A definite price was set by the Commissioners of the Revenue on wolves' heads, ranging up to £6—no small sum in those days—for the head of a bitch : while a regular pack of wolfhounds was established in Co. Meath under the terms of a lease made in 1653.[20] The wolves were steadily reduced after peace was restored, but we find many notices of their existence after the Restoration. Rawdon, writing in 1665, mentions the efforts of keepers and " gun men " to destroy a wolf which was giving them such trouble. Nearly twenty years later, but in the more remote

[17] Rawdon to Conway, C.S.P. Ire., 2 Sept., 1665.
[19] Decoys were not an innovation ; Sir Wm. Brereton's *Travels* contains several descriptions of them.
[20] Prendergast, *Cromwellian Settlement*, pp.284 and 310 ; O'Flaherty, *Iar-Connaght*, p.181. Cf. MS. Nat. Lib. 663, p.374 and *Analecta Hibernica*, No. 15, pp.275 and 314.

county of Leitrim, Tadhg Rody says " the wolves which were very numerous in this county are now very few, occasioned by the care of the justices at the Quarter Sessions who always give unto those that kill one 2d. a hearth out of every hearth in the barony where the service is done "[21] and even as late as 1698 in a return of the stock of Wm. Conyngham in Co. Down the loss of a two-year-old from his stock of black cattle is noted as " killed with the wolf " without any indication that the incident was particularly remarkable[22]. Bishop Downes in his *Visitation* notes Mount Gabriel (Schull) and Berehaven as still the haunt of wolves in 1699. The last wolf in Co. Cork is said to have been killed by Brian Townsend in 1710.[23] Wild beasts and birds, long extinct in England, lingered on in the remote parts of Ireland as the golden eagle did in the highlands of Scotland. Pine-martens, for example, are still to be found in the West of Ireland,[24] though as far back as 1638 Strafford complains of their scarcity and, having promised to send Laud a quantity of this valuable fur, apologizes to him for being able to send him only 92 skins.[25]

Though the vast woods which had been a feature of the Irish landscape and a safe retreat for hard-pressed fighting men in the days of more or less incessant guerilla warfare were already devastated, little of the ground they had occupied was reclaimed for agriculture. Rough scrub which grew up among the stumps of the old forests formed splendid cover for woodcock, pheasants, and other game.

[21] MS. T.C.D. I. 1. 2, p.137.
[22] Doneraile Papers (*Analecta Hibernica*, No. 15, p.361).
[23] T. A. Lunham in Cork Arch. Journal, 1908, p.143.
[24] I remember when I was a boy a trapper in Co. Clare one day brought me three pine-martens which he had caught in rabbit traps.
[25] J.R.S.A.I., Vol. IV., p.235-6.

They had been extensively felled, first as fuel for the ironworks and industrial enterprises of Richard Boyle, Earl of Cork, and other lesser men of his type, and later as a means of providing ready cash for the new Cromwellian owners. The latter were for the most part devoid of the traditions of land-ownership, of which a due regard for silviculture is one, and apart from that they were for some time exceedingly nervous about their prospects of re-taining their recently acquired estates, and so had an incentive to make quick profits. As for the re-maining woods, though they were still plentiful enough to be spoken of in England as if they contained an inexhaustible supply of timber,[26] in Ireland itself there echoed throughout the country the poet's lament for their disappearance:

" Cad a dhéanfamuíd feasta gan adhmad
    Tá deire na gcoillte ar lár."

It is interesting to note that swans, which have always been plentiful in Ireland, were killed regularly in the seventeenth century,[27] so that the traditional belief that it is unlucky to shoot a swan, still current in most parts, is not as ancient as is generally thought, or, if it originated in the legend of the Children of Lir, it suffered an eclipse in early modern times.

The absence of rooks or crows, however, except squall-crows, is noted by Dineley, and before his time by Fynes Moryson and others. Colonel

---

[26] Daniel Defoe, *Tour* (E.L. Edn.), Vol. I., p.141. A considerable quantity of timber for the rebuilding of London after the Great Fire came from Ire-land. Cf. C.S.P. Dom., Oct. 17, 1667. The regular export of Irish timber to England continued throughout the century. See Cal. Treas. Papers, Vol. XLI., No. 30, 1696, Customs Books, etc. ; also MacGillicuddy Papers, folios 116 and 138.

[27] *Advertisements for Ireland*, p.34.

Solomon Richards describes the arrival of the first
magpies from Wales on a bleak easterly wind about
1672, and states that ten years later they were
breeding all over Co. Wexford and in the neighbouring counties. " The natural Irish," he adds,
" much disgust them, saying they shall never be rid
of the English while these magpies remain."[29]
Ravens were not uncommon nor were they confined
to the remoter districts since one is noted in 1655 as
building regularly in a tower in the town of Kells.[30]

Among the steps taken to combat the wolf menace
in 1652 was an official order prohibiting the export
of wolf-dogs from Ireland. These dogs were much
valued : they are often mentioned in contemporary
correspondence as forming most acceptable gifts,
and among the recipients of wolf-hounds from
Ireland we find names so diverse and so eminent
as Cardinal Richelieu, the Shah of Persia and the
Great Mogul,[31] and the Irish gentry, who were very
much attached to them, found it a hardship to have
to leave them behind in Ireland when they left the
country. It is generally considered that love of
animals has never been a trait very strong in the
Irish character, and the Irish people have often
been accused, not without some justification, of
cruelty towards them, or at least of indifference to
animal suffering. Yet men at least thought highly
of those wolf-dogs ; and that the love of a man for
his canine companion is no modern emotion can be
seen from the charming poem written by a Kerry

[29] MS. T.C.D. I. 1. 2, p.284. About a hundred years later they were so
numerous that an Act (27 G. III., c. 35) prescribed rewards for their
destruction.
[30] *Analecta Hibernica*, No. 8, p.426.
[31] P. Gardner, *The Irish Wolfhound*, Dundalk, 1931. See also Appendix B,
p.336. The State Papers—those calendared as *Domestic* as well as *Ireland*—
contain frequent references to Irish greyhounds as valuable gifts to eminent
people.

poet about 1675 on the death of his little spaniel.[32] Pets such as monkeys were quite common in country houses in the seventeenth century, but I have no evidence of how they were treated.[33]

The wolf-dog had reached its highest state of development: it declined with the extermination of its natural quarry, but retained its fierceness long after it was required for hunting wolves. Thus Rawdon, apropos of looking out for a wolf-dog for Conway, says that he thinks " the Irish breed will be all catt after kind and I think it not so important to any Englishman to be concerned that an English mastiff be the Conqueror,"[34] and on June 16th, 1670, Evelyn describes how at the Bear Garden an Irish wolf-dog " beat a cruel mastiff ". Gabriel Beranger, a visitor to Ireland a century later thus describes them as seen in Connacht: " They are amazing large, white with black spots, but of the make and shape of the greyhound, only the head and neck somewhat large in proportion."[35]

Greyhounds, a name which may possibly be derived from the Irish word for hare, were evidently a robuster breed than those of the present day. In fact, the word seems to have been synonymous with wolf-hound. Hear what Lord Orrery has to say : " I have prepared for you three Irish greyhounds. Two of them are white and shagged,[36] which is a great rarity. Last week I was sending them to you

[32] *Dánta Sheafraidh Uí Dhonnchadha an Ghleanna*, Dublin, 1902, p.20.
[33] The introduction of parrots as pets, if pets they can be called, dates from the discovery of the West Indies and the opening up of trade with that part of the world and with the West Coast of Africa. See Wright, *Domestic Manners*, p.491.
[34] C.S.P. Ire., 9 Nov., 1667.
[35] J.R.S.A.I., Vol. XI. p.148. Cf. *London Gazette*, 27 Mar., 1684 ; " A great Irish wolfdog, all his back of a sallow colour, his belly white."
[36] The *London Gazette* of 26 Nov., 1681, contains the following advertisement : " A very large Irish greyhound being of a sullied white with some pale yellowish spots about him and his chops of a black colour was lost on Thursday."

but am by a disaster forced to stop my intention for a mastiff running through the streets which flew at men as well as dogs the brace of shagged dogs fell on him and killed him."[37] Before sending them to London with a man specially detailed for the job he physicked them for fear of rabies.

New forms of sport encouraged the breeding of dogs to suit them, and the forerunners of the present-day foxhound and setter came into prominence about this time. The Game Law already referred to earlier in this chapter,[38] which it is interesting to note also introduced the principle of the protection of wild fowl, prohibited the keeping of setters by persons of less substance than £100 per annum, while hounds and even spaniels could not legally be kept by the ordinary small farmer or cottier. Good sporting dogs fetched high prices, and Lord Ossory paid £6 for a "setting dog" in 1685 before going to a shoot at Badminton, and £10 for another the following year. His dogs, in fact, cost more than his guns, for two of which and a flask he was charged £12 18s. 4d.[39] A rich man to-day would not object to giving £50 for a gun, but few setters would change hands at £40 or more, which is about the modern equivalent of the figure paid by Lord Ossory.

The value of money in the time of Charles II is often stated to have been ten times as great as at the present day. It is true that farm stock[40] and produce could be bought, and farm workers hired,

---

[37] Orrery to Bennet, C.S.P Ire., 1663, p.291.

[38] See note 7 *supra*.

[39] J.R.S.A.I., Vol. I., p.417.

[40] Cheap as livestock was in 1678 wool made up to 8s. a stone at a time when sheep could be bought for less than 5s. each and cows for £1. (See *Cal. of Orrery Papers, passim*).

at about one-tenth of the present rate ; and food and drink generally were very cheap, especially in rural Ireland where both labour and food were not much more than half what they cost in England or even in Dublin. On the other hand, once we turn from the barest necessities of life, prices approximate quite nearly to those of the present day. Clothes, for example, which of course were of good material and well made, were dear, while travelling, postage and other such services were very expensive and so only used when absolutely necessary. If a man went to the barber he paid at least 4d. for a hair cut, and dinner at a good tavern normally cost about 1s. 6d. In short, after making a list many pages in length of the prices of various articles and services, noted down from time to time in the course of reading, I have come to the conclusion that, so far as it is possible to make a satisfactory comparison at all, the value of money can be regarded as four or, at most five, times as great in the period under consideration as it is to-day.[41] In this connexion it may be of interest to recall that Macaulay, in his Essay on Temple, speaks of £500 a year as a sum which at the time of the Restoration was sufficient for the wants of a family mixing in fashionable circles.[42]

Well-bred horses, like dogs, fetched high prices. Lord Ossory paid £129 for one in 1687 which may

[41] This passage was written before the Second Great War which has resulted in a further depreciation in the value of money.

[42] Cf.Gregory King's Table of average incomes comprising all grades of society in England in 1688. His estimate for " esquires " is £450 and gentlemen £280, eminent merchants £400, lawyers £154 and farmers and shopkeepers about £45 ; naval and military officers, eminent clergymen, as well as " persons in liberal arts and sciences " are given as a mere £60 to £80. At the top of the scale peers, whose households are estimated to consist of as many as 40 persons, are credited with £3,200 a year. This Table is printed in Trevelyan, *English Social History*, Second Edition (London, 1946), p.277.

be compared with the price of an ordinary nag a few years before—from five shillings to one pound, " unless prime pad pacing nags."[43]   Ireland is now so famous for its horses that it is not generally realized that this pre-eminence is of comparatively modern date.   The Irish work-horse though small was " full of mettle, exceeding hardy, and will carry burdens the greatness whereof would startle any man's belief."[44]   The ordinary Irish nag, indeed, was held in esteem from the earliest times, but in the seventeenth century Irish horses had not made a reputation and were regarded as inferior to English. After the Restoration the attention of country gentlemen was seriously directed to the breeding of bloodstock and high-class hunters.   Rawdon's letters contain many references to this phase of rural activity, and in 1670 Colonel Daniel O'Brien, writing from County Clare to Arlington, remarks : " I begin to be the greatest breeder of horses in the King's dominions for I keep about my house 16,000 acres for my mares, colts, and deer " ; of very poor barren land, he adds.   He sends the Secretary " a gelding that I have some time tried after the hounds, and though he be of an Irish breed, I think he will not be left behind by any company that hunts in England."[45]

If the Irish horse had yet to make his reputation Irish horsemen were already famous.   That the Irish, having many miles of coast-line, have never been a maritime people is curious, but if as a nation they have not taken kindly to ships[46] they have always

[43] Rawdon to Conway, C.S.P.I., 1666/69, pp.365 and 463. See also Books of old Corporation of Ross, 1691, printed in J.R.S.A.I., Vol. XXXI.
[44] Wyndham-Quin, *The Foxhound in Co. Limerick*, p.13. Cf. *The Western Wonder*, p.22.
[45] C.S.P. Ire., 1670, p.205.
[46] Cf., however, *Cambrensis Eversus*, Vol. II., p.179.

been at home on horseback. No Irish horseman at the time of the Battle of Kinsale used stirrups.[47]

Racing usually took the form of matches between the chosen horses of two or three gentlemen, who frequently rode their own mounts. The principal public racecourse was the Curragh : the Curragh, " so much noised here," writes Dunton, " is a very large plain covered in most places with heath. It is said to be five and twenty miles round. It is the Newmarket of Ireland where the horse-races are run, and also hunting matches made : there being here great stock of hares, and moor game for hawking ; all of which are carefully preserved. . . . " His majesty for encouragement to breed large and serviceable horses in this Kingdom has been pleased to give £100 a year out of his Treasury here to buy a plate, which they run for at the Curragh in September. The horses that run are to carry twelve stone each . . . There is another race run yearly here in March or April, for a plate of a hundred guineas, which are advanced by the subscription of several gentlemen ; and the course is four measured miles." There were races there " in April, 1634, when Lord Cork backed Lord Digby's horse against one of the Earl of Ormond's and lost a new beaver hat to Mr. Ferrers, one of the Lord Deputy's gentlemen."[48] A generation later stakes were more substantial. Apropos of making a successful bet against the horse of his colonel, Lord Arran, " in the great match which was run for £200," Sir Nicholas Armourer, in a letter to

[47] Fynes Moryson, *Commonwealth*, p.285. Cf. ninety years later, Sir A. Conyngham complains that the Irish do not know how to make saddles and the shops do not provide them. Clarke Papers, MS. T.C.D. K. 5. 4. cccii.
[48] MS. note by the late Dr. Grattan Flood in his copy of C.S.P.I., now in my possession.

Joseph Williamson, makes this characteristic remark : "We northern men know no commander
nor own no friends but which they take to be the
stronger side."[49]

Society ladies of the Restoration period were to
be seen attending race meetings ; but violent
exercise for ladies was unfashionable in the seventeenth century.[50]   Horsemanship, however, was
among the normal accomplishments of a society
lady, particularly in France, where the delicate
Louise de la Vallière was remarkable for her skill
in riding bareback. They sometimes took an active
part in other sports, too. Another famous French-
woman, Ninon de l'Enclos, whom we naturally
associate rather with the boudoir than the chase,
is said to have been a very good shot. In a letter
written in 1642, Urbanus Vigors says of Lady
Broghill, an Englishwoman resident in Ireland :
" I know but few men in the land will shoot off a
fowling piece better or nearer the mark than her
ladyship."[51]   An early number of the *Spectai r*
notices the appearance soon after 1700 of t e
masculine, fox-hunting, swearing type of woman,
and Strutt tells us that society ladies frequented
far less reputable sporting gatherings than race-
meetings. His quotation from Sir Richard Steele[52]
in the *Tatler*, of February 16, 1709, will give
us some idea of the nature of the popular entertainments patronized by fashionable ladies in England.
" Some   French   writers   have   represented   this

[49] C.S.P. Ire., 1663, p.91.
[50] There is an uncomplimentary reference in Moffet's *Hudibras* to women
riding astride (canto v. line 20), but Lynch says that this method was only
practised by an occasional humble peasant woman, and was regarded in
the seventeenth century as improper. (*Cambrensis Eversus*, Vol. II., p. 151).
See also *Anatomy of Melancholy*, Pt. 2, Sec. 2, Mem. 4
[51] 1641 Depositions MS., T.C.D. F. 2. 11. Letter No. 21, p.248.
[52] Steele was born in Dublin in 1672.

diversion of the common people much to our [i.e. English] disadvantage and imputed it to a natural fierceness and cruelty of temper, as they do some other entertainments peculiar to our nation. I mean those elegant diversions of bull-baiting and prize-fighting, with the like ingenious recreations of the bear-garden. I wish I knew how to answer the reproach which is cast upon us and excuse the death of so many innocent cocks, bulls, dogs, and bears as have been set together by the ears, or died an untimely death, only to make us sport."

The following graphic description of bull-baiting in 1699 by Henri Misson, coming as it does from a Frenchman who was, on the whole, an admirer of England, though rather long, is sufficiently interesting to quote in full.

" They tie a rope to the root of the horns of the ox or bull and fasten the other end of the cord to an iron ring fixed to a stake driven into the ground ; so that this cord being about 15 foot long, the bull is confined to a sphere of about 30 feet diameter. Several butchers and other gentlemen that are desirous to exercise their dogs stand round about, each holding his own by the ears ; and then the sport begins, they let loose one of the dogs : the dog runs at the bull ; the bull, immovable, looks down upon the dog with an eye of scorn, and only turns a horn to him to hinder him from coming near : the dog is not daunted at this, he runs round him and tries to get beneath his belly, in order to seize him by the muzzle, or the dewlap, or the pendant glands, which are so necessary in the great work of generation : the bull then puts himself in a posture of defence ; he beats the ground with his feet which he joins together as close as possible, and his chief aim is not to gore the dog with the point of his horns, but to slide one of them under the dog's belly (who creeps close to the ground to hinder it) and to throw him so high in the air that he may break his neck in the fall. This often happens when the dog thinks he is sure of fixing his teeth, a turn of the horn, which seems to be done with all the negligence in the world, gives him a sprawl 30 feet high, and puts him in danger of a damnable squelch when he comes down. This danger would be unavoidable, if the dog's friends were not ready beneath him, some with their backs to give him a soft reception, and others with long poles, which they offer him slantways, to the intent that, sliding down them, it may break the force of his fall ; notwithstanding all their care, a toss generally makes him sing to a very scurvy tune, and draw his phiz into a pitiful grimace : but unless he is totally stunned by the fall, he is sure to crawl again towards the bull, with his old antipathy, come on't what will. Sometimes a second frisk into the air disables him for ever : but sometimes too he fastens upon his enemy, and when once he has seized him with his eye teeth, he sticks to him like a leech and would sooner die than leave his hold. Then the bull bellows, and bounds, and kicks about to shake off the dog : by his leaping the dog seems to be no manner of weight to him, though in all appearance he puts him to great pain. In the end either the dog tears out the piece he has laid hold on, and falls, or else remains fixed to him, with an obstinacy that would never end, if they did not pull him off. To call him away would be in vain ; to give him a hundred blows would be as much so ; you might cut him to pieces joint by joint before he would let loose. What is to be done then? While some hold the bull, others thrust staves into the dog's mouth, and open it by main force. This is the only way to part them."[53]

In his very full description of the popular amusements of Kilkenny,[54] Mr. Prim states that bull-baiting began to fall into disrepute among the wealthier classes of society by 1687, but that it remained popular with the lower orders for a long time after that[55]: it was kept up by the butchers in the town of Kilkenny until the year 1837. The decline of bull-baiting as a society entertainment did not, however, connote a change of heart on the part of the upper classes, for its place was taken by cockfighting. This pastime had long been beloved of English kings, for Henry VIII and James I were both keen patrons of it, and Charles II often diverted himself by watching a cock-fight while on holiday at Newmarket. It was so far organized as an aristocratic pastime to succeed bull-baiting that matches between teams of cocks representing Kilkenny and the neighbouring counties were regularly arranged, often lasting three or four days ; and in 1747 a cockpit was officially built by the Corporation of Kilkenny town—the site of which was apparently in the churchyard of St. Mary's.

There is no doubt that these sports involved cruelty, and they approximated somewhat to bull-fighting in modern Spain as a public spectacle, though danger to human life was lacking. An

[53] Henri Misson, *Memoirs and Observations in his Travels over England with some account of Scotland and Ireland*, 1699.
[54] J.R.S.A.I., Vol. II.
[55] In 1714 The Corporation of Kinsale ordered that no butcher should slaughter a bull without its first being baited and imposed a penalty of 20s. for failure to do so. *Analecta Hibernica*, No. 15, p.181.

attempt was made in 1683 to introduce bull-fighting into England, but according to a news-writer[56] of that date it failed to appeal to the London populace because with English bulls it did not prove sanguinary enough for their taste. When they saw that there was no prospect of men or even horses being killed the people went home in disgust.[57] Most sport, indeed, involves cruelty in some degree, and at the present day, whatever we may think of fox-hunting, there is a good deal of cruelty in the artificial sport of hunting a stag previously captured and liberated for the occasion. The cruelty, or I would rather say the callousness, of our seventeenth century ancestors was not, however, peculiar to Ireland. Ruthlessness in waging war was as much a characteristic of the Cromwellian soldiers as of the exasperated native Irish they came to conquer. It is rather the characteristic of an age than of any particular nation : a survival of the dark ages in fact, not yet wholly dead. Two hundred and fifty years ago criminals, and men condemned for political offences too, were executed in public, and a hanging was always sure to collect a big crowd of spectators ; but I can hardly imagine that the populace of London would shun Tower Green if the execution of some notorious murderer were to be advertised to take place there to-day.

We have seen above that cruelty to animals was a trait in the English character noticed unfavourably

[56] Newdigate-Newdegate, *Cavalier and Puritan*, p. 243. (London, 1901).
[57] It may be noted that Lady Fanshawe, who spent several years in Spain between 1650 and 1666, frequently mentions her attendance at bull-fights, but never refers to cruelty in connexion with them. That this is due to the normal callousness of all classes in the seventeenth century, and not to any want of ferocity in the Spanish national sport, as practised in her day, is attested by two lengthy contemporary accounts of these popular entertainments given in the Appendix of the 1907 edition of her *Memoirs*.

by a French writer, and the Irish were certainly
no more tender-hearted than their neighbours
in this respect. In Moffet's *Irish Hudibras* we have
a picture of the cowardly bully Bruno practising
on an inoffensive cow the thrust which he would
like to have given to Redmundo. He used a
" dung-fork " which, it is interesting to note, was
then a two-pronged implement, and the ghastly
fate he wishes her, when she not unnaturally resents
his unprovoked assault and attacks him with her
horns, does credit to his inventive powers if not to
his humanity. Here is the description of the contest
which led to Bruno going to skulk in a barn :

> " The gaping crowds, who still delight
>   To be spectators at a fight,[58]
>   To see a scuffle at a fair,
>   And who from meat and drink forbear
>   Or see two rival dogs engage
>   About a bitch in mighty rage,
>   Pressed on apace, to feed their eyes,
>   And see the issue of their prize.
>   And Gillo, master of the treat
>   And revels, made them all retreat,
>   And leave those champions room enough
>   To wrestle, scratch, to kick and cuff.
>   Sometimes with close embrace they hug,
>   With art they grip, with strength they tug ;
>   And when the hardness of their skulls
>   They try like rams, or pushing bulls
>
> *   *   *   *   *
>
>   And now they both together fall
>   To ground, and in strange postures crawl :
>   Then up they start in mighty rage
>   And like fierce mastives do engage.
>   The ring where they the fight maintain'd
>   With purple gore was all disdain'd
>   And slippery made . . ."

[58] Cf. Misson's description of the interest shown in England by spectators
in any chance fight of schoolboys or workmen in the streets. He was struck
by the way in which they " kept the ring " and did not interfere as long as
the combatants observed the " rules ". *Memoirs* (English Translation),
p.305.

and so on : it reads like an account in doggerel verse of an " all-in " wrestling match to-day between Gouging George and the Yellow Tiger or some such heroes at Chicago or Kansas City.

I believe there are practically no rules in that form of athletic contest to-day. Wrestling was a recognized form of public entertainment in the seventeenth century : it appears to have provided a living for its successful exponents and to have been governed by at least one or two accepted rules. " Now this," writes Dr. Douglas Hyde in his perhaps too literal translation of his own Irish original " was the way it was customary with them to make a wrestling at this time ; that was, to bind a girdle or belt of leather round the body of the two men, and to give each man of them a hold on the other man's belt and when they would be ready and the word would be given them they would begin wrestling." He goes on to describe how young Thomas Costello, confident in the strength which subsequently earned him the sobriquet *láidir*, accepted the challenge of a certain champion who, according to the custom of the time, was living at the expense of the town of Sligo until the towns-people could find someone to beat him. This particular champion was of the bully type and having already killed several men in previous contests, was much feared. We are then given a vivid picture of the scene in the square of the country town as the astonished crowd, breathless with anxiety a moment before, see the 10 to 1 odds-on-chance man defeated in the first minute of the contest—his neck broken. The victor had, of course, no fear of immediate arrest to answer a charge of manslaughter, but found himself a popular hero.[59]

We are not told whether this event took place on a Sunday or not, but as Connacht was the province most remote from the influences of Puritanism, it is more than likely that it did.

Up till the middle of the century Sunday was the chief day for popular pastimes, which we must not forget were infrequent outside the larger towns ; but Cromwell's Sabbatarianism put an end to that. In places like Kilkenny, even the mystery and miracle plays, which rivalled bull-baiting in their ability to draw the crowd, were discontinued about 1650,[60] savouring no doubt in the eyes of the victorious Cromwellians of idolatry and papistry. It is true that there was a real reaction against Puritanism in England, which was reflected in Ireland, though not very noticeably, because the supporters of Cromwell—Broghill,[61] Coote, Clotworthy and the rest—remained the most powerful section of the population after the Restoration, having been indeed very largely responsible for bringing it about. But in England itself, however much the excesses of Puritan zeal were disliked, the people as a whole remained unswervingly Protestant and a Protestant atmosphere was imparted to all legislation in Ireland. We have noticed in an earlier chapter among the presentments at the sessions and assizes in Co. Cork reference to a harper playing " on the Sabbath day contrary to the Act,"[62] and in

[59] *Amhráin Cúige Connacht*, pp.46-48.
[60] Prim, op. cit., p.327.
[61] In spite of what his confidential secretary, Thomas Morrice, says of his motives in his preface to *The Orrery State Correspondence* Broghill may, I think, be fairly so described.
[62] 7 Wm. III., c. 17 prohibited sports, games and pastimes on Sunday but not till 1787 was Sunday shooting forbidden by Statute.

the same manuscript we read that an order was made—and no doubt this was no isolated case—that " prophaners of the Sabbath " should be punished.[63] In the remoter parts of the country, however, Sunday remained a day of leisure and amusement, such English-made social laws having little force when repugnant to the feelings of the people. Contemporary corroboration of this is afforded by the passage quoted above on p.36 By the Act just referred to, alehouse keepers were prohibited from opening or supplying liquor during the hours of divine service on Sundays ; drovers and carriers were forbidden to travel or enter inns on Sundays. To make this Act more effective the constables were enjoined to enter taverns frequently to apprehend offenders.

The number of holydays observed by the people in the same way as Sundays was very considerable even after the passing of the Act of 1695, which limited them to thirty-three[64]. The motive in this case was not Sabbatarian but economic : labourers and servants refusing to work on Holydays other than the 33 specified were to forfeit 2 shillings and constables who failed to enforce this regulation were liable to a fine of £1. On the other hand there appears to have been no legal objection to the employment of artisans on Sundays since we know from certain seventeenth century account books that this was sometimes done.[65]

Athletic meetings are, of course, not a modern idea, since the ancient Greeks organized them so successfully and permanently that we still use the

[63] MS. T.C.D. N. 3. 20, 1676-1702. (July, 1695).
[64] A memorandum printed at p.261 of C.S.P.I., 1666/69 states that at that time Holydays " observed more by Papists than by Protestants are a tenth part of the whole year."
[65] Eg. Arthur MS. fo.

terminology they invented ; and in Ireland's heyday we had our Tailteann Games, but as far as my researches have gone not even a feeble shadow of these survived in the days we are studying. But if the Games themselves were but a dim memory, the athletic feats of the old time champions were not forgotten. In his elegy on Diarmuid O'Leary of Killeen, Egan O'Rahilly extols the dead man for his prowess in the manly exercises of the heroes whose blood flowed in his veins. He excelled " in stone-casting, in dancing, in running, in riding strong spirited horses, in lifting the race-rings on roads . . ." As late as the beginning of the seventeenth century Irishmen had a great reputation as runners— runners, that is, with a purpose unconnected with games and athletics: as light troops, messengers, and so on. But their speed and stamina in this respect disappeared with the abolition of Irish dress. Dr. Lynch speaks of the obstinate adherence of the humbler orders to their traditional dress, and the retention in use of the " braccae " in some places in Ulster after the upheavals of 1641 and following years. " The chief motive," he thought, " for their obstinate adherence to this dress is the facilities it affords for the full exercise of their natural fleetness. They can generally keep pace with the courser galloping at his greatest speed . . ."[66] In the interesting letter of Urbanus Vigors preserved among the 1641 depositions, he says of the " rebels" : " for they are nimble swift footmen they usually march as fast as their horse." He also describes rather vividly the part played in the skirmish near Lismore by " Fennell's choice shot, an old fowler

[66] *Cambrensis Eversus*, Vol. II., p.211. See also Green, *The Making of Ireland and its Undoing*, p.81.

which did usually run by his horse side, with his fowling piece."[67] Yet Petty, in 1672, states that the "footmanship" for which the Irish had been so famous a generation before, "is now quite lost among them".

The modern conception that games are played as much for the enjoyment of the spectators as of the players would not have entered people's heads in 1680. But I think we may assume that games began to have a spectacular aspect not so very long after, because any organized contest between the representatives of rival towns, parishes or counties is sure to arouse local patriotism, and we know that by 1768, if not much earlier, hurling matches often took place between the gentlemen of Counties Kilkenny, Tipperary, and Leix, or Queen's County as it was then invariably called.[68] Though it does not come within the period covered by this book, it is of interest to note that about 1775 Irishmen in London hurled regularly in the fields at the back of the British Museum, and the game as played then does not appear to have differed materially from that played in Ireland at the present day.[69] Direct references to hurling in the seventeenth century are infrequent, but it was certainly played: Dunton describes very vividly hurling as he saw it played, and Orrery, in a letter dated July 9, 1667, mentions a great meeting of Irish Catholics " under pretence of a match at hurling." Football appears to have been less popular than hurling in Ireland in the seventeenth century, but the fact that both these games are specified in the Act prohibiting Sunday

[67] MS. T.C.D. F. 3. 11, p.248.
[68] R.S.A.I., Vol. II., p.332.
[69] Strutt, *Pastimes*, p.78.

pastimes suggests that they were generally played. Misson, writing of England, alludes to it as a " useful and charming exercise," and mentions that the ball used was " of leather, as large as a man's head and filled with wind ; it is tossed with the feet in the streets."

The practice of making the spectators of outdoor contests pay—of charging " gate-money "— is quite a modern idea ; but stage performances, of course, were not free and quite considerable sums were sometimes asked for admission to travelling shows ; the elephant, for example, which was burnt in its " booth " in Dublin in 1681 [71] had been seen by very few of the populace because they objected to the high charge made by the proprietor for viewing it.

Games, like sport, were a matter not for the populace but for the aristocracy, who in the period of peace following the Restoration began to take a certain amount of interest in them. Indoor games had long been in existence to while away the tedium of wet days, cards and dice being the most universal. L'ombre [72] was the fashionable card game in the reign of Charles II, in Ireland at any rate. Chess, which of course figures in Irish legendary tales dating from before the dawn of history, is mentioned in the *Anatomy of Melancholy*, as also is the game called " tables". This word may be occasionally used to denote something like billiards, but is more often associated with dice, as in Burton's list of indoor amusements, in which billiards is separately

[71] See p.219, note 84.
[72] For a description of this and other card games of the period see *The Compleat Gamester*, London, 1674 (by C. Cotton, published anonymously).

mentioned.[73] " Playing at tables " was included among the pastimes of the Earl of Tyrone in Co. Waterford in 1678.[74] Games like billiards and shovelboard were an occupation for the leisured class by day. Cards and chess were suitable to long winter evenings. Music and story-telling were the recreations of the old Irish by night, but where English ideas and customs had established themselves it was not unusual for the host to hire jugglers, acrobats, fire-eaters and such like entertainers for the diversion of his guests after a dinner or a supper party.[75] Bodley in his entertaining account of his visit in 1620 to what was in most respects really an English country house, though actually at Lecale, Co. Down, describes how one night " certain maskers of the Irish gentry " called to the house and " contributed to their hilarity." These maskers wore fantastic costumes, including masks and paper noses. Bodley and his friends also derived much amusement from watching two of the domestics

[73] *The Anatomy of Melancholy*, Pt. 2, Sec. 2, Mem. 4. " The ordinary recreations which we have in winter, and in most solitary times to busy our minds with, are cards, tables and dice, shovelboard, chess-play, the philosopher's game, small trunks, shuttlecock, billiards, music, masks, singing, dancing, Yulegames, frolics, jests, riddles, catches purposes, questions, commands, merry tales of errant knights, etc." This book, first published in 1621, was revised several times by the author up to the 6th (1652) edition, from which, reprinted in the Everyman Library, the foregoing list has been taken. Cf. also Misson, *Memoirs and Observations*, p.304 ; and Appendix B, Letter IV. T. Lucas, in his account of Patrick Hurley (*Lives of the Gamesters*, 1930 edn., p.174) mentions tipcat, cricket, skittles, span-farthing and trap-ball as boyish recreations in Ireland towards the end of the seventeenth century. Shuttleboard, as it is called in a Kinsale presentment of 1658 (*Analecta Hibernica*, No. 15, p.176), is indicated as the " ruin of many poor tradesmen and apprentices." " A payer of tables with men " are mentioned in the inventory of household goods at Castlemartyr. *Orrery Papers*, folio 280, (not in printed edition).

[74] Printed Tracts on the " Popish Plot " (Nat. Library), *Informations of Hubert Bourk*. Tyrone's other amusements were hunting, fishing and reading Irish. This Earl of Tyrone was a Poer and had no connexion with the famous Earl of an earlier generation, to whom the reading of Irish might have been regarded as a normal relaxation.

[75] Geocaigh, meaning travelling jugglers or showmen, are mentioned by O'Bruadair : see *Dánaire*, Pt. I., p.108, and cf. Quennell, *History of Everyday Things in England*, 4th Edn., Vol. II., p.157.

engage in a contest of "skiver the goose," a pastime popular in Ulster for two hundred years after Bodley's time though in a somewhat less rough form, the defeated combatant being no longer prodded with a sharp stick in his posterior. In England in the time of Charles II, and on into the next century, people got a great deal of amusement out of elaborate practical jokes, often of a kind which must have been very disconcerting to the victims of them.[76] It is probable that wherever English ideas then prevailed in this country the same thing was true of Ireland, though no diarist like Celia Fiennes has recorded her enjoyment of them here.

The tennis played by kings and courtiers was played under cover. According to Mr. Prim, tennis was introduced from England by Ormond.[77] Bowls certainly became a fashionable game in Ireland after the Restoration. Dublin naturally led the way in this new outdoor pastime. "The green at Oxmantown," says Rawdon, "is a most noble place and every evening my Lord Deputy bowls there, and the ladies at kettlepins which spoils the playhouse"; and again, another Dublin letter remarks: "Alderman Tye's new bowling green (played upon so airy a ground) so fans the nobility and gentry of both sexes every day that no immoderate heat offends them or putrifies their blood."[78] In the sixth of Dunton's letters, printed in Appendix B, he says that the bowling green at Oxmantown is "the only thing that Dublin exceeds or equals London in; it much surpasses the green at Marrow-

[76] The same thing is true of France where cases are on record of practical jokes even resulting in the victim's death. Bradby, *The Great Days of Versailles*, p.72.
[77] Dunton mentions a tennis court in Dublin, situated in Winetavern Street. (*Dublin Scuffle*, p.368).
[78] Rawdon to Conway, C.S.P.I., 1665, pp.589 and 591.

bone." The game, however, was not confined to the city. Bowling greens were found in the provinces, north and south.[79]

The participation of both sexes in a game was something of an innovation. Dunton, who was a keen player himself, remarks : " The bowling green above all has charms for me : I think it no improper recreation for ladies ; and where men, who are desirous to civilize themselves in ladies' companies, might partake with them there. The only difficulty is there are very few bowling greens in private families, they are so chargeable to keep : and all public meetings for diversion soon grow scandalous in this corrupt age."[80]

I would like to be able to say how these greens were kept. If their surface was in any way comparable to the smooth sward now considered essential for the game of bowls it is difficult to understand how this could have been produced at a time when lawnmowers were unheard of. A heavy stone roller would, of course, have rendered the ground sufficiently level, but how to keep the grass evenly cut must have been the problem. Many operations we now perform by mechanical devices, clipping horses for example, could be done effectively by simpler though slower means, but I confess I have often wondered how a really smooth bowling-green was produced, in any place where sheep could not be let in to graze down the herbage. We may assume that the scythesman of the day had attained a very high degree of efficiency. Dr. Johnson once compared Pope's verse with " a velvet lawn shaven by the

[79] MS. T.C.D. I. 1. 3 ; and Rawdon to Conway, C.S.P. Ire., July 1, 1665. A bowling green was laid out at Trinity College in 1684 and a fives court built soon after. These represented the first attempt to provide regular games for the students.
[80] Second answer to Citizen's Wife—*Dublin Scuffle*, p.525.

scythe and levelled by the roller." The skilled
rural worker, however, only received a few pence
for his day's work, and his labour was classed as
" unskilled," as that of the cleverest ploughman or
the most experienced shepherd is in our present-day
world of anomalies. According to Petty, the wage
of a labourer in Ireland, about the year 1676, was
4d. a day, as compared with 8d. in England,[81]
though fully a hundred years earlier a Dublin
labourer received 7d. per day,[82] showing that
city wages, then as now, ruled much higher than
rural. Petty's figures are corroborated by another
contemporary writer who, referring to a country
clergyman whose benefice was worth 18s. per annum
remarks, " and therefore all the rest of the week he
was forced to thatch, thresh or wrought other ways
for three pence a day."[83] With such slender incomes it is no wonder that sport played little part
in the daily lives of the working classes.

Sometimes for the sake of a few shillings they were
prepared to play the part of victim in the rough
rural pastimes which were got up to divert the
"quality", and no doubt entertained the rustics,
too, when they did not happen to be awaiting their
turn for rough handling. A case is recorded of a
butcher named Harris, of Mallow, being killed as
a result of blanket-tossing. His widow made a
claim on the Dowager Countess of Clancarty on
the ground that Harris was " barbarously
murdered " by the Countess's son. In her defence
the Countess says : " There was a custom (though
an inhuman pastime) in that part of Ireland, to
toss men in blankets that the country people would

[81] *Petty Papers*, ed. Lansdowne, Vol. II., p.58.
[82] Jnl. of R.S.A.I., Vol. XXXI., p.104.
[83] *The Western Wonder*, p.34.

come freely to offer themselves to be tossed for half crown a piece, that the said butcher was unfortunately tossed, and for want of care died soon after ; that the said Earl was no otherwise accessory than as a spectator as he was to others tossed the same day."[84] This was probably true as several troopers were tried in 1687 for the manslaughter of Harris and acquitted.[85]

As I have already noted, dancing was almost the only amusement to which the poor were addicted, if we except gambling. A somewhat unsavoury feature of the life of the time was the association of dancing and mumming with wakes and even with religious pilgrimages. Indeed, the abuses connected with wakes were more serious than the mere indecorum of merrymaking on a solemn occasion : the merrymaking was frequently not of an innocent kind, for it involved not only excessive drinking but also practices which were always coarse and very often actually licentious. A great deal of evidence of this has already been collected in print, all pointing in the same direction. While some writers charitably designate as " this jovial crew", or as " revellers as if at one of the feasts of Bacchus " the

[84] Cal. Treasury Papers, Vol. XXV., Dec., 1, 1693. It may be of interest to add that one of the papers in this case is a receipt from Mrs. Harris for £100, dated 30 April, 1687, acquitting the Earl from all further demands. The Treasury Papers do not inform us whether she managed to extract any further dole from the Countess, but the case has an additional interest because it is a reminder of the varying fortunes of the great families in Ireland at this period. The young Earl was an ardent Jacobite. In 1687 James was king and the MacCarthys were still wealthy and influential. In 1690 Clancarty found himself a prisoner in the Tower of London, and the butcher's widow (no doubt regretting that she had made in '87 what she subsequently counted a bad bargain) decided that it would be worth while trying again in the very different circumstances which obtained six years later.

Cardinal Mazarin's nephew and heir is said to have met his death in the same way while a schoolboy at a Jesuit College in France.

[85] Cal. Orrery Papers, p.337. Harris's death is described in *Ireland from the Restoration to the Present Time* (1716), p.57. In the same book (p.203) blanket tossing is mentioned as a not unusual method of " punishing " clergymen of the established church !

participants in what others describe as orgies, that abuses existed is denied by none. The anonymous gentleman who was entrusted with the chorographical survey of the barony of Forth in Co. Wexford in 1683, himself a Catholic, as I mentioned when quoting from him in an earlier chapter, contradicts the usual allegations of " rude emulations or clamourous but counterfeit resentments of seeming sorrow," but he is silent in regard to the more serious charges. Archbishop Brenan alludes to abuses, but contents himself with saying that his clergy were endeavouring to eradicate them,[86] and in *Cambrensis Eversus* a whole page is given to the extravagances of the keening women at wakes and the efforts of the priests to discourage them, yet Dr. Lynch makes no mention of drunkenness or unseemly conduct in this connexion. Probably, therefore, the idea of regarding wakes as a source of entertainment, which led me to embark on this subject in a chapter devoted to the people's sports and amusements, was not common until the very end of the seventeenth century, and the scenes so graphically described by eighteenth and nineteenth century writers were a subsequent development of it not properly belonging to the period we are considering.[87]

The allegation that pilgrimages were made the occasion for a popular outing of the modern bank-holiday type is not general. I will quote one, for what it is worth, my authority being Sir Henry Piers, who, I may observe, shows throughout his writings a pronounced anti-Catholic bias. Having

[86] *Letters*, p.50.
[87] For a full discussion of this subject, embodying quotations from several reliable witnesses, see Dineley, *Observations*, notes pp.20 to 35.

described the pilgrimage itself, which took place to a spot of great natural beauty and involved much physical hardship on the pilgrims, who completed the journey over a stony path at the edge of a precipice on their naked knees, he goes on : " their devotions done they return shod and merry, no longer concerned for the sins that were the cause of that so severe penance but as if they now having paid the score longed to go on in them again they return with speed to a certain green spot of ground and here fall to dancing and carousing ; for ale sellers in great numbers on these days have their booths as in a fair and to be sure the bagpipes fail not to pay their attendance. Thus in lewd and obscene dances with excess of drinking the day of their devotion is ended, so as now one who should see them would think they had been celebrating a feast of Bacchus, or oftentimes it falleth out that more blood falls on the grass from their drunken pates when the pilgrimage is ended than was before shed on the stones from their bare feet and knees during their devotions."[88]

This description of the end of a pilgrimage to St. Kevin's Chapel suggests a faction fight, which phenomenon was generally a form of spontaneous popular recreation. Those ebullitions were not unknown in the seventeenth century. Father White in his MS. history of Limerick records a fracas between the members of certain trade guilds in 1669,[89] and we have an account of what may be called a faction fight in Co. Kerry given by Egan O'Rahilly as a witness in a case tried before a

[88] MS. T.C.D., I. 1. 2, p.306. Sir H. Piers wrote from Co. Westmeath.
[89] MS. R.I.A. 24.D. 21., p.191.

judge.⁹⁰ They were not, however, very frequent and, like the customs associated with wakes, belong to a somewhat later time. All these abuses were discouraged by the Church, but the difficulties surrounding the Catholic clergy in the performance of their duties, even before the Penal Code was enforced in its full vigour, were so great that it was many a long year before their efforts were attended with any success.

⁹⁰ Irish Texts Edn., p.285. O'Rahilly's evidence is given in Irish and contains a number of obscure words. The editors have not attempted to translate this document. It is difficult to do more than get the general drift of it, but from that it is obvious that he is describing what may be regarded as the typical " faction fight." The date, however, may be somewhat later than 1700.

CHAPTER VI

Life on the Land

IN dealing with cognate subjects I have already given many particulars relating to agriculture.[1] It would therefore be redundant to devote a full length detailed chapter to the farming community ; but at the same time since farmers and farm workers were, at least numerically, the most important element in the population, this scattered information should, I think, be supplemented by a short sketch of life on the land.

To-day we use the term ' farmer ' indifferently to denote the pastoral grazier of Co. Meath, the extensive grower of corn and root crops in Co. Wexford, and the small crofter on the mountain sides of Kerry or Connemara. In the second half of the seventeenth century there was much the same diversity in acreage and prosperity but less difference in the methods and system followed by the various classes of agriculturist. Indeed the word ' agriculturist ' is a misnomer in speaking of those times : it was not until towards the end of the eighteenth century that scientific principles were first introduced into Irish agriculture ; and England was little further advanced, for there the system (if such it may be called) was also backward and rudimentary before the influence of Arthur Young and Coke of Norfolk revolutionized English methods.

Arthur Young, who was for several years a land agent in Ireland, is often referred to as the father of modern agriculture. It is significant that Olivier

[1] The various references to the subject are classified in the Index under the word ' Agriculture.'

de Serre, the man who in his own country is described as " the father of French agriculture", lived more than 150 years before Young and Coke. Seventeenth century France was well ahead of England in agriculture as in most other arts and sciences. Henri IV and Sully, and later Colbert, definitely encouraged attempts to put agriculture on a more scientific basis ; but Ireland, already in economics (as it was later to become in culture) virtually a satellite of Great Britain, remained unaffected by French progress.

There is evidence to prove that before the devastating wars of the sixteenth century the Irish were, comparatively speaking, not backward in agriculture ; but we are concerned here with the generation which followed the Cromwellian settlement, and we will confine our attention to the fifty years which saw Charles II, his brother and nephew on the throne of England, and Louis XIV in his heyday on that of France.

Agricultural production in Ireland has always consisted primarily of live stock. We have already noticed the absence of fences and enclosures in the countryside[2] ; and this involved the employment of large numbers of herdsmen whose constant work was to keep their masters' little black cattle[3] from straying too far afield. Every evening they had to be rounded up and brought in to the bawn for the

[2] See also Chapter VIII., p.243.
[3] There are two distinct native breeds of cattle still extant in Ireland : the Kerry and the Irish Maol. The latter is usually brindle in colour and, as its name implies, hornless. I think that the black cattle of which we read were horned and of the type we now call Kerries. The cow which appears in Dineley's illustration of a woman milking is a horned one, and Head refers to the smallness of the joints of meat. A proclamation issued by Ginckell in Co. Galway in 1691 refers to " sheep, black cattle and horses," apparently implying thereby that no other cattle were to be found in the west. Reference to the " English " breed of cattle is occasionally met with, e.g., J.R.S.A.I., XVI., p.342.

night, and at dawn of day released and driven to their appointed pastures and there minded. In summer it was customary to take them far from the homestead, and the herdsmen would remain out at night with them, sleeping for the few hours of darkness in hastily erected shelters made with the branches of trees.

In some cases not only the herdsmen accompanied the cattle to their summer pastures : the owner and his family went with them and stayed for awhile in the rude timber dwelling attached to the booley, or enclosure where the cows were milked. This was a survival or development of the old Irish custom of creaghting, but was only practicable so long as the country was thinly populated.

An Order of 1655 requires the creaghts[4], which were the subject of repeated complaints by English authorities in the previous century, to settle in villages. Creaghting, however, which in fact survived in remote places well into the nineteenth century,[5] as did its counterpart the rundale system of tillage,[6] disappeared gradually not in obedience to Government Orders but as a result of the increase in population and the establishment of personal tenure under English law; and it survived in most parts of the country only in the transfer of livestock to some holding at a considerable distance from the homestead. Creaghts (*corruidheachta*) are repeatedly mentioned in O Mellan's War Journal of 1641-47[7] and up to the last decade of the

[4] For a description of early seventeenth century creaghts see J.R.S.A.I. Vol. III., p.423 *et seq.*
[5] Evans, *Irish Heritage*, p.50.
[6] *Ibidem.* Chapter VI of that work contains a valuable description of the rundale system.
[7] MS. R.I.A. 23 H7.

century in time of peace[8] as well as of war[9] they continued to be a source of trouble to the Government and its supporters.

The word " creaght " was frequently employed in a wrong sense by English and even Anglo-Irish writers in the second half of the seventeenth century : Archbishop King, for example, in his Diary[10] equates it with "rapparee," while it is used in some official documents to mean " wicker habitations."[11]

It must be understood that the modern idea expressed in the term " baby beef " was still undreamt of : it involves, of course, intensive feeding from calfhood so as to bring cattle specially bred for the purpose to maturity at two years old or less. The practice then was to slaughter animals at anything up to seven years old, in many cases after using them for awhile as draught oxen. As the seventeenth century advanced garrons (small draught horses) continued steadily to displace oxen for draught purposes though the latter were still extensively used.[12] The restrictions on the shipping of live cattle introduced by the Cattle Acts of Charles II led to the growth of an export trade in beef, but

[8] Orrery to Ormond, 15 Jan. 1666[7] : " I can assure your Grace that Dably Costlelogh (*sic*) with but two men with him was about ten days since seen in the woods of Tomgrinny in the Co. of Clare. It is believed his coming into those parts was to raise above 1,000 Ulstermen which with their crafts last summer came to settle themselves in a mountain which makes the border between the counties of Clare and Galway. I know not what to do with those vagrant Ulsters. They commit no offence which might give me a legal rise to secure them or drive them out of this province." (*Orrery State Letters*, Vol. II., p.120).

[9] Lord Longford, to Patrick Kenny, 29 March, 1690, ordering him to look into the preservation of the meadows and pastures from the destruction of the " keiriaghts " and also into the " villainous proceedings of the rapparees." (*Analecta Hibernica*, No. 15, p.112).

[10] J.R.S.A.I., Vol. XXXIII., p.402. Adrian Adornes in his Narrative of his experiences in Connacht in 1690 and 1691, a manuscript (Rawl. c.439) of 65 closely written pages, frequently mentions the depredations of the " kirriaghts " by which, like King. he appears to mean a band of rapparees. though he occasionally uses this word also in the same sense.

[11] J.R.S.A.I., Vol. III., p.430.

[12] Teams of ten oxen were used regularly in the 1660's on the Orrery estates for hauling timber. *Cal. of Orrery Papers*, p.24 and *passim*.

before that an animal which was intended solely to be converted into meat was not considered saleable before its fifth year. This is easily intelligible when it is remembered that comparatively little hay was saved.[13] The limited supply of fodder was allocated to cows, draught oxen and horses, the bullocks and dry heifers being wintered on withered grass left ungrazed and uncut during the summer. The mild Irish winters made this possible, though on farms where no hay was available during periods of hard frost or snow, many cattle, especially in the north, actually perished from starvation, and all normally lost condition to such an extent that it took until the month of June each year before they began to thrive again.

It can be seen from this that the work which had to be done on an Irish farm was very different from what it is to-day. On a modern farm the dead period of the year is short : the digging of potatoes and the pulling and clamping of mangolds and turnips is not completed till November is far advanced, and by February the plough is often again at work preparing for the spring crops ; even on a farm with a minimum of tillage there are fences and ditches to be repaired, meadows to be grass-harrowed and rolled, top-dressing to be carted on to the fields, and a dozen other jobs besides the daily round of foddering cattle. In the second half of the seventeenth century the beneficial practice of applying lime to grassland as a fertilizer, regarded in 1650 as an innovation, began to be widely adopted.[14] This provided much employ-

[13] The more progressive farmers cut it in good time. Rawdon, for example, had his mowers at work by June 19th in 1665 (C.S.P.I. 1663/65, p.602).
[14] See Boate's *Natural History* in connexion with the customary treatment of Irish land.

ment for farm workers in many districts at times when they were not otherwise busy ; for apart from the labour of distributing the lime itself, limestone had first to be quarried and burnt in a kiln.

Tillage, though ample to supply the limited needs of the country, was not extensive. The rudimentary methods then in vogue did not involve the manuring of tillage crops. An area of grassland was ploughed up in the early spring, and when the corn had been removed the following autumn the field was either ploughed again and allowed to lie fallow, or the stubbles were left untouched : in either case it reverted to grass in the course of time by a process of natural regeneration, though the pasturage thus produced was, except on the richest land, of inferior quality. An attempt, it is true, was sometimes made to add a temporary fertility to land intended for corn crops by burning the surface sod. The after effects of this—" bettimore,"[16] as it was called in County Wexford—were very deleterious, and all progressive farmers condemned it as well as ploughing by the tail, plucking the wool off live sheep, and burning corn in the straw as barbarous practices. The Act of 1634[17] which made them illegal was largely a dead letter for many years.

The fact that there were few fields permanently enclosed meant that every cornfield had to be specially fenced off in such a way as to keep cattle from entering it between the month of April, when it would be sown, and the end of September, when the harvesting would be completed, though in some

[16] Irish, beiteáil
[17] 10/11 Ch. I., c. 15. This statute also prescribed penalties for breaking or cutting fences.

places, of course, where booleying was practised
the bulk of the cattle would have been removed
and such as remained were kept in control by means
of fetters[18].   The preparation of these temporary
fences, which had to be made with whitethorns
and the like cut from the surrounding scrublands,[19]
provided more work for the labourers in the winter,
as did the cutting of firewood for the homestead.
The unsubstantial character of the dwelling houses
and offices, most of which were still made of timber,
involved fairly constant work in repairs and re-
newals ; and of course the timber so used was not
obtained in the form of planks and slats and posts
ready for use, but had to be cut from tree trunks by
two men working in one of the old-fashioned
sawpits which were still common in Co. Clare and
in other remote parts of the country scarcely forty
years ago.

Above all, the thatcher's trade had an important
place in the rural economy. Practically every house
which made any pretence to be a permanent
structure had a thatched roof, and this was usually
made of the strong reed which grows on the margin
of inland lakes. The principal corn crop was oats,
but the straw of this, like the common rush, makes
an inferior thatch compared with wheat or the
"Shannon reed".   In the seventeenth century
Ireland was not a bread-eating country to any
extent, but in certain parts, notably around Dublin
and Kilkenny and in Counties Wexford and
Kildare (all places where the natural reed was not
plentiful) a certain amount of wheat was regularly
sown and the straw of this was available for thatch-

18 Evans, *Irish Heritage*, p.55.
19 See note 17 *supra*.

ing purposes. It must be remembered, too, that thatched houses were still common in towns, or at least in their suburbs, as we know from the attempts made by the urban authorities to abolish them on account of the danger of fire where they existed.[20]

In the winter, then, the people had work enough to do to keep them occupied. By March the lambing began, and before the end of April it was time to think about the shearing of the great flocks of sheep which were to be seen on every grassy hillside. Sheep were usually shorn, or at least clipped, twice in the year—in spring and early autumn. Wherever this practice was not followed shearing would be postponed till May.[21] The Irish sheep was of the long-woolled type. Therefore wherever flocks had access to land overgrown with rough scrub—and few sheep-runs were free of this bugbear of the shepherd —the animals lost a great deal of wool by getting entangled in thickets and briars. This, not mere barbarous ignorance, was the real reason for shearing twice annually.

Once the drying winds of spring came there was much ado about the little plots of tillage. Nowadays a good ploughman, with a pair of lively Irish Draught horses, will plough nearly a statute acre in a day—a matter for surprise to farmers accustomed to the heavy, slow-moving Shires and Clydesdales of England and Scotland. But on the average Irish farm in the seventeenth century ploughing was an operation attended with something like the bustle associated with threshing time in our own day. The

[20] See Assembly Rolls—Dublin and Limerick, *passim*.
[21] The difference between the 17th century calendar and that in use to-day must not be forgotten in considering questions relating to climate and seasons. When the change from Old Style was officially made in the middle of the next century (1752) the error was eleven days : see Cheney, *Handbook of Dates* (London, 1945) pp.10-11.

barbarous practice of ploughing by the tail long persisted in spite of laws passed to put an end to it : instances of fines being executed for this practice are met with in the 60's[22] and it was not unknown in remote districts even at the end of Charles II's reign. This involved the hitching of six or eight garrons to a rough and cumbersome swing plough. In addition to the ploughman himself there was a man or youth to lead each horse[23]; and it is not hard to imagine the shouting and swearing and the constant stops and restarts which marked the slow progress of the plough as it turned its uneven furrows. Ploughing by the tail was defended by its advocates on the grounds that, to avoid hurting themselves, the horses stopped instantly whenever the soc of the plough struck against anything solid, whereas when more humanely tackled they were liable constantly to break traces and even the ploughshare itself. By modern standards this usage is indefensible, but the undoubted cruelty and economic wastage involved can be explained, if not excused, by a fact overlooked by those who most vehemently condemn it. This was the nature of the land which had to be ploughed.[24] Apart from the numerous large stones, which in course of time have since been removed from arable land, there were then innumerable stumps and roots of trees still below the surface of the ground, relics of the woods which had but recently covered a great part of the country and against these the ploughshare was liable to strike at any moment.

[22] C.S.P.I., 1660/62, pp.387, 481, etc. See Moody, *The Londonderry Plantation*, for the prevalence of this custom in Ulster.
[23] In contrast to this we may note that in Arthur Young's time it was customary for one man to manage several horses drawing separate carts.
[24] Apologists of this practice at the beginning of the century did in fact use this argument. Moody, *The Londonderry Plantation*, p.342.

Even where more up-to-date methods were employed—and a reference to Appendix A will show that in districts where tillage was at all extensive and traditional Irish ploughmen and horses were skilful enough—ploughing was not quite the solitary job it now is.

The seed, of course, was sown by hand, broad-casted from a sack or apron, as it still is on small farms to-day ; and rude home-made harrows, drawn by several garrons, covered it in. The harvesting, too, was an operation requiring many hands : reapers with their sickles, binders, stookers, gleaners ; and later on there was threshing and winnowing to be done with no better instruments than the flail and the bellows. Every farm, indeed, was, at certain seasons at least, a centre of ceaseless activity : inside the house itself as much as on the land outside, for on all important occasions there were many mouths to be fed, and even when work on the farm was comparatively slack there was nearly always some outsider—thatcher, itinerant tailor[25] or the like—to be catered for as well as the family and its regular dependants.

The ladies of the upper classes, though they were very early risers, did not do any manual work more strenuous than sewing and embroidery or the making of preserves and cordials ; but the ordinary woman's duties were not confined to cooking and housework. The cows and calves, and of course the

[25] The country tailor is one of the tradesmen mentioned in *Pairlement Chloinne Tomáis* as belonging to the unprivileged servile class. Others in the same category are fullers, cobblers, sievemakers, chimney-sweeps, weavers, mill-hands and smith's helpers, with whom are included collectors of customs excise and hearth-money. Commenting on this, and particularly the addition of tithe-proctors to the list, Dr. McAdoo, in the essay referred to on p.85 *supra*, remarks that it is typical of Clann Tomáis that this despised and hated oppressor of the poor is nevertheless accepted as one of themselves.

dairy, were their special care. Milk and milk products were the staple diet of the people from time immemorial and, even when the introduction of potatoes provided a cheap and easily produced form of sustenance, they served to supplement rather than displace the traditional food of the people in all except the very poorest classes of the community. Two hundred and fifty years ago, and indeed until quite recent times, milking cows and feeding calves was counted as essentially a woman's job as darning socks is to-day ; though it is hard to know why, since the milking of a refractory cow involves the risk of a violent kick if only when spancelling her, and for that matter the operation of milking itself requires considerable strength in the hands and wrist of the milker when he or she has to deal with a cow with a really " tough " udder. Farmers' wives, daughters and maidservants, whose day's work, like that of their menfolk, always began at dawn, had no time to think of wearing silk stockings or cultivating the feminine graces. And in addition to their ordinary work there was the business of bearing and rearing children. Women of all classes married young and normally had very large families, at least half of which, however, might be expected to die in infancy.[26]

In the days we are dealing with the countryside was accessible to all. The citizens of Dublin could easily get away from streets and houses, and this was true even of London, for one reads of wildfowl being shot where Regent Street now is. In Ireland the sights and sounds of the farm were quite familiar to the average man. On an important and ceremonial

[26] Infant mortality appears to have been even greater in France. See Bradby, *The Great Days of Versailles*, p.61.

occasion, in the course of an address to the Duke of Ormond on a purely political topic, Sir Audley Mervin, the Speaker of the House of Commons, saw nothing indecorous in making use of a simile taken from the farmyard. " In the north of Ireland," he said, " the Irish have a custom in the winter, when milk is scarce, to kill the calf and reserve the skin, and stuffing it with straw they set it upon four wooden feet, which they call a puckcan (*sic* = pocán) and the cow will be as fond of this as she was of the living calf. She will low after it and lick it and give down her milk so it stand but by her."[27]

There was a practical reason for the custom he here refers to. Many things, however, were habitually done on and about the farm whose origin can be traced back to pagan times and whose continuance was due to the superstitious beliefs of the country people added to their innate conservatism.

Some of these, indeed, have survived in a harmless form right down to our own times.[28] When, for example, a person enters a house where butter is being churned he or she is expected to take a turn with the churn, though a present-day housewife is not likely to believe that some supernatural agency will cause her butter to vanish if this custom is not observed. In the seventeenth century, and much later than that, the country people had an implicit belief in the existence of fairies, whose malign influence, particularly on the work of the dairy and the health of the live stock, had constantly to be propitiated. On St. John's Eve it was customary to make small bonfires in the principal gaps and tracks

[27] Speech, 13 Feb. 1662 [3] (Pamphlet, Dublin, 1662 [3]).
[28] A few of our remaining popular superstitions are not very ancient : those connected with the magpie, for instance, cannot have been general among our seventeenth century ancestors, for the simple reason that in their day the magpie was practically non-existent in Ireland.

frequented by cattle to prevent the fairies passing there ; on May Day the pails of milk were adorned with garlands of flowers ; and rings of mountain ash were often attached to cows' udders to safeguard them against the spells of fairies. Similarly the people sought to protect their houses against evil spirits by nailing a horse-shoe on the threshold, and against fire by tying two burnt embers in the form of a cross and sticking this in the thatch. The belief in supernatural cures for sick animals was also very widespread. Nicholas Dowdall in his contribution to the chorographical survey promoted by Petty and the Dublin Philosophical Society, describes one which he admits was generally supposed to be effective, though he laughed at it himself and preferred something more up-to-date prescribed by his English dairywoman. The conagh worm was believed to be the cause of a prevalent cattle disease which was probably what we now call blackleg or blackquarter. " The common sort," he says, " do believe when they find one of these worms by making an auger hole in a tree and putting the worm alive in it [being careful not to hurt it, he says on another page] and close it with a wooden pin, the leaves then have healing properties when boiled . . . "[29]

It would be tedious to multiply examples of this kind. Many books exist which deal at length with the subject of fairy lore and superstitious beliefs and practices.[30] These were by no means confined to the poorer and more ignorant classes. Many of the

[29] MS. T.C.D. I. 1, 2. pp.147, 148. A little treatise on cattle diseases was published in Dublin in 1673—*The Herdsman's Mate*, by Michael Harward.
[30] The volumes of the J.R.S.A.I. and the more recently established *Béaloideas* contain many articles of interest on this subject. Much information in a more accessible form is to be found in T. Crofton Croker's *Researches in the South of Ireland* and in E. E. Evans's *Irish Heritage*, Chaps. 17, 18 and 19. For conagh worm superstitions see J.R.S.A.I., Vol. VIII., p.323.

noblest families, Anglo-Irish as well as Gaelic, had no doubt of the existence of banshees, and the aristocratic huntsman was as much put out as the humblest fisherman by meeting a red-headed woman as he left his gate in the morning. Superstition, however, meaning something ever present in men's minds—not a mere cult or affectation—was part of the daily lives of the working people far more than was the case with their employers and social superiors.

In composing our picture of farm life we must not overlook the numerous cottier class. We have already considered in some detail[31] the wretched hovels in which they, and usually their animals, lived ; or it would be more accurate to say, sheltered themselves by night. Dunton's description, quoted in Appendix B, gives an idea of the wretched patches of " garden " which were attached to these :‾ it is easy to imagine a gloomy November day and to visualize the pool of foul green water outside the doorway, the rotting potato stalks and the scattered heads of cabbage half eaten by the solitary goat or starveling calf ; but the picture will be a distorted one unless we also recall those May evenings with the scent of whitethorn in the air when the young people found time to dance by the roadside while their grandparents sat and watched them or walked slowly home among the fragrant golden furze-bushes, their brogues or unshod feet wet with the dew of the fresh green grass. Or if this sounds a trifle too idyllic we may balance Dunton's sordid scene (which I do not wish to suggest was in

---

[31] See Chapter IV. So far as housing was concerned, there was little to choose between a labourer's cabin and that of the man who, in his own and his neighbour's estimation, might be regarded as a small farmer.

itself much exaggerated) by reflecting how many of the more industrious small holders grew a square of hemp or flax, the latter the raw material for a home industry which employed thousands of women in spinning and weaving and in making their own and their families' clothes.

The poor labourer was probably not consciously affected by his surroundings. Psychologically we know very little about him.[33] He was inarticulate: *Pairlemint Chloinne Tomáis*, though it is valuable as a picture of the lowest stratum of seventeenth century society, is a satire quite devoid of sympathy with its subject. It was not until the next century that the worker in the fields gave expression to his thoughts and feelings in verse ; and then a poet like " Eoghan an Bheoil Bhinn "—best known by the anglicized form of his name, Owen Roe O'Sullivan—outwardly indistinguishable from his fellows in equally humble circumstances, was not of the true cottier class. The Gaelic poets of the seventeenth century, who were still influenced in some degree by the bardic tradition, showed a keen appreciation of the beauties of nature, and of the natural beauties of Ireland in particular, but they do not give us those intimate glimpses of daily life in the country which we get in the eighteenth century peasant poets and which have something in common with the early work of Robert Burns, though nothing could be more different than the fate of their poetry. David O'Bruadair, it is true, was reduced for a time to earning his living by manual work, but so far from describing this episode of his life as an interesting experience, he dismisses it contemptuously as a thing only to be mentioned as showing to what a

[33] See note 25 *supra* and Index under Cottiers and Labour.

sorry pass the Ireland which traditionally honoured its poets had been reduced.

O'Bruadair, when he was down and out, may well have turned his hand to cattle droving. Men sometimes went great distances with their drovers to buy cattle. Sir George Rawdon, for instance, mentions a visit to Mullingar fair[34] as nothing out of the ordinary, though the distance from that midland town to his home at Lisburn is about 120 miles.

Rawdon, of course, was progressive and up-to-date in his farming, as he was in all his rural activities, whether he was making roads, planting orchards or improving the sporting amenities of his own and Lord Conway's demesnes. Though he died in 1684, forty-seven years before the Royal Dublin Society was founded, it was his example and that of a few others like him, which opened men's eyes to the need of such a body, one of whose principal objects has always been the advancement of agriculture. As I have already said, few improvements of a fundamental scientific nature were introduced in this field of activity in the seventeenth century. It was in agriculture, as in agrarian, political and social affairs, a period of transition. The better type of English Protestant settler, exemplified by Sir George Rawdon, certainly did much to promote agricultural progress, within the limitations of the knowledge possessed by the men of their time. While giving them due credit we should not forget that a commendable spirit of enterprise in this respect had been shown before their day by the Cistercian monks.[35] Nevertheless, traditional

[34] Fairs other than those held from time immemorial were established by Letters Patent. See for example, the King's letter of 14 Jan., 1670, in reply to the petition of the sovereign and burgesses of Athy, for leave to hold fairs twice yearly in that town. C.S.P.I. 1669 /70, p.66.
[35] *Cambrensis Eversus*, Vol. II., p.277 n.

Gaelic Ireland, whose outlook was expressed by the surviving bards of the old school, hated such innovations as " fairs held in the places of the chase" and " the open green crossed by girdles of twisting fences " ; and the beginning of a more settled and productive country life, though no doubt it would have come in any case in due course, must be accounted a direct result of the final English conquest of Ireland in the seventeenth century.

CHAPTER VII

Dublin and Town Life

THE striking difference between the almost mediæval conditions of the early years of the seventeenth century and the comparatively modern conditions of post-Restoration times is particularly marked in the towns. Dublin has always been the principal city in the country, but the increase in its population and extent has been much more steady and gradual than that of Belfast, or of many towns in England which owe their expansion, if not their existence, to the industrial revolution dating from the end of the eighteenth century. Dublin has now a population of 520,000 and Belfast is also about half a million. In 1706 the population of Dublin was estimated at 60,224, which is probably rather less than the correct figure. At the same time the only town in Ulster given by the same authority is Derry, with a mere 2,848, Belfast not being large enough to be mentioned at all.[1] These figures are based on the hearth money returns.[2] Dublin, however, expanded in a most remarkable manner after the Restoration,

[1] MS. T.C.D. I. 1. 3. pp.320-330. It is difficult to reconcile the figures given by various authorities for the population of Dublin. Petty's own estimates, or the estimates attributed to him vary: (see *Political Anatomy*; *Petty Papers*, ed. Lansdowne ; and *Calendar of the Records of the City of Dublin*, Vol. V., preface, p.xxxii.). Probably this is due to the inclusion or exclusion of certain suburbs in the total. The highest estimate for the period 1680 to 1700 I have seen is 69,090—for 1682 (Journal of the Cork Hist. and Arch. Soc., Vol. III., p.25), and the lowest, 40,508 for 1696 (MS. T.C.D. I. 1. 2, p.74). In an article on this subject in the Journal of the R.S.A.I. (Vol. XXXI., p.28) the estimate for 1728 is given as 146,025.

[2] Houses with one hearth in Dublin were taken as equivalent to $4\frac{1}{2}$ and in the country to 5 persons ; in the case of those with more than one hearth the figures were: country 7, Dublin $8\frac{1}{2}$. The total population of Ireland is given in the manuscript mentioned in note 1 as 1,620,901 in 1706, which may be compared with Sir William Petty's estimate for 1672 in his *Political Anatomy* of 1,100,000. Elsewhere (*Petty Papers*, Vol. I., p.57) he puts it at 1,260,000, two thirds of these being Irish Papists. Orrery in a letter to Ormond dated Dec. 14, 1666, estimates the number of men in Ireland fit to bear arms as 600,000, four-fifths of them Papists (*Orrery State Papers*,

comparable indeed to what has taken place during
the past thirty years, and this continued for about
half a century : thus in the short space of four years,
from 1701 to 1705, there was an increase of no less
than 765 houses in the parishes of the city and
liberties. In the first half of the seventeenth century
Dublin was a mediæval town, lying to the north
and west of the Castle on the south side of the river
and not extending far beyond the city walls. Though
the records of the City Assembly tell a tale of
constant shortage of money, the citizens themselves
appear to have had both the enterprise and the
capital to carry out schemes of development, and
even the Corporation,[3] as we would now call it,
managed to find the money or the credit to build
several bridges across the Liffey, to make embank-
ments along the riverside, and to erect some
important buildings. The Government, too, did its
share, by the establishment of the Phoenix Park
and the Royal Hospital at Kilmainham, towards

Vol. II., p.95), clearly an overestimate. Seamus Pender (J.C.H.A.S.,
Vol. XLIV, No. 160, p.82) believes that the population fell to about half-a-
million after the Cromwellian war and devastation. Little reliance, however, can be placed on the actual figures given in the so-called Census of 1659
(where the total is as low as 360,000 and Dublin and Liberties are returned
as a mere 8,780) since the arguments against it being a census, in the sense
of a full enumeration of the people, appear to be convincing. Archbp.
King states in his remarks on Dr. Willoughby's Observations (MS. Nat.
Lib., not yet catalogued—ref. *pro tem*. S.1.) that according to a return
made by the clergy in 1690 there were in Dublin 8,300 Protestant men
between 16 and 80 years of age.
[3] Officially the city Corporations, as we would now call them, were
termed Assemblies. The minute books of the bodies governing the
civic affairs of Dublin and Limerick are called the Dublin Assembly
Roll and the Limerick City Assembly Book. The former was edited
by Sir John Gilbert and published under the title of *Calendar of the City
of Dublin Records*. The Limerick City Assembly Book, covering the years
with which this book deals, is preserved in the National Library, Dublin,
and is catalogued as MS. No. 89. For brevity I shall refer to them in these
notes as " Cal. Dub. Rec." and " Nat. Lib. MS. 89." The use of the word
' Corporation ' in the modern sense of city council is seldom if ever found
in the Dublin Assembly Roll, but it occurs here and there in the Limerick
City Assembly Book, and Dineley occasionally uses it in the same way,
as does Dr. Arthur as early as 1626 (Arthur MS. fo. 5 recto). Cf. *Orrery
Papers*, ff. 349, 495, 613 and 683. *Analecta Hib*. No. 12, p.124, *et seq*.

making Dublin the nucleus of a modern capital, and one which in Dunton's time at the end of the seventeenth century was recognized as a city second only to London in size and importance in the king's dominions. It is interesting to notice incidentally that London, then as now, was more than ten times as large as Dublin,[4] but there was no other city in England or Scotland as large as Dublin. Even thirty years earlier, when it had not recovered from the set-back of the Cromwellian wars, M. Jouvin de Rochfort, the French traveller who visited Ireland in 1666, remarked that Dublin with its suburbs was one of the greatest and best peopled towns in Europe. A good idea of the extent of the city at the end of the reign of Charles II can be obtained by studying the map made by T. Phillips at the time : a reproduction of it appears in Falkiner's *Illustrations of Irish History*, where the streets, none of which were marked by name in the original map, are as far as possible identified. Including the suburbs, where the land was not yet fully occupied by buildings, the city by this time covered the space bounded by a line drawn approximately from Trinity College— which had hitherto been described as " Near Dublin "[5]—up Grafton Street to Stephen's Green, thence by St. Kevin's Street past St. Patrick's Cathedral to St. James's Gate, across the Liffey at Ussher's Island ; then on the north side including Oxmantown Green, where the Collins Barracks now stands, and eastwards a little to the north of the

[4] Dr. Arthur Bryant gives the population of London in 1660 as between 500,000 and 600,000. At the same time he says that Bristol and Norwich, the next in importance among English cities, had each about 30,000 inhabitants. (*The England of Charles II.*, pp.13 and 137).
[5] It is so referred to even by Dunton, but by his time the space between the College and the nearest city gate was extensively built upon. Cf. Dixon, *Trinity College*, p.13.

present North King Street to a point somewhere near O'Connell Street. The bridge nearest to the mouth of the river was Essex Bridge, at the bottom of Capel Street. This was built in 1676. It is difficult to realize that all the large part of Dublin now lying between O'Connell Bridge and Sandymount was then, with the exception of a narrow neck of land at Ringsend, covered by the sea twice daily and could only be traversed at low tide.

In point of population, though Dublin was a very considerable place according to the standards of the time, its position relative to the rest of the people of the country was by no means so disproportionate as it is to-day ; for if we accept the figures I quoted above only about one in 28 persons in Ireland were resident in Dublin as against one in 9, or less, to-day.

Dublin was an English city so far as its institutions and its leading citizens were concerned. Perhaps I might use the word ' British ' here, and add that it was nevertheless un-English. It was, in fact, English in rather the same way as Hong Kong is now, with its British institutions and governing class and a subordinate native population. Of course the analogy is not quite perfect, because even the strongest Gaelic influences could not produce an atmosphere so un-English as that of the Far East, and moreover, the Chinese hinterland is independent of Great Britain ; but with that reservation the parallel will serve.

Town life had no place in Gaelic Ireland. In early times such small towns as existed were Scandinavian settlements, and later these fell into English hands. By degrees, however, the native Irish penetrated into the towns and became indistinguishable from the early settlers who remained

OBJECTS IN EVERYDAY USE

(Photographs of Specimens supplied by the National Museum of Ireland)

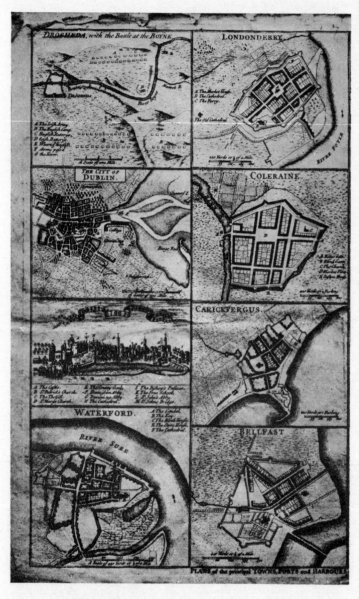

PLANS OF THE PRINCIPAL IRISH TOWNS AT THE END OF THE 17th CENTURY
(From Tindal's Continuation of Rapin's "Histoire d'Angleterre")

Catholic; so that in the seventeenth century Galway, and to a large extent Limerick also, were essentially Irish, even though by the end of the century the control of their affairs had passed into alien hands. This process took much longer in the case of Dublin which has only become an Irish city during the past half century, and even yet retains a good deal of its English character.

The better class of those Irish who in mediæval times went to live in the towns became merchants.[6] Commerce abhors war except to the limited extent that it can profit by supplying the combatants with the materials of warfare. So inevitably the towns, in which of course there was always a considerable proportion of men of English blood, were loyal to the English connexion as being the most likely to mean a strong central government and to preserve settled conditions favourable to commerce. The Irish in the towns were therefore more friendly to English pretensions to rule the country than were the Gaelic countrymen from whom they sprang. This attitude of the towns was traditional. Speaking of them in Elizabethan times, Standish O'Grady, in his preface to *Pacata Hibernia*, says : " Without exception the walled towns and cities, inland and seaboard, held by the Crown in all those wars, including the Nine Years' War—Tyrone's war. It is useless to endeavour to upset this cardinal fact by reference to State Papers in which the disloyalty, etc., of townsmen is animadverted upon. The fact remains that not one of the walled towns, inland or seaboard, declared at any time in favour of any of the insurgent lords ; no

---

[6] From their families the professional class was recruited. Later on penal legislation closed all the regular professions, except medicine, to Catholics, so that by the end of the century the proportion of Catholic doctors became very high.

more than did the walled towns and cities of the Continent when the same controversy of Crown versus the great feudal dynasts was being fought out there. And for the same reason. The walled towns represented commerce ; and commerce cares little for right and wrong, but cares a great deal for peace, law, and order. The cause of peace, law, and order —of despotism, too, had men been able to see a little beyond their own noses—seemed to the mercantile interest to be bound up with the cause of the Crown. Europe felt that and so did Ireland. The walled towns went hotly with the Crown throughout the whole course of the controversy between the Crown and the territorial autocracies. Nor can it be pretended that they were coerced, for the walled towns were self-governed and self-defended. The townsmen manned their own walls and towers and held their own gates. Each had its own armed force and every substantial burgher was a soldier, and owed his first duty to the town of which he was a citizen ; and in war-time all such towns sent forth their legal quota to fight for the Crown—never to fight for any great lord." This political orientation was gradually turned to hostility by the attempts, begun in Elizabeth's reign, to force Protestantism on the citizens : their so-called loyalty was not deeply rooted, particularly in Limerick, whose stubborn resistance both to Ireton and to William of Orange is famous.

Limerick was usually considered the second city of the kingdom up to Cromwell's time, but it suffered very severely as a result of the destruction wrought by the long siege which only terminated in 1651 and, after making a rapid recovery, it was again devastated by the sieges which followed the battle of

Aughrim in 1691 and ended with the famous Treaty of Limerick. In this siege practically all the extensive suburbs outside the walls were razed to the ground.[7]

Boate places the first six towns of Ireland in 1652 in this order : Dublin, Galway, Waterford, Limerick, Cork, Derry ; and he considers Drogheda, Kilkenny and Bandon worthy of mention. Forty years later Lawrence Eachard, in his *Chorographical Description of Ireland*, states that seven places in the country might be called cities, naming the six mentioned by Boate and adding Kilkenny. Eachard counts Drogheda, Kinsale and Athlone the most important towns after the seven cities. Dineley thought very highly of Limerick, and a few years later Stevens remarks that it was inferior to none but Dublin. Sir Thomas Molyneux, on the other hand, describes Galway as the best town he had seen after Dublin, well-built,[8] and distinctively Catholic. He adds that the inhabitants were all " Old English-Irish."[9] In the first of his unpublished letters, written about the same time, Dunton mentions that Galway was almost entirely Papist.

In the period we are considering, the number of towns in Ireland was not great, and the population even of these, except Dublin, to which I have already referred, was quite small. Kilkenny was the only place of importance, which was anything approaching its present size.[10] Its population (now 10,000)

[7] Begley, *History of the Diocese of Limerick in the* 16*th and* 17*th Centuries*, Chapter VI.

[8] Cf. *Cambrensis Eversus*, Introd., p. v., and Green, *Making of Ireland and Its Undoing*, *passim*. The well-built stone houses of Galway are frequently mentioned by travellers. These are well illustrated in Thos. Phillips's unpublished Military Survey of Ireland, 1685. MS. Nat. Lib. 660.

[9] MS. T.C.D. I. 1. 3. pp.80-81.

[10] Kilkenny in 1681 is described by Dineley as " the most pleasant and delightful town of the kingdom." It was in its heyday a generation before Dineley visited it, when it was the Confederate capital. Cf. p.30 *supra*.

was then about 7,000. According to the authority quoted at the beginning of this chapter, in the early eighteenth century Cork had about 25,000 inhabitants,[11] Limerick 11,000, and Waterford and Galway 6,000 each. The rest were little more than villages, though some like Kilmallock and Kinsale retained something of their urban character by reason of their former strategic importance, and others like Bandon and one or two in the north were newly built with a definite sectarian object. Ennis, for example, the most important town in Co. Clare, had not at the most more than 600 inhabitants.[12] In considering urban life, therefore, as distinct from rural, I may confine myself principally to Dublin and one other place of less importance, such as Limerick.

In trying to reconstruct the scenes which would have met my eyes had I been going to visit Dublin towards the end of the seventeenth century, it is natural for me, being a Munsterman, to think of approaching the city along the Naas road and entering it by way of St. James's Gate and Thomas Street, and so passing straight into the heart of the old town. If the visitor were from outside Ireland

[11] See note 1. Sir Richard Cox remarked about that time that there were over 20,000 people in the suburbs of Cork, which had grown bigger than the city itself. (Jnl. of Cork Hist. and Arch. Soc., 1902, p.160). This was, however, no more than an expression of opinion. How inaccurate such can be is illustrated by Dineley's remarks that Kilkenny was about the size of Orleans, which city at the time had a population of 31,000. (*Obs.* p.52, note 1). Sir R. Cox died in 1733, aged 83, and in his old age he is reported to have said that " Ireland was so much improved of late years that if a person could but rise from the dead, who was intombed 40 years, he would not know the spot where he was born or the surrounding neighbourhood, for the face of nature with the help of art had entirely altered every feature." (*Tour through Ireland by Two English Gentlemen*, Dublin, 1746, p.98).
[12] MS. T.C.D. I. 1. 2, p.237. Eachard describes Killaloe as " once a very considerable place, now decaying, though still counted the chief of the county." Sixmilebridge was about equal to Ennis in population. Dineley's illustration shows Ennis to have been a poor enough place in 1681.

his ship would probably anchor off Ringsend, unless he had made the passage in a small craft of not more than six feet draught, in which case she might make her way up the river at high tide as far as the Custom House,[13] and tie up close to the quay, heeling over later on, of course, when she grounded as the tide went out. According to Sir Frederick Falkiner, such small seagoing craft could go up the river as far as Merchant's and Wood Quays. The same authority states that gabbards or barges were used to transfer cargoes from ships anchored at Ringsend to the quays.[14] Actually we know from a minute of the Dublin Corporation in 1684 that the quaying of Wood Quay to Essex Bridge was only under consideration in that year.

It was decided that the major part of this work was to be undertaken by the riparian tenants. This was the ordinary arrangement at the time, so far as the lower reaches of the Liffey were concerned, with the result that parts of the riverbank were quayed and parts were not, like the foot-pavements in the streets of Johannesburg a few years ago, when each householder was responsible for the space between his house or shop and the roadway. Thus in 1683 a lease was granted to one Hawkins (no doubt Hawkins Street took its name from this family), and by its terms the lessee was ordered to continue the quay already built on the adjacent property, and a provision was inserted declaring the lease void if the quay was not finished within 21

[13] The Custom House was just below Essex Bridge, near where Dollard's printing-house now stands.
[14] *Foundation of the King's Hospital*, p.4. In 1685 it was decided that the drawbridge on Essex Bridge be arched over and that gabbards should strike their masts there. (Cal. Dub. Rec., Vol. V., p.361).

years. Further up the river a whole section was
sometimes undertaken by one man.[15]

The advantages of quaying were partly negatived
by the fact that the channels at the mouth of the
river were becoming blocked up, and the necessity
for some properly constituted authority to control
the affairs of the port was recognized soon after
settled conditions were restored and the development of the city on modern lines began. It was not
until 1673, however, that the first steps were taken
towards the promotion of the body which eventually
became the Port and Docks Board of the present
day.[16] Influence, corruption and incompetence
retarded the advance in this direction for a number
of years.

The passenger disembarking at Ringsend would
find little or no accommodation in the isolated group
of cottages which stood on that tongue of dry land,
and as soon as the tide receded he would have to
take one of the peculiar cars described by Dunton[17]
in which he would be driven at a fast speed and
with much jolting across the firm strand to a point
not far from Trinity College and so into the city.
They would drive along what is now Dame Street,
or Damas or Dam Street, as it was called even as
late as the early nineteenth century. It was then a
rough road outside the city proper, bordered by large
houses recently built for prominent people such as
Anglesey, Temple and Eustace, whose names are

[15] In the transaction concerning the quaying of the stretch from the Old
Bridge to Park Gate, it was provided that the petitioner should suffer such
common sewers as were necessary to pass through the premises into the
river. At that time the word ' sewer ' was used to denote any drain or
watercourse.
[16] Falkiner, *Illustrations of Irish History*, p.186 and R.I.A., Proceedings,
XXIV, c, p.133 *et seq.* See also *Analecta Hibernica*, No. 1, p.157 (Rawl.
b. 492), on establishment of pilot service in the same year.
[17] Yarranton stated in 1675 that £500 per annum was earned by these carmen. Cal. Dub. Rec., Vol. V., p.574.

perpetuated by those of the streets now occupying the space where the houses of these magnates originally stood in their own grounds. The most conspicuous of these mansions was Chichester House where the Parliament of 1661 was convened. It occupied the site of the present Bank of Ireland, erected in 1728, which was, of course, used as the Parliament House until the Union. In 1674 among the holders of seats in the new Protestant Church of St. Andrew, situated on the south side of Dame Street, besides those just mentioned, were Henry Aston and John Rogerson, The Countess of Clancarty was also a seat-holder : this is interesting for a different reason, as the MacCarthys were one of the leading Catholic families and the Dowager Duchess a staunch adherent of the old faith ; in fact a rumour got about in 1681 that her brother, the Duke of Ormond, had received the Sacrament, according to the Catholic rite, one evening at her house in College Green.[18] The Duke, though he had no leanings towards the religion professed by most of his family, knew enough about it to be able to point out that Mass is not celebrated after noon and that the sacrament of Communion is administered only at Mass, except in the case of sick persons. The young Countess brought up her son a Protestant but, unlike his illustrious kinsman, this young man (the fourth earl) at the age of seventeen reverted to Catholicism, and although he himself ended his days in comparative affluence and happiness on the Continent, the family estates in Ireland were thus lost for ever.[19]

[18] Gilbert, *History of Dublin*, Vol. III., p.19.
[19] For an account of his romantic career see Webo's *Compendium*, p.304. This is the same Lord Clancarty who figured in the incident related on page 162.

Perhaps the narrow old Blind Gate would be no longer at the entrance of Dame Street, as it was removed during the reign of Charles II, but the Dams Gate nearer the Castle was not demolished until 1698.[20] Once through this the traveller was in the old city, and the business of finding accommodation would be his next consideration. He might, as Dunton did, arrive at eleven o'clock at night if the time of low tide so ordained, thus making his task more difficult.

There was no lack of taverns and coffee-houses in Dublin[21] : the number of taverns and ale-houses is given as over 1,500 in the minutes of the Corporation for 1667 ; but inns in which travellers might find shelter for the night were both scarce and bad. Jouvin, it is true, found the Mitre Inn at Oxmantown tolerable, but few travellers had a good word to say for them, and it was customary to take lodgings with some housewife who made it her business to accommodate visitors.

The jolting experienced crossing the firm strand from Ringsend was slight compared with that in the badly paved streets, though if the journey were undertaken in the daytime the congestion in the narrow streets effectively prevented horse-drawn vehicles from proceeding at more than walking pace. The Assembly Roll contains frequent refer-

[20] Gilbert, Vol. II., p.257. My facts regarding Dublin at this period are principally obtained from this work, from the Calendar of Records referred to in note 3, from the State Papers, from Dunton's " Conversation in Ireland " (printed in his *Dublin Scuffle*), and from his unpublished letters.

[21] The names of a number of the better-known Dublin inns are to be found in the State Papers (C.S.P.I. and C.S.P. Dom.) indexed under " Dublin City." They had signs in the English fashion to correspond with such picturesque names as " The Bear & Ragged Staff " " The Nag's Head," " The Sugar Loaf " and " The White Hart." A list of some of them is also given in J.R.S.A.I., Vol. XLI., p.33. Kilkenny inns, not however with special reference to the seventeenth century, are the subject of a paper by J. G. Prim in J.R.S.A.I., Vol., VII., p.153. See also Dub. Hist. Rec. II. 3. 119.

ences to the crowded condition of the streets, and efforts were made from time to time to check the more flagrant causes of it, such as the practice of bringing in large loads of hay for sale in the streets instead of in the recognized market places.

A cause of complaint which has recurred at intervals down to our day was the number of hucksters who exposed their wares for sale in the streets. They were a constant annoyance to the regular shopkeepers as well as a serious obstruction to the traffic. Many of them were people in from the country with poultry, wild-fowl, rabbits, etc. A minute of June, 1669, is quite graphic: " The streets are much pestered with hucksters sitting under bulks and stalls in the streets whereby the streets are made so narrow that coaches or carts cannot well pass or turn." Another minute of April, 1684, describes the street from Essex Gate to Wood Quay, "commonly called Blind Quay". This, though very narrow, with hardly room for two coaches to pass, was a great thoroughfare always full of coaches, cars and carts, and is described as not only congested with traffic but actually dangerous to life.[22] A detour nearer to the river was proposed, and it was eventually made, but whether " at no great charge", as its sponsors believed, is not recorded. The abuse of street trading was not due only to country people flocking into the city and disregarding the regulations : complaints were made of freemen setting up stalls in the streets " to the annoyance and harm of shopkeepers."[23] As early as January, 1660/1, an attempt was made to

[22] Early in the 18th century a law was passed making it obligatory on carmen to lead their horses in the streets of Dublin and Cork instead of riding on their carts as theretofore.
[23] Jan. 1667 /8, Cal. Dub. Rec., Vol. IV., p.439.

abolish street-sellers, except those duly licensed, but the regulations had little effect. Seven years later it was decided that street-selling should be allowed only on public fair-days.[24] Sellers of victuals, however, were permitted to continue on the streets, and later on we find a tendency to encourage country people to come in in order to keep down city prices.

The loud street cries which were a feature of London life are not mentioned as a nuisance in Dublin, though no doubt they were equally to be heard there. Street-singers, too, must have added their contribution to the general hub-bub. The Corporation, indeed, encouraged music in its proper place, as their pay-roll included a number of musicians who formed a permanent city band.[25] Whether they in any way fulfilled the function of a modern municipal orchestra I do not know ; but they were required, like the town bands of Holland at the same date, to perform in public on certain occasions, and were specifically ordered " to go in and through the city and suburbs with the city waits every usual night from October 5th to February 5th yearly."[26]

Many of the pictures conjured up by the prosaic minutes of the Dublin Assembly in the time of

[24] The dates of these were to be fixed by proclamation, but custom had already firmly established several of them. In Limerick there were " two fairs a year, viz., that of St. John the Baptist and St. James, the latter whereof is after the manner of Bartholomew Fair, London, and continues a fortnight during which time no arrest can be made in the town for debt, in signal whereof a white glove is hung out at the prison." Dineley, *Observations*, p.120.

[25] In the year 1658 Kilkenny had several officially appointed city musicians who were paid a salary of £5 a year each, but by 1709, though there were four scavengers, there was no musician on the payroll. In the next generation, however, the Corporation again officially recognized music as an element in municipal affairs by appointing a salaried organist. J.R.S.A.I., Vol. XXXIII., p.209.

[26] O'Bruadair refers to sreanga sraidéigse in his poem on Patrick Sarsfield.

Charles II and James II would have made fine material for an artist like Hogarth, had one been commissioned to illustrate those ponderous volumes. Imagine the life he would have put into the somewhat colourless description I have just given of the crowded streets. What pictures he would have made of the disembarkation of passengers at Ringsend ; of the great brewers' drays ; of horses being driven to water through narrow alleys scarce five feet wide to the danger of the ragged children playing in them ; of the better-class children in the City School crowding into the small kitchen below it for want of warmth in their class-room ; of the importunate chairmen on Cork Hill and their allies the tavern waiters ; of street brawls after dark ; of prostitutes outside the theatre in Smock Alley ; of the public drawing and hanging of a condemned rapparee ; of the indescribable horrors of the Newgate goal ; or, if he turned his hand to less gruesome subjects, of the Bowling Green on a fine day in summer ; of the citizens taking the air on Stephen's Green ; of fireworks, and wine flowing in the streets on such occasions as the State arrival of the Duke of Ormond[27]; or of the ceremonial observed when the Lord Mayor[28] entertained the aldermen and burgesses to dinner.

At night, of course, the whole city was almost in darkness. In 1687 a resolution was passed by the City Assembly " for the prevention of many mischiefs and inconveniences in the streets in the dark nights " that lanterns and candles be hung out from selected houses every night in the winter season from 5 to 10

[27] Cf. Limerick on 10 June, 1687, when the Mayor celebrated the birth of James II's heir by distributing three hogsheads of wine among the populace at his own expense. (Begley, *Diocese of Limerick*, Vol. II, p.356).
[28] The Mayor of Dublin became Lord Mayor in October, 1665. This dignity had previously been refused on the grounds of expense.

p.m. The cost of this was to be borne by the inhabitants of each street and the position of the lights determined by the Lord Mayor and Sheriffs.[29]

Limerick was quite up-to-date in this respect according to the standards of the time, for as early as 1678 the Town Clerk, Recorder and Comptroller of the Corporation were appointed as a subcommittee to devise methods "for keeping of candle-light" on dark nights,[30] and for improving the cleanliness of the streets.[31] At first the responsibility for street-lighting was placed upon the householders but in 1696 "lamps to enlighten the streets at night were for the first time fixed up in Limerick by Alderman Thomas Rose at his own expenses"[32]. The conditions in London at the same time were not much better, until about 1690 a new form of lamp superseded the old lanterns there. Misson describes them as having a very thick convex glass which caused them to "throw out great rays of light and illuminate the path for people who go on foot tolerably well." These were only lighted from 6 p.m. till midnight between Michaelmas and Lady Day from the third day after full moon to the sixth day after new moon, so even in London the streets were often in darkness before midnight. In this connexion it should be

[29] See *Dublin Historical Record*, Vol. V, No. 4, p.130, article by P. Meehan on "Early Dublin Public Lighting."
[30] Even some of the smaller towns took steps in this direction. In October 1680, for example, keepers of alehouses, taverns and brandy shops in New Ross were ordered to hang out their lights on dark nights from 6 p.m. to 9 p.m. under penalty of a fine of 6d. "for every neglect." Old Corporation Book of Ross : J.R.S.A.I., Vol. XXII., p.290.
[31] R.I.A. MS. 24. D. 21, p.213.
[32] Nat. Lib. MS. 89. By a resolution of Aug. 15, 1673, for instance, the inhabitants were ordered not to keep any swine within the walls nor to allow dogs to be loose in the streets after 10 p.m. This was no idle threat as the beadle had to hough any pigs found. Several regulations were made governing refuse and other "nuisances" in the streets. Cf. Kinsale Presentments printed *Analecta Hibernica*, No. 15, pp.172 to 180.

remembered that in English towns the working day began before dawn and the citizens were accustomed to regard the afternoons as a time for recreation.[33] No doubt this was also the case in Dublin, for the great bell of Christchurch Cathedral was rung regularly at 4 a.m. and 9 p.m.,[34] by which hour the ordinary citizen would have been retiring to bed. He was not, however, dependent on this bell as a timekeeper. The morning bell served to arouse the citizens for the new day's work but the ordinary alarm clock which now usually fulfills that function was not unknown in the seventeenth century,[35] and of course pocket watches were carried by people who could afford them. In Dublin there was a public clock on the Tholsel, to attend to which a clockmaker was officially appointed in 1667 at an annual salary of £5, later raised to £6.

To his remarks on street-lighting, Misson adds as worth special mention a note saying : " on each side of the street there is almost all over London a way better paved than the rest for foot passengers." The paving of Dublin was still very bad, but a definite improvement was made as the century drew to a close, and the unskilled paviers who had been considered good enough to do this important work were no longer tolerated and men trained to the trade were employed.[36] By 1681 there was a separate Paviers' Corporation in London : in Dublin paviers were accepted as a " wing of the masons."

[33] Bryant, *The England of Charles II.*, p.35. In Ireland working hours were of course very long and nothing in the nature of a regular eight, or even ten hour day had yet been introduced.
[34] Cal. Dub. Rec., IV., p.447. In Limerick the Cathedral bell was rung daily at 4 a.m. and 8 p.m. (MS. Nat. Lib. No. 89, Sep. 15, 1673).
[35] Jnl. R.S.A.I., Vol. I., p.418.
[36] In the smaller towns the duty of paving devolved upon the house-owners who were responsible for the portion of the street lying before their doors. See, for example, Kinsale Presentments, *Analecta Hibernica*, No. 15, p.172, *et seq.*

Not only were the streets rough and uneven and, in wet weather deep in mud, they were also dirty by reason of the inadequate scavenging system. There is no evidence that the almost incredibly filthy conditions described by Professor Maxwell[37] as existing in the slums of Dublin in the eighteenth century disgraced the seventeenth century city, foul though it was in many respects. A regular system of scavenging did exist and was to some extent carried out, but its weakness lay in the fact that this work, like most of the public services at the time, was farmed to a private contractor,[38] who very seldom did more than he was absolutely obliged in carrying out his side of the bargain.

The water supply of the city was one of the few services under the direct control of the Corporation and this was managed by a committee ; but though the usual cause of inefficiency was thus absent, lack of funds prevented much progress being made in the provision of water, beyond the main conduits and cisterns which had been in existence from very early times ; citizens were allowed, under licence, to connect their houses with these cisterns, but the pipes might not be larger " than a quill."[39] As might be expected in a densely populated town like the old city of Dublin, the provision of a water supply was an affair of primary importance, yet considerable periods had often to be

[37] *Dublin Under the Georges*, Chapter IV. The sanitary conditions in London as described by Dr. A. Bryant in his *England of Charles II*, particularly before the Great Fire, were appalling.

[38] In Dublin he was remunerated by the grant of the market tolls and received no cash except when he was required to do work outside his contract. In Limerick, on the other hand, the scavengers were paid employees at a salary of about £6 per annum. See account of the Mayor's quarterly disbursements, Jan. 14, 1674 (O.S.), Nat. Lib. MS. 89. See also Kinsale Presentments referred to in note 36 and Arthur MS. fo. 4 verso.

[39] Gilbert refers to their having been there in the 13th century. (*Hist. of Dublin*, Vol. I., p.213).

endured during which one or more of the regular sources failed : once a district was without water for a whole year owing to the decay of the lead in the ancient conduit and shortage of money on the part of the civic authorities, though the whole job was eventually done for £47. The financial difficulty, however, was overcome, so far as water supplies were concerned, by the introduction of a water rate with specially appointed collectors and a surveyor to supervise the whole system.[40]

The abuses which rendered the old city of Dublin an offensive place to live in were gradually removed. As I have said, improvements were made both in street-cleaning, public scavenging and paving; and slaughterhouses and the fish market with their attendant strong smells were confined to certain specified places,though complaints of contraventions of the slaughtering regulations and of the inefficiency or carelessness of public scavengers are a commonplace in all seventeenth century municipal records. In this, as in other things, the smaller city of Limerick kept pace with the capital. The last of these reproaches on the fair name of Dublin, the smell of the Liffey, was not obviated till the modern main sewer was constructed to carry all the city drainage far out to sea ; but in the seventeenth century if the river was noisome it was because it was a convenient place for people to dispose of all kinds of objectionable rubbish, for

[40] There are many references to this question in the Dublin Assembly Roll. It would be tedious to go into details here, but the particulars given in the minute for Dec. 10, 1663, are very interesting and afford much useful information about the various types of citizen—wholesale brewers, inn-keepers, water-carriers, private housekeepers, and so on—who used the water. A valuable paper on the Dublin Water Supply may be mentioned : " The Water Supply " (13th century to 1670) by H. F. Berry, J.R.S.A.I., Vol. XXI., p.557.

there was as yet no regular system of public sewerage draining into it.

The exceptionally broad streets of the modern city of Dublin owe their existence to the Wide Streets Commissioners of the eighteenth century. Before their time they were narrow and dirty, crowded and congested by day and dangerous by night. There was no regular police system, and such police duties as were considered necessary were carried out either by the watch or by the military, the constables being easily bribed and more easily intimidated, the soldiers seldom available at the moment they were required.

The laws of the seventeenth century, with their sectarian bias and the savage sentences imposed for minor offences, differed vastly from those under which we now live, but the legal system itself was the same in general principles, certain elements of modern practice originating in Stuart times, when, for example, the "rules of evidence" first arose in the civil courts, passing thence to the criminal courts.[41]

The abuses of the system were no doubt more marked in Ireland where instead of being the outcome of a natural and gradual development it had been imposed ready-made only two or three generations before. In civil actions the legal devices whereby justice might be defeated (which were so vigorously denounced by Lord Justice Cook in a letter printed in full in Appendix O)[42] were more flagrantly availed of in this country; while in criminal cases, particularly where the accused were poor men, miscarriages of justice were more frequent. There was no Habeas Corpus

---

[41] Kenny *Outlines of Criminal Law*, p.359.
[42] See p.417 *et seq. infra.*

Act in Ireland.[43] But the framework of the system, with its judges, barristers and solicitors, its grand juries and common juries, was the same.[44] The same procedure obtained in the equity side of the Courts of Chancery and Exchequer[45]—in which civil litigation was then for the most part conducted—with their Bills and Answers and the rest of their cumbrous machinery,[46] and the same legal fictions such as those involved in Fines and Recoveries and associated with the names John Doe and Richard Roe complicated the proceedings relating to property.[47] In this connexion it may be remarked that the ecclesiastical courts still retained some of their mediæval importance in the national life : the civil courts had no jurisdiction, for example, in purely matrimonial affairs and it was the episcopal authorities—diocesan and prerogative—who exercised the functions subsequently transferred to the Probate Court. Even the English Courts Leet and Baron had their counterpart in Ireland wherever manorial rights had been granted to the new owners of property.

[43] I am indebted to Dr. Séamus Ó hInnse, of the Dublin Institute for Advanced Studies, for the following note. Ireland never had a Bill of Rights. In 1692, in the first Irish Parliament that was held after the Revolution, the heads of a Bill containing the chief provisions of a Bill of Rights were sent to England. They were, however, never returned to Ireland. The heads of a Bill extending the provisions of the Habeas Corpus Act to Ireland had again and again been transmitted to England, but were never returned. Indeed the Irish Privy Council were told to transmit the Bill no more. It was not till 1782 that an Irish Habeas Corpus Act (21 & 22 Geo. III Ireland, c.11) was passed. The English Habeas Corpus Act had been passed in 1679.

[44] See C.S.P.I. Indices sub " Ireland : Law Courts."

[45] In one respect the Exchequer Court was then important, viz., it was the only one from which no writ of error lay in England (Bagwell, Vol. III. p.155).

[46] This is illustrated in the cases reported in Part IV. of the *Kenmare MSS.* and in *Analecta Hibernica*, No. 15, p.17, *et seq.*, and also in MacLysaght, *Short Study of a Transplanted Family, passim.*

[47] There were many differences in practice between the two countries : see, for example, letter from David Duane, printed *Kenmare MSS.*, p.38.

The same procedure as in England was followed in the case of debtors, who might spend the greater part of their life in prison if unable to discharge their liabilities,[48] and the horrors of the London Newgate were repeated and indeed excelled in the Newgate gaol in Dublin, where prisoners who could not or would not yield to the entirely illegal extortions of the head jailer and his myrmidons were stripped naked, even when ill and in the depth of winter, and subjected to every imaginable form of degradation. Occasionally even deaths from starvation are recorded and many cases of long incarceration without trial appear in the official and semi-official documents of the time[49]. Many famous men were confined there from time to time, including Archbishop Oliver Plunket, who spent as long as ten months within its walls. That it had no lack of inmates, legitimately consigned to it, is not remarkable, having regard to the semibarbarous conditions of life in the slums of the period.

The numerous poor of Dublin were almost entirely uncared for, except the few favoured Protestant old people who were admitted to the very meagre relief scheme in operation.[50] Towards

[48] Even though they might not be morally responsible for them. Cf. The Case of Robert Browne, *Orrery Papers*, p.334. An attempt was made in 1698 to alleviate the worst abuses of the prison system. See C.S.P. Dom., 1698, p.371. See also *London Gazette*, 20 June, 1666. Mr. Patrick O'Connor of the National Library kindly lent me his MS. of extracts relating to Ireland from the *London Gazette* from which I have taken the various references thereto in this chapter.

[49] Vide e.g. *Analecta Hibernica*, No. 2, p.22, and No. 15, p.213.

[50] The system of poor relief in Limerick, prior to the reign of James II., when the first serious attempt was made to deal with the problem in the capital (see note 57 *infra*), was superior to that in Dublin. (See MS. Nat. Lib. 89, Apl. 5, 1679, *et passim*). Cork had two asylums for the aged poor in which sectarian distinctions were not too strict (MS. T.C.D., N.3.20), and almshouses were to be found here and there throughout the country supported by the voluntary contributions of the charitable. For remarks on beggars in Cork and the proposed workhouse there, see *Alexander the Coppersmith*, p.57. Almshouses and hospitals were exempted from hearth-money by an Act of 15 Ch. II.

the end of the century we come across some references to the numerous beggars[51] who became
such an ugly feature of Ireland under the four
Georges, but they were not yet a serious blot on
the national being outside Dublin[51a]; there they
were subjected to special regulations, and in 1682
two whole-time beadles were appointed to see that
the regulations were carried out and offenders duly
punished. There was little sentiment wasted on the
poor. The views of Sir William Petty on this subject,
as expressed in his will, were not peculiar to himself.
" As for legacies to the poor," he wrote in that
document,[51b] " I am at a stand. As for beggers by
trade and election I give them nothing ; . . . as
for those who can get no work the magistrate
should cause them to be employed, which may
be well done in Ireland where is 115 acres of
improvable land for every head ; prisoners for
crimes by the King; for debt by their prosecutors."
Even in his last will and testament Petty is still
the surveyor ; and after all he does leave £20
to the most wanting in the parish in which he
should die " to answer custom and take the surer
side."

The poor of the towns were, of course, entirely
without education, being mostly Catholics, and as
such increasingly debarred as time went on from
religious instruction or influences of any kind. The
Protestant poor were in little better case as it was not
their children but those of the middle class who got
their education at the City School. This school was

---

[51] Irish beggars with false passes and certificates are named in the *London Gazette* of 7 Oct., 1670.

[51a] For a valuable article on beggers and poor relief see that by T. K. Moylan in Dub. Hist. Record, I .1. p.11 and *ib*. I.2. p.41.

[51b] *Tracts Relating to Ireland*, Dublin 1769, p.xi.

intended for the children of poor freemen, but it numbered many among its pupils who did not come in this category,[52] notably the twelve-year-old child afterwards world-famous as the Duke of Marlborough.[53] Begging, prostitution, and especially petty thieving, became increasingly common, being perhaps the only ways of living open to many of these wretched people.

Side by side with this semi-criminal slum-life existed Society: the entourage of the vice-regal court, the landlords with estates in the country (confiscated estates, of course, in almost every case) whose presence gave distinction to the audience at the theatre, and a few very successful or outstanding professional men such as Sir William Petty or the Molyneux brothers, whose scientific activities gave to Dublin a cultural aspect which its many book-shops seem to confirm. I have already referred to the fondness of the same aristocratic set who patronized the stage for the game of bowls. They had a splendid bowling green at Oxmantown which I mentioned in a previous chapter.[54] It was situated near the Bloody Bridge, a wooden structure erected in 1670, and so called from the fatal ending to a disturbance created by a crowd of apprentices and presumably instigated by the ferrymen who feared with reason that the completion of the bridge would

[52] Though known officially as the Free School its master was in 1654 ordered to board and teach the son of Col. Bagnall for £20 per annum. (Commonwealth State Accounts, *Analecta Hibernica*, No. 15, p.267).
[53] The Free School is not to be confused with the Bluecoat School to which I shall refer later. The Free School was then (in 1662) under a Dr. Hill, who resigned because, like so many other officials, he could get no pay, though the salary was very small. Even in 1676, when it had been very substantially raised, it was only £80 p.a. His place, however, was eagerly sought for, and his successors were fully qualified men, one of whom subsequently became a bishop. Cal. Dub. Rec., Vol. IV., p.191 ; Vol. V., p.106 ; and Sir F. Falkiner, *Foundation of the King's Hospital*, p.38.
[54] p.159 *supra*. It was described in 1665 as " Alderman Tye's (i.e. Tighe's) new bowling green." C.S.P. Ire., 1663/65, p.591.

deprive them of their livelihood. Up to that time there had only been one bridge over the Liffey in Dublin—the Old Bridge built as far back as 1210.[55]

The patrons of the bowling green for the most part had their own carriages and chairs, but in a capital city like Dublin, with its floating population, there were many " persons of quality," to use the phrase employed at the time, who were not so equipped and required to be conveyed from place to place expeditiously and without exposing themselves to the dirt of the streets. This need eventually resulted in the establishment of public transport in the form of hackney cars and sedan chairs. Judging from the frequent references to this subject, not only in the Dublin Assembly Roll but also in the State Papers, it must have been considered a matter of considerable importance and, quite in keeping with the ways of the time, a monopoly was granted in 1667 to René Mézandière—not an Irishman, of course—in respect of public passenger transport in the city. Previously the Corporation had licensed a certain number of hackney car drivers themselves and devoted the proceeds to special purposes such as paving the streets ; and again in 1681, when Mézandière's monopoly had apparently expired, the proceeds derived from the very much increased licence fees were allocated to a fund for the upkeep of the proposed workhouse, though it had not yet been built. The carmen were hedged round with quite a number of restrictions and regulations governing their numbers, the fares they could charge, the hazards[56] they might stand

[55] Limerick, situated on a river much broader than the Liffey, had two handsome stone bridges long before the dawn of the 17th century.
[56] This word is of more recent introduction.

at, the badges they must wear, and so on. Even the type of horse was specified, for nothing under fifteen hands was supposed to be used, though apparently they were generally passed if over fourteen hands. At first it was considered that thirty of these cars would be ample to supply the public needs, but in spite of fears expressed about increasing the density of the traffic, the Corporation had on successive occasions to give way and license more cars, till in 1687 there were eighty of them on the hazards, besides a certain number of pirates who managed to ply for hire unlicensed.[57]

It was an easy matter to get out of Dublin. A certain number of these very carmen were authorized to drive you by private coach outside the seven mile limit within which the city cars could ply ; or indeed if you had a mind to walk you could get out into the country in a quarter of an hour or so. If your lodgings were in the heart of the city you were not very far from St. Stephen's Green, which was only laid out between 1666 and 1670, and though the plots surrounding it were allocated at that date, many of them were not built on till a considerable time after. The west side, however, was occupied, for we find Whalley publishing his almanacs and pamphlets " at the Sign of the Blew Posts next door to the Wheel of Fortune " there.[58]

Dunton had a preference for the North Side of Dublin. He was really happy when lodging with Mrs. Orson at Arbour Hill, though while there he

[57] For full details see Cal. Dub. Rec., 30 Apl., 1667. The licence fee was still 50/- in 1687, and the funds so raised were not deflected from the purpose to which they had been assigned in 1681 The workhouse was built in 1688 on the road to Kilmainham. Dunton says there were also up to 100 " Ringsend " cars plying for hire ten years later.
Cf. MacGillycuddy MSS., folio 107.
[58] Webb, *Compendium of Irish Biography*, p.560.

" fell sick of the bloody flux, the usual distemper of the country and many times fatal."[59] Even when he was staying in the quarter of the town where the bookshops were, in and around Castle Street and Skinner's Row, he used to walk out, often before his breakfast, to the strand—not far from where Amien Street Station now stands, I take it. He describes how leaving the strand one summer morning " he walked up a hill into the fields by the side of Ballybough Lane, which I thought one of the best prospects about Dublin " ; and again : " at other times I would walk through those green meadows from the end of Stoneybatter to the Cabragh, about a mile from my lodging, full of stately trees." His lodging in this case was, of course, the Orsons'.

Pleasant expeditions might be made to such places as Malahide, then renowned for its oysters, if you had a whole day to spare. One of these is described by Dunton in his Fifth Letter.[60]

By the end of the century, though we hear little of tea being drunk,[61] coffee-houses were numerous in Dublin and were also to be found in other towns, not only Limerick, Cork, Galway and Kilkenny, but even Clonmel and Wexford being mentioned by Dunton in this connexion. They met the need for a place where men might turn in at any time and converse over a little light refreshment, and became very popular. They were the precursors of the modern restaurant, but when he wanted a solid

[59] *Dublin Scuffle*, p.366. See p.222 *infra*.
[60] p.363 *et seq.*
[61] In 1658 tea was known as " china drink," chocolate being advertised as " an excellent West India drink " in the London coffee-houses. Considering the importance of tea in the national diet of Ireland to-day, it is interesting to note that it was still a rarity in 1764 (Jnl. R.S.A.I., Vol. IV., p.140 n.), and even in 1808 Dutton in his *Survey of Co. Clare* (p.160) remarks : " happily as yet little money is thrown away on tea or sugar."

dinner Dunton went to one of the cook-shops. The modern club may also perhaps be regarded as a development of the seventeenth century coffee-house, which to some extent fulfilled its function[62] : the mere business of eating and drinking was only one of the needs for which it catered. It was at Pat's Coffee House that Dunton wrote most of his *Conversation in Ireland*,[63] so evidently they offered some opportunities of privacy. There was nothing disreputable about coffee-houses. The Rev. Rowland Davies, Protestant Dean of Cork, tells us in his diary how he frequented them and regularly read the news there when he was in England in 1689. For the most part they were patronized by persons of leisure with little to do but cultivate the art of conversation, and by professional men and university professors who made them serve the purpose of a modern club smoke-room to discuss political and scientific questions. Indeed it was in a coffee-house that the Dublin Philosophical Society held its informal meetings for the first ten years of its existence. Business men, too, often made use of them to transact their deals. The well-known usurer, Joseph Damer, perhaps because his business was established before coffee-houses became popular, used the London Tavern as his office. Dunton, whose primary business in Ireland was to dispose of a large quantity of books by auction, made use of the famous Dick's Coffee House for this purpose. It seems to have become the recognized place for

[62] Pepys on one occasion speaks of going to the " coffee club." *Diary*, Jan. 17, 1659.

[63] *Dublin Scuffle*, p.304. Throughout my notes I have referred to this volume, of which I have made such frequent use, as " Dublin Scuffle." It will be understood that the " Conversation " was included with the *Dublin Scuffle* when it was published in 1699, though actually quite a separate work. Nearly all my references are to the " Conversation." I might add that the word ' conversation ' is here used in its old sense of " method of living."

the holding of important auctions. Probably one of the most noteworthy of these was the sale in 1704 of over 30,000 acres of land belonging to the Earl of Thomond—or rather of 99 years leases thereof—" to be disposed of by cant," as the advertisement puts it, at Dick's Coffee House in Skinner's Row, between the hours of 9 a.m. and 12 noon and 3 and 6 p.m., every Tuesday, Thursday and Saturday till finished.[44]

Bookselling had already become a very important and lucrative trade[45] before the close of the seventeenth century. It was even possible to make a fortune at it, if we can believe Dunton, who states that a Mr. Wilde made £40,000 in the book trade in London. There was a Joseph Wilde who had a bookshop in Castle Street in 1670 ; and in 1695, after Cork House had been given up as the municipal headquarters when the new Tholsel[46] was built, one Richard Wilde occupied part of it as a bookshop, another part being converted into Lucas's Coffee House, which became so popular a year or two later. I assume that it was a mere coincidence that the very successful bookseller just mentioned was also named Wilde. Certainly the number of

[44] The original advertisement and the documents containing details regarding the lands to be disposed of are among the papers in the Bradshaw Collection. Those here referred to are item 4118 in the Bradshaw Collection Catalogue. They contain much information of great value to the student of family history in Co. Clare and part of Co. Limerick. The names of the tenants of the large farms, as well as the small, are nearly all Irish, and land was evidently fetching high prices at the end of the 17th century, judging from those obtained in 1704. No names of cottagers are given, and in most cases even the number of cabins on each lot is only given approximately.

[45] Publishing, on the other hand, was a precarious business on account of the absence of any general copyright law. Occasionally copyright was granted to individuals, e.g. Samuel Butler for his *Hudibras* : see C.S.P.I. 1663 /65, p.298.

[46] An illustration of this building showing a great deal of detail is to be seen in the Dineley MSS. in the National Library, Dublin. The portion of the MS. dealing with Dublin was not included in the edition of his Irish tours published in 1870, and frequently referred to by me under the short title of " Observations."

booksellers in Dublin increased rapidly at this time. Dunton mentions several by name, and a very complete list of early Irish booksellers and printers is to be found in the Bradshaw Catalogue. Much of their activity was devoted to the production of pamphlets, the second half of the seventeenth century and the first half of the eighteenth being the period when this form of publication attained its greatest popularity. They seem to have served the purpose now met by the correspondence columns of the daily press or by articles on controversial subjects in weekly and monthly periodicals, and varied as much in length. The majority are sectarian in character, those published in London and Dublin being for the most part strongly, often scurrilously, anti-Catholic. They were much used as a means of getting publicity, but probably most of these pamphlets, where no sectarian motive prompted their publication, were issued with a view to catching the pence of the citizens, just as a stop-press edition of the evening papers was put on the streets in pre-war days when the latest news of some *cause célèbre* came to hand. Thus the subject of many is trials for murder, coining and other crimes. Stories connected with famous or notorious rapparees were especially popular, and the pamphlets describing the death of Redmond O'Hanlon in 1681[67] were probably best-sellers, as I am sure was the last speech of Charles Callaher some years later, with its exceedingly gruesome footnote recounting in vivid detail the horrors which followed after he had, in accordance with his sentence, been cut down from the gallows while still alive. The best known of the longer pamphlets of a serious

[67] See Chapter VIII., note 93.

nature published in Dublin at the time we are considering was William Molyneux's *Case of Ireland being Bound by Acts of Parliament of England Stated*, published by Joseph Ray in 1690.

The use of advertisements was only just beginning towards the end of the seventeenth century and the very word had scarcely acquired its present meaning even in a secondary sense. In 1623 Sir Henry Bourchier was able to call his treatise on the state of the country "Advertisements for Ireland," without any thought of being misunderstood. However, the modern meaning gradually came into use, and we find it employed by the auctioneers who announced the sale of the Earl of Thomond's property, referred to above, and sometimes in the earliest editions of newspapers about the same time when people wished to regain lost property or draw attention to some personal matter. Absconding apprentices and servants were frequently the subject of these advertisements,[68] their clothes being sometimes described in detail and any peculiarity which might assist identification being added. One of the facts mentioned, for example, in the case of a Dublin servant, of Scottish nationality, who was said to have disappeared after robbing his master in 1686, was that he was a speaker of Irish.[69]

Dunton advertised his book auctions by distributing handbills about the town, but as I have not seen one of these I do not know whether he actually used

[68] E.g. advertisement for a runaway joiner's apprentice in the Dublin *Flying Post*, Mar. 7, 1699. Several examples of such advertisements are to be seen in the *Dublin Intelligence*, a weekly paper established in 1689 or 1690. Probably the very earliest newspaper of any kind was the short-lived *Irish Monthly Mercury*, printed and published in Cork in 1649, referred to in Jnl. of Cork Hist. and Arch. Soc., 1897, p.139. See also Chap. IV., p.126.

[69] *London Gazette*, No. 2200. The earliest advertisement in the modern sense I have come across is an English one seeking information regarding a lost greyhound in Westminster (*London Gazette*, 18 July. 1667).

the word ' advertisement ' or not. The earliest
form of advertisement—one still in use in many
country towns in Ireland—was the announcement
of matters of public interest such as the date of an
athletic contest, public meeting, the loss of cattle,
and so on, by a bellman or crier, who attended
places where people resorted in large numbers.[70]

The comparatively high level of culture in Dublin
indicated by the number of bookshops there and by
the activities of the Dublin Philosophical Society
is confirmed by the success of the new theatre in
Smock Alley, whose players even presented plays in
Great Britain[70a]. This replaced the original play
house in St. Werburgh Street, which was ruined during
the war of 1641-52. Early in the eighteenth century
the talent of Dublin actors and actresses was recognized outside Ireland, and several of these, such as Peg
Woffington, became famous in London. There were
but two theatres in London at the close of the
seventeenth century, when that in Smock Alley was
the only one in Dublin. This theatre was opened in
1662[71] and the players were accustomed to play to
full houses, so full indeed that on one occasion in
1670 the overcrowded upper gallery collapsed and
three people were killed as a result.[72] This evidently

[70] Cf. instructions to advertise Tyrconnell's proclamation in 1686 *re*
salmon fishing in Co. Kerry " with sound of trumpet and beat of drum in
full market and publicly fixed up in all the markets and other public places
throughout that county." MacGillycuddy MSS., folio 130.
[70a] See article entitled " Irish Players at Oxford and Edinburgh, 1677-
1681," by W. J. Lawrence in *The Dublin Magazine*, Vol.VII (N.S.), p.49 *et seq*.
[71] According to Rev. S. C. Hughes (*Pre-Victorian Drama in Dublin*, p.2)
this theatre measured 139 ft. x 63 ft. A considerable amount of useful information concerning the theatre in Dublin will be found in C.S.P.I.: see
Indices *sub* " Dublin City, theatre in."
[72] Referring to this incident, Bagwell does not mention that fact, but he
tells us that Lady Clanbrasil, who was present with the vice-regal party, was
hurt by the fall of the gallery. He gives some interesting particulars in
connexion with this theatre. (See his *Ireland under the Stuarts*, III., p.104 ;
Adair, *Presbyterian Church*, ch. xviii. ; Hitchcock, *Irish Stage*, pp.16-17.)
According to the *London Gazette* (27 Dec. 1670) there were seven or eight
lives lost on this occasion.

did not deter the proprietors from re-erecting this gallery, as when Dunton was there more than a quarter of a century later, he mentions that the theatre consisted of stage, pit, boxes, two galleries, lettices, and music loft. It cost £2,000 to build, a modest enough sum even allowing for the value of money at the time. Most of this sum, however, was evidently expended on the interior, for Dunton speaks highly of this as being equal to those in London, describing it as " a place very contrary to its owners," who made the best show outside. Dunton's strictures on individuals were often made with no more basis than personal prejudice, so that we need not deduce anything from this remark beyond the fact that the exterior of the playhouse befitted the rather mean street in which it stood. His comments on its location are illuminating, but were considered too indelicate to be reprinted in the 1818 edition of his works.

In considering the Dublin associated with Petty and Molyneux, with Whalley the astrologer and Father Peter Walsh of Remonstrance fame, the Dublin which knew the great Duke of Ormond at the end of his career and in which Jonathan Swift grew to manhood, we must remember that the spacious and dignified Dublin of to-day is essentially Georgian. Excepting a few in the neighbourhood of the Coombe, hardly a building exists to remind us of what it looked like when the Stuarts still held the throne. We can get no help from the Castle most of which was rebuilt in the 18th century, or from the two cathedrals, St. Patrick's and Christ Church, for they have stood almost unchanged,[73]

---

[73] In 1871 Christ Church was in a very ruinous condition and £200,000 was spent on its restoration, but of course the main lines of the ancient fabric were unaltered.

like oaks in a forest of short-lived pines, while the town around them was more than once demolished and rebuilt. In Limerick some of the tall stone houses mentioned by Dineley in 1681 have remained until our own time.[74] The house in Nicholas Street where Ireton died, probably of typhus, was still to be seen about thirty years ago.[75] The fine stone houses of Galway were admired by every traveller who went there. Probably there were some buildings of that type in Dublin also, but the greater part of the streets of the city consisted of houses mainly built of timber, presumably of the type still preserved here and there in old English cities, with the upper storeys projecting over the lower. Thatched houses were numerous, and one of the first acts of the Dublin Corporation[76] after they began to reorganize the affairs of the city was to prohibit any such, even in the suburbs, because of the danger of fire.[77] In Limerick, too, a few years later a number of small thatched houses were demolished by order of the Corporation. In a description of the Cornmarket in Dublin towards the close of the seventeenth century, we read of a Catholic convent being in that street, as well as an old castle four storeys high, and "large timber houses, on the ground floor kitchen and one lodging room, second and third three rooms each, and fourth two garrets, being the sign of the George." Another house in this street

---

[74] Dr. Arthur mentions a number of stone houses as well as some of "cadge-work" in the section of his manuscript (B.M. Addl. 31885) devoted to his financial transactions. The house he built for himself in 1626 was of stone. The houses of Drogheda are also described in the Down Survey as being built of stone. (*Analecta Hibernica*, No. 8, p.424).

[75] A good illustration of this is given in Begley's *Diocese of Limerick in the 16th and 17th Centuries*, p.338. See note 78.

[76] See Proclamation of 2 Sept., 1670 (C.S.P.I. 1669/70, p.249).

[77] Misson in 1699 mentions the Society of Fire Insurers in London (*Memoirs*, p.148), but I have come across no record of any similar body in Dublin at that date.

was called the Frying Pan. The London Tavern in 1667 is thus described : " A timber house slated, a base court, a back building more backward and a small garden in Fishamble Street," and again, the Post Office in 1668 was a " timber house in High Street, with a large backside and garden plot reaching to Back Lane."[78]

The practice of numbering houses in city streets was of later date and it was the custom to distinguish them by signs.[79] The barber's pole and the three balls of the pawnbroker are still familiar to us, but the signs I speak of were chosen as arbitrarily as the names of the villas in a Victorian suburb, if not quite so fantastically. These signs were commonest on inns and taverns, a practice still common in England, though not much in use in modern Ireland. The residences of the townspeople were also sometimes so distinguished. The tendency of the better-class citizens to move out into the suburbs did not become general till a later date, and many gentlemen of the highest standing lived in the most densely populated part of the city, such as Back Lane, Castle Street, and Skinner's Row, and some of their houses had signs like the sign of the Golden Key at the residence of Lawrence Saul in Saul's Court. Shops, too, especially booksellers, often used signs like those associated with inns. Thus John Foster did business at " the Dolphin," Patrick Campbell at " the Bible," and Samuel Helston

[78] Gilbert, *History of Dublin*, Vol. I., p.234. A very good idea of the appearance of the city of Limerick is given by the illustration of it in Thomas Phillips's *Military Survey* of 1685. This shows the thatched houses referred to : all those remaining at this date are shown as quite substantial and have chimneys. The fine stone houses of Galway, so often referred to by travellers, are to be seen in Phillips's illustration of that place. He also shows clearly the " half-timber " type of house mentioned in the text. MS. Nat. Lib. No. 66, p.660.
[79] According to Macaulay the original reason for this was that the common people could not read.

at " the College Arms." Many of the signs used
were picturesque, like " the Bear and the Ragged
Staff,"[80] or " the Wandering Jew," others grotesque,
like " the Whalley's Head."

The " Whalley's Head," of course, belongs to a
somewhat later time, since the sign was only used
after the death of that celebrated impostor. Though
he lived on till 1724 he was born in 1653 and was a
true product of the seventeenth century. He was
very unpopular with the native Irish, who one day
in 1688 seized the opportunity of the astrologer's
being put in the stocks to show their dislike of him by
pelting him with rotten eggs. John Whalley was not
without rivals with the dupes who bought his
almanacs and swallowed his necromancy. A priest
named James O'Finaghty had a tremendous vogue,
especially among the rural poor, as a miraculous
healer, though he quite failed to substantiate his
alleged powers when put to the test by Petty.
Valentine Greatorex was another man of the same
type, but his quackery was less outrageous.[81]
Legislation was still required to control the activities
of these "empirics" as they were called at the time.[82]

The popularity of these quacks in some quarters
did not interfere with the steady progress of the

[80] See note 21 *supra.*
[81] Greatorex, or Greatrakes, was successful for a time as a professional
healer in London also, where some of his cures were certified by the newly
established Royal Society. Another Irishman, who set up as a doctor in
Chester but relied chiefly on theatrical effects for his " miraculous " cures,
attained considerable notoriety about the same time. His methods are
described in a letter dated Aug. 17, 1663 (printed in C.S.P. Dom.). The
dangerous and unprofessional practices of the quacks of Cork, " with
whom this city swarms " (i.e. in 1737) are recounted in *Alexander the
Coppersmith*, p.127 *et seq.* For other examples of the claims of quacks, see
Fitzmaurice, *Petty*, p.71. Even respectable practitioners were very crude in
their treatment of patients, as the well-known account of the death of Charles
II testifies. For a curious but typical prescription see *Orrery Papers*, p.61.
[82] See two letters of Sir Patrick Dun (1697 and 1698) referred to in *Analecta
Hibernica*, No. 2, p.10. Dun was one of the earliest doctors in Ireland to
devote attention to anatomy. He bought bodies for dissecting. Belcher,
Memoirs of Sir Patrick Dun, p.20.

medical profession, though it caused the College
of Physicians to seek some protection against
unqualified practitioners, to which end they obtained a new charter in 1692. The College was
established in the reign of Charles I, nine years later
than the similar institution in London, and properly
qualified doctors had long practised in Dublin and
other cities. Dunton, however, did not think much
of the Dublin doctors, and he remarks that there
was only one of them, a Dr. Smith, whom he would
consult if sick. Nevertheless there were several
distinguished physicians in Dublin at the time,
notably Drs. Belton and Molyneux and Sir Patrick
Dun.

Though still rudimentary the science of medicine
underwent a great change in the period under
review. Up to the beginning and even the middle of
the century the hereditary *fir leighis*, belonging to
such families as the O Hickeys the O Lees and the
O Ferguses, continued to practise in much the same
way as their forbears did right back to pre-Christian
times.[83] Very different were the comparatively
modern methods[84] of a man like Dr. Thomas
Arthur, one of the best-known Irishmen of the
seventeenth century who had studied at Bordeaux
and Paris, where he took his degree.[85]

[83] See John Windele, Irish Medical Superstition, J.R.S.A.I., VIII., p.308
et seq.
[84] An interesting example of the scientific activity of the period is to be
seen in a booklet of 72 pages written by a graduate of Trinity College,
Dublin, published in 1682. Its full title is " An Anatomical Account of the
Elephant accidentally burnt in Dublin on June 17, 1681, sent in a letter
to Sir Will Petty, F.R.S., together with . . . anatomical observations in the
eyes of animals communicated in another letter to Hon. R. Boyle, F.R.S."
Unfortunately the circumstances of the death of this elephant, as rather
graphically told on pp.4 to 6 of the text, handicapped scientific observation.
[85] The reputation of French doctors was not high (Bradby, *op. cit.*, p.285).
There is much evidence available to shew they had advanced but little
from the days referred to by Molière in his well-known jibe : " Clysterium
donare, postea seignare, ensuitta purgare ; reseignare, repurgare, reclys-
terisare "—emetics, bleeding and purges, and then more.

A close examination of Dr. Arthur's accounts, which cover the period 1619 to 1666[86] and give in many cases not only the patient's name and the fee received but also the nature of the complaint, enables some idea to be formed of the daily life of a seventeenth century physician. Dr. Arthur started as an unknown young man in Limerick and when over fifty years of age began to practise in Dublin, though he did not sever his connexion with his native city where he had property and diverse interests unconnected with the profession of medicine, his notes upon which are of considerable value in forming a picture of other aspects of the social life of his time.

Throughout the whole half century during which he practised medicine, whether as a beginner in Limerick or as a man of established reputation in Dublin, he seldom saw more than one patient each day. It would appear that in those times the doctor always visited the patient at his or her home and did not have consulting hours in his own house as a modern physician has. Many of his calls were made to " big houses " at a considerable distance from town. His fee for a visit was usually 10s. though he sometimes charged as much as £1 and now and then he was satisfied with a mere half crown from the less well-to-do, who are dismissed anonymously in some such phrase as " quidam rusticus." From time to time after his reputation was made he would be summoned to attend some important personage such as the Earl of Antrim or Lord Clanrickarde who lived far from Dublin and as much as three weeks including several days' journey each way was

[86] He died in January 1675, not in 1666 as has often been stated. His will was proved the same month (1674 O.S.) G.O. MS. 224, p.163. See also article referred to in the next note.

sometimes spent in visiting one such patient. These were the " plums," for not only was he paid about £1 per day for all the time he was away from home but he also made a considerable additional sum by treating other patients who lived in the neighbourhood he was visiting and were glad to avail themselves of the opportunity of consulting him. Nevertheless his total receipts from fees seem comparatively small : in Limerick in his best year he made over £300, but his average in Dublin was little more than half that sum,[87] which would be equivalent to hardly £1,000 a year in present (or rather in 1939) values.[88] Dr. Arthur's income in fact was derived as much from the results of his successful speculation in land as from his earnings as a doctor.

Such other evidence as I have been able to discover on the subject of doctors' fees tends to corroborate the conclusions to be drawn from the Arthur MS. In 1684, for example, a Dr. Morris received £40 for constant attendance during a period of five weeks on Lady Inchiquin, " never leaving the house ".[89] The doctors who attended Lady Ossory in 1685, when she had smallpox, received eighty guineas, but their number and the period of their attendance is not recorded.[90] Her midwife and nurse on another occasion were paid twenty guineas.[91]

Nothing but a perusal of the fee-book can convey an adequate idea of the variety of the complaints

[87] Dr. Richard Hayes in the course of correspondence which resulted from my comments on his interesting article on Dr. Arthur in the North West Munster Archaeological Journal (Vol. I, No. 3, p.113 *et seq.*) suggests that the doctor may have had reason to complain that he was not always paid the fees which were due to him. Petty's income from his medical practice in 1652 was £400 per an. *Petty Papers* Vol. II, p.155.
[88] See p.143.
[89] *Orrery Papers*, p.293.
[90] J.R.S.A.I., Vol. I., p.418.
[91] *Ibidem.*

for which Dr. Arthur treated his patients.[92] Among the commonest of these were gallstones and gout, usually the result of overeating. Venereal disease was fairly prevalent, especially during the Cromwellian period. Dysentery, colloquially called the " bloody flux "[93], appears to have been an illness particularly associated with Ireland and is mentioned by Boate and other writers as such. As might be expected, considering the insanitary conditions of life, the country suffered very severely from this disease, especially during the war years, when it accounted for more deaths than the fighting itself, ruthless though it was. Dr. Willoughby, writing in 1691,[94] ascribes the decline of dysentery to the widespread reclamation of bogs which followed the Restoration.[95] The epidemic of plague which devastated London in 1665 was not very seriously felt in Ireland[96]—no doubt the wise precaution of enforcing quarantine regulations for incoming passengers from England to Dublin[97] was a contributory cause of this comparative immunity. The disease which was most general, however, being in fact endemic throughout Europe and regarded by most people as almost inevitable, was smallpox. It was often fatal—Mary II was one of its most distinguished victims ; it left its mark on high and low—it was the cause for example of Carolan's blindness and disfigured many a young seventeenth century beauty.

[92] He does not tell us that he conducted many post-mortems. These were sometimes carried out voluntarily .

[93] See page 209 *supra*.

[94] MS. Nat. Lib. not yet catalogued ; see p.184, note 2, *supra*.

[95] An interesting discussion on the prevalence of dysentery, typhus and bubonic plague at that time will be found in the *British Medical Journal* for August 28 and Sept. 11, 1937.

[96] See *London Gaz.* 10 Dec., 1665, and Murphy MS. (N.L. ref. *pro tem.* Box 183), p.31.

[97] Dublin Assembly Roll, 25 July, 1665. See also J.R.S.A.I., Vol. XXXIII., p.230, and 30th Report of D.K.R.I., p.51.

Dr. Arthur's manuscript,[98] while it usually specifies the diseases and disorders he was called upon to deal with, throws no light on his methods of treatment, though the addition of the word " percuratus " from time to time after a patient's name suggests that, in spite of the elementary state of medical knowledge in his day and the lack of such primary essentials to the modern physician as the stethoscope and the clinical thermometer, he had a fair amount of success, as indeed may be deduced from the fact of his having been consulted by numbers of prominent people many of whom regarded his religion—for he was an uncompromising Catholic—as anathema.[99]

The hereditary Gaelic *fir-leighis* being extinct, the people who were remote from cities—that is to say in those days the majority of the population—had practically no medical aid available. Even the comparatively well-off had therefore to depend on home remedies, some of which no doubt were simple and proved by long experience to be efficacious in ordinary cases of illness, and it is not altogether surprising in the circumstances that quack cures were often recommended and tried by men and women whose outlook was otherwise enlightened.[100] Similarly there were no hospitals. The suppression of the monasteries a century earlier had eliminated the only body of men who had made any attempt, however feeble, to supply this need and no step was taken in this direction by the authorities if we except the provision in

[98] For a brief description of this MS. (B.M. Addl. 31,885) see my note thereon in J.R.S.A.I., Vol. LXXX, Pt. I.
[99] He frequently attended Archbishop Ussher, for example, whom he invariably describes as " pseudo-episcopus " or " pseudo-primas."
[100] Some typical examples of "cures" are to be found in J.R.S.A.I., Vol. III., p.171, *Ossory Papers*, pp.61, 62, 97, *Kenmare MSS.*, pp.106, 107 and *Illustrations of Irish History* (Sir William Brereton's Travels), p.371.

wartime of some wards for sick and wounded soldiers.[101] The need, however, was recognised by Petty.[101a]

The science of surgery was still quite in its infancy : in fact it was regarded almost as a trade rather than a profession[102] and was practised in a very rough and ready way, generally by barbers as a sort of spare time job, much in the same way as smiths in remote country places sometimes act as amateur veterinary surgeons to-day. This connexion between hairdressing and surgery was indeed accepted and officially recognized, for there was a Guild of Barber-Chirurgiens duly incorporated,[103] and among the examples of guilds not restricting themselves to their particular trades which were brought before the Assembly we meet a complaint, in 1682, that surgeons were taking vintners and apothecaries as apprentices, contrary to the rules of their corporation.[104]

By that date practically every trade had its organized guild or corporation, which was governed by strict rules and protected by royal charter. The tradesmen and artisans of Limerick

---

[101] See e.g. J.R.S.A.I., Vol. I., pp.37, 38. The " hospitals " which were exempted from hearth-money were institutions of the almshouse type not hospitals in the modern sense of the word.

[101a] *Treatise of Taxes & Contributions* (London, 1667) p.11.

[102] Chirurgeons were, however, not unnaturally regarded as a necessary part of the military establishment, especially in wartime, and army surgeons usually received the same pay as the junior officers, viz. 4s. a day between 1642 and 1656, an army physician getting 5s, and an apothecary 2s. 6d. at the same period, the chaplain (or " preacher ") being thought worth 6s. or 6s. 8d. a day. A little later (1663) the salary of the Physician-General to the Army was fixed at 10s. a day. (*Analecta Hibernica*, No. 4, p.21 ; No. 15, p.230, *et seq.* ; C.S.P.I. 1663 /65, pp.93, 106). There were cases of men practising both as physicians and surgeons : see the interesting petition of John Meagher, printed *Analecta Hibernica*, No. 1, pp.112, 113.

[103] It was not until the middle of the 18th century that the surgeons severed their connexion with the Barbers' Guild. Cameron, *History of the Royal College of Surgeons, Ireland.* Second edition, 1916, Ch. I.

[104] A few years later in a charter of James II apothecaries were declared to be an integral part of the profession. See also Dub. Hist. Rec. IV 4, p.150.

and other cities had their own separate corporations but, as might be expected, the list of those in Dublin was more extensive than it was elsewhere.

While there was no real industrial activity in Ireland under the Stuarts, commerce, primary production and a certain amount of manufacture were carried on without the continuous interruptions of the war-ridden Tudor period and free from the stagnation of despair which gripped the country in the eighteenth century till the efforts of Grattan partially dispelled it. The trade in provisions which grew up as a result of the prohibition by England of the export of live cattle from Ireland continued to flourish for some time. William Bolton in his business letters from Madeira often refers to foodstuffs from Ireland : a sharp decline in prices in March, 1700, was due to their " being over-glutted with all sorts of provisions from Ireland." These provisions for the most part took the form of beef, but corn was also exported. Thus on 19 April, 1696, Bolton mentions a cargo of wheat from Youghal.[107] Cork was the most important port through which this export trade was carried on. Francis Rogers, himself a merchant, thus describes that place :

" Here runs a strong tide in the middle of the harbour ; ships that come to load here generally run higher up to Cove or Passage, or right up to Cork, the river running through it. Here are handsome quays where the smaller ships lie and load. This is a large and populous city, having many merchants and tradesmen in it. It is encompassed by a good

---

[107] *Bolton Letters*, ed. Simon, London, 1928.

wall of stone, but not many guns. They drive a very great trade to the West Indies with their provisions, chiefly by Bristol men who flock hither to load about September and October for Jamaica, Barbadoes, Antegoa, and the other islands of the West Indies, with beef, pork, butter, candles, etc. The inhabitants drive a pretty smart Gillycranky trade to France. This city is accounted the first in Ireland for trade ; it has a very large market ; the people are generally given to hospitality, civil and courteous to strangers ; follow pretty much the French air in conversation, bringing up their children to dance, play on the fiddle, and fence, if they can give them nothing else."[108]

The commodities exported[109] were all products derived from the land. Professor George O'Brien has pointed out that no sign of the industrial revolution had begun to appear in the seventeenth century, that the period under review was not marked by any noticeable advance in the methods of production, and that the relations between employer and wage-earner were very much the same in 1760 as they had been in 1600. He quotes the following passage from Hewins's *English Trade and Finance*, which is equally applicable to Irish conditions : " In the seventeenth century the advantages of the division of labour were widely recognized. In the towns there was a combination of the domestic with the manufacturing system, i.e. certain operations were carried on by handicrafts-

[108] Journal of Francis Rogers, printed in *Three Sea Journals of Stuart Times*, p.196.
[109] The State Papers of our period contain many useful references to the export trade of Ireland to America, the West Indies, the Canaries, France and other countries, which will be found in the indices of the volumes of C.S.P.I. and C.S.P. Dom. covering the years 1647 to 1700 under " Ireland Exports " ; the headings " Dublin," " Cork," " Limerick " and other ports should also be consulted.

men grouped together in families or workshops while subsidiary processes were performed in the homes of the people. In the more rural districts the usual industrial group was the family. The dealer gave out raw material to be worked up by the craftsman and his wife and children. But there was no deep line of division between dealer and artisan or merchant and employed."

No citizen who was not a freeman could belong to one of the trade corporations. The freedom of the city was occasionally presented with considerable ceremony to some distinguished person as a mark of the city's respect and honour, but in those times to be a freeman was not a mere honorary and formal title. It meant the enjoyment of definite privileges as well as involving certain responsibilities. To the craftsman it was almost essential, because his brother tradesman could make it difficult for him to get work at all if he were not a member of their corporation. Though at certain periods in Cork no one could open a shop unless he were a freeman,[110] to shopkeepers it was not so generally important, but in normal times the privileges attaching to freedom were enough to induce a citizen to apply for it if he did not already possess it.[111] At times, however, there was a tendency to regard the advantages as doubtful. There was the initial fine or fee, which was often as much as £1, though payable in instalments. The benefit of free education

[110] O'Sullivan, *Economic History of Cork City*, p.100.
[111] It would appear that the son of a man who already enjoyed the freedom of a city did not automatically become a freeman himself, but had to pay the customary fine for admission. Abraham Jackson, for example, is recorded as going through the customary formalities of admission in Limerick, though described as " son and heir of Tho. Jackson, a freeman of this city." (Nat. Lib. MS. 89. 15 Sept., 1673). See also Old Corporation Book of Ross, J.R.S.A.I., Vol. XXII., p.288 and *History of the Dublin Bakers*, pp.355-357.

in a school designed to take only twenty pupils was obviously not of general application ; and the freeman never could be sure that his privileged position would continue. Thus in Dublin the double water rate collected from alien and non-free citizens was abolished in 1675 as the result of an agitation by that class of the community. In Limerick the free-men were frequently called upon to forego their privileges. In 1673, for example, they were required to pay the petty duties from which they were usually exempted. In this case the extra money so collected was wanted for the repair of the Thomond Bridge and the walls.[112] Again in 1679 they had to pay customs—like any Tadhg or Diarmuid from the country. The special fund so raised over a period of two years was required to meet the heavy costs incurred in the protracted litigation with Sir George Preston about the Corporation's salmon weir.

These petty customs were levied on goods as they passed through the city gates, both inwards and outwards. The rates ranged from one farthing on a sheep to threepence on a barrel of wine or aquavitae, a pack of cloth or a dozen hats. Horseloads of skins, timber-work, etc., paid fourpence, while a boatload of rape seeds coming to the quay was charged a shilling. The Corporation did not, as a rule, collect these customs directly but in accordance with the usage of the times they farmed them, as they did the net-fishing, by cant to an individual citizen.   In

[112] The walls of Limerick, which in Dineley's time were paved, were retained as fortifications long after those of Dublin had lost their military usefulness. So the gate-houses in Limerick continued to perform their origi-nal function. Crofton Croker in his *Researches in the South of Ireland* (p.48) states that Limerick was long regarded by the English Government with watchfulness and distrust on account of the loyalty of the citizens to the Stuart cause. Sixty years elapsed after the second siege before this strictness was relaxed and the gates were thrown open. In the middle of the 18th century there were seventeen gates guarded and locked regularly every night.

Limerick the offices so purchased included that of " common measurer," who had the right to prevent any private merchant from using his own measures when buying or selling corn, etc., or any but the public " beames " for weighing heavy weights.[113] These " farmers " or contractors were very prone to bid more than the thing was worth, and rebates were often allowed when a farmer could show that he had actually lost money on his contract.

We hear much talk nowadays about the curtailment of individual liberty and the interference with trade by government regulation and control ; but the idea that business men should be allowed to conduct commercial affairs with little or no restrictions belongs to the nineteenth century. In the seventeenth, merchants and shopkeepers had to conform to very definite rules and were liable to legal prosecution if they did not. I have already referred to the charters of the various trade corporations, and an example of the rules and regulations governing the conduct of business in the city of Limerick in the time of Charles II can be seen from the extracts given in Appendix G.[114]

Although Dublin was a more English city than Limerick, indeed it may have been because of that fact, much more latitude was allowed in regard to admitting Catholics to the freedom of the city in the capital than in the smaller city. Apart from the few years after the accession of James II, when Catholics were naturally in a strong position, the Dublin Assembly on several occasions, notably in 1672, 1676 and 1678,[115] made provision for Catholics

---

[113] For weights and measures see Ware, Vol. II., p.222.
[114] See also records of the Town of Limavady, J.R.S.A.I., Vol. XLI., p.162 *et seq.*
[115] Cal. Dub. Rec., and J.R.S.A.I., XXXIII., p.230.

becoming freemen. In Limerick, on the other hand, once the control of the city passed finally into Protestant hands, Catholics were discouraged, and in the end excluded altogether, so that we find in the Assembly Minute Book, under date Oct. 4, 1675, a significant resolution reluctantly agreeing to the admission of one Thomas Lysaght, a Catholic, to the freedom of the city " at the request of the present Mayor . . . this to be no precedent for the future, nor any Mayor hereafter shall move the Council for making any Papist free on account of his privilege."[116] This man, with one Creagh, was the last Catholic to be admitted in Limerick, except, of course, during the reign of James II. In Kinsale, which may be taken as an example of a smaller corporate town, it appears to have been found almost impossible to prevent Catholics trading there.[117]

No doubt one of the reasons why Catholics were not excluded too rigidly in Dublin was the shortage of money which so continually hampered the Assembly's civic activities. Catholic fees and fines were as useful as Protestant money in helping to fill the city's depleted treasury.

In the seventeenth century the city of Dublin had incurred practically no public debt. In 1668 arrangements were made to raise as a loan secured on the city the £300 required to pay for the water-pipes imported in that year—which it is interesting to note were made of elm trees, being of too large a diameter for lead. By 1686 the total indebtedness

[116] Though the trades and shops were kept as far as possible in Protestant hands the inhabitants of the towns were largely Catholic and there was, of course, a great influx of Catholic country people on market-days. See Orrery to Ormond 25 Jan., 1678. *Orrery Papers*, p.193.
[117] See MSS. of the Old Corporation of Kinsale. Some of the Presentments on which this statement is based are printed in *Analecta Hibernica*, No. 15.

under this head was £1,100 plus £200 for interest
due. These precursors of the modern municipal
loans were not, of course, offered to the public as
an investment but negotiated with an individual
" to pay off their most craving debts." It was
money well invested, for the security was sound and
the rate of interest up to eight per cent., so that
some delay in its payment was taken with equani-
mity. Limerick, on the other hand, as we have seen,
when money was wanted for a particular purpose,
called for a special sacrifice on the part of the freemen or made a special collection for a definite object.

The financial system of the country was rudimentary. Though the establishment under State
auspices of a regular bank was seriously proposed as
early as 1623, such banking as was done in the
seventeenth century was in the hands of brokers,
who were usually goldsmiths. In the period of
increased prosperity enjoyed by Dublin after the
Restoration, the banker-goldsmiths became a
recognized class in the community. They were to
be found in one particular part of the city, and the
parish of St. Werburgh's was crowded with their
places of business, where they received deposits and
issued notes.[118] Dunton in 1698 employed a certain
Mr. Lumm,[119] of Castle Street, whom he describes
as " one of the chief bankers in Dublin " to transmit
the proceeds of his book sales to London. He does
not mention how much he lost on the exchange.
After the Restoration the rate of exchange was very
unfavourable to Ireland, and Petty mentions that it
cost about seven per cent.[119a] Inland large sums

[118] C. M. Tenison in J.C.H.A.S., Vol. III 1894, p.17.
[119] Elnathan Lumm. G.O. MS. 238, p.332.
[119a] Ormond to Bennet, C.S.P. Ire. 1663/65, p.150 ; *Petty Papers*, I., p.58.
Cf. Southwell MSS., 16 July, 1688 (T.C.D. I. 6. 11) and Abdy MSS.
passim (Nat. Lib. No. 325).

were often sent by road in cash. Rawdon, for example, in one of his letters refers to £900 which he had sent " well guarded " to Lord Conway in Dublin but no doubt the necessity for this cumbrous procedure was gradually eliminated by the development of the banking system. The distinction of having the first bank in Ireland is claimed by Cork, where Hoare's Bank was established in 1675,[120] but there were probably institutions of a very similar nature in Dublin at the same time. The notes of the banker-goldsmiths and the traders' tokens[121] which were issued by substantial merchants in the larger towns had only a local circulation, and the risk of carrying actual cash from place to place was usually met, even early in the century, by the issue of bills of exchange and letters of credit to their friends and acquaintances by rich men such as the Earl of Cork. The coinage itself was in a state of hopeless confusion. There was no mint in Ireland till James II established two—in Dublin and Limerick—the issue of whose debased coinage, though only intended as a temporary measure, served to make confusion worse confounded. All sorts of foreign coins, both gold and silver, counterfeit as well as genuine, were in circulation, known as pistoles, rix dollars, ducatoons, Portugal Royals, Mexican pieces-of-eight, and other romantic sounding names, their value being determined by weight,[122] which in turn led to much fraud and uncertainty.[123]

---

[120] J.C.H.A.S., Vol. I., p.221.

[121] For Traders' tokens see J.R.S.A.I., Vol. XXI., p.209.

[122] Dineley has a drawing of the instrument commonly used for this purpose. (*Observations*, p.36). He says that the Spanish cobs, half-cobs and quarter-cobs were the coins most frequently met with. See also Ware, Vol. II., p.219 ; J.R.S.A.I., Vol. III., p.162 for the value in 1689 of other coins not mentioned above, e.g. Broad Carolus, half Edward, etc. ; and Proclamation (C.S.P.I. 1660 /62, p.197) making various foreign coins legal currency and stating their value, in addition to those already mentioned the list specifies the ducat, ducatoon, golden rider, French Louis, old Peru and cardecu.

[123] See O'Brien, *Economic History of Ireland in the Seventeenth Century*, p.205.

The bulk of the wealth of the country was still in the hands of the landed aristocracy, if we can so describe a class which, as a result of the territorial upheaval following the advent of Cromwell, consisted largely of people whose origin was by no means aristocratic. There were successful business men, of course, who made a good deal of money : William Yorke, for example, a Dutchman who had settled in Limerick and became its Mayor, and who was well enough off to build an Exchange for the citizens entirely at his own expense.[124] The Revocation of the Edict of Nantes gave a great stimulus to the immigration of the Huguenot tradesmen, but twenty years before that event they were already being encouraged to come to Ireland. An Act To Encourage Protestant Strangers to Settle in Ireland was passed in 1662.[125] Trade jealousy prevented a similar measure from being made applicable to England. These men and their descendants in due course became some of the foremost merchants, manufacturers and bankers in Ireland. The earliest Huguenot immigrants who settled at Cork were goldsmiths. These are said to have influenced Irish style in their art and to have given it a decidedly

[124] I presume this Yorke was one of the Dutchmen referred to by Orrery in his letter to Bennet (C.S.P.I., 26 Jun., 1663) when he says of Limerick, where he had had some of his arrears satisfied by a grant of houses : " This city being the most considerable in all Ireland for strength and situation . . . I have already got above 80 Dutch thither who have set up considerable manufactures and trade by sea, and I am daily increasing the numbers of those who are likely to beautify and enrich it." Three years later, however, an original letter contained among the Orrery Papers informs us that so far as weavers were concerned only one of these was then left in Limerick. MS. Nat. Lib., No. 32. folio 67.
[125] Individual attempts to implement this Act continued to be made by " improving " landlords for many years after its introduction. The Lane Papers (Nat. Lib. MS. not yet catalogued) under date 3 June, 1692, record the settlement of French Protestant families at Dromahaire, Co. Leitrim. See also *London Gazette*, 2 May, 1681, for similar scheme, at low rents, for Lanesborough, Co. Longford. The Palatine settlement in Co. Limerick belongs to the early eighteenth century.

Continental character.[126] Among other successful merchants the Quakers were beginning to attract attention not so much because of their commercial acumen and substantial fortunes,[127] but rather on account of their determined resistance to any law or custom which ran counter to their principles. They suffered much persecution in Ireland, as in England, for they refused among other things to take oaths, pay tithes, contribute to churches, observe religious holy-days or remove their hats in court. At a later date their persistence was rewarded by the modification of the law in many respects, notably in the matter of oaths and marriage ceremonies.

Among the methods adopted by the impoverished Corporation of Dublin to obtain ready money, besides such expedients as public lotteries, was the granting of leases of the more or less waste land adjacent to the city for a fine and a small rent. The land on all four sides of St. Stephen's Green was parcelled out in this way in 1664 when the first steps were taken to lay it out as a public pleasure ground[128]; and it is interesting to note that provision was made that the houses to be erected should conform to a certain architectural standard. Oxmantown Green had already been extensively built on : the bowling green there was protected from encroachment, but Ormond had to arrange for the drilling of the troops at Stephen's Green

---

[126] Lee, *The Huguenot Settlements in Ireland*, p.48, *et passim*. See also Brigid O'Mullane in Dub. Hist. Rec. VI. 3. 110 *et seq.*
[127] Among the extracts from the Council Book of the Corporation of Cork (quoted p.159 of Rev. Rowland Davies' *Journal*) is : " 12 Nov. 1690— That application be made to the Quakers and other moneyed men."
[128] The year 1670 is usually given as the date of the establishment of St. Stephen's Green as a public park. It is true that the Green itself was not levelled till 1670, and references to tree planting and improvements there are to be found in the Assembly minutes at various later dates. The minute for the year 1664 on which I base my statement is to be found in Cal. Dub. Rec., Vol. IV., p.298.

because the open space at Oxmantown had become too restricted. A similar development scheme at the North Strand, on the way to Clontarf, was attempted in 1664, but we learn from the minutes of a meeting held two years later that this fell through.

The Phoenix Park was the most extensive of the public works undertaken in Dublin after the Restoration. It was almost lost to the city when the King's mistress, the Duchess of Cleveland, attempted to obtain a grant of it for herself. Her influence with the King, however, was not strong enough to induce him to carry through such an outrageous proposal, to which, be it said to his credit, Essex offered most determined opposition. It is still one of the largest public parks in any city in the world, and as originally laid out it covered an even greater area, since it then included the land on the south side of the river now occupied by the Kingsbridge Railway Station and by the Royal Hospital at Kilmainham, which was itself built on ground taken from the Phoenix Park not long after the park was established. At this time the vice-regal residence was removed to Chapelizod which was then, of course, well outside the suburbs of the city.

In this brief sketch of Dublin in the second half of the seventeenth century I need not refer to any other public institution or building, except perhaps the Bluecoat School[129] which, like the Royal Hospital, was a foundation dating from the reign of Charles II.

In this chapter on town life we have lost all touch

[129] The history of this has been told by Sir Frederick R. Falkiner in his *Foundation of the King's Hospital*, Dublin, 1906. The papers and documents preserved there are calendared in *Analecta Hibernica*, No. 15. See also Chart's *Story of Dublin* (Mediaeval Towns Series), London, 1932. For the Royal Hospital see *Story of the Royal Hospital, Kilmainham.* (Childers and Stewart). Revised edition, London, 1921 ; and MS. Nat. Lib. No. 87.

with the Gaelic and Catholic Ireland which still survived in the country. Dublin especially was essentially Protestant and Anglo-Irish, if not actually English. Any list of names will tell its tale at a glance. Take for instance the Bluecoat School. Out of the original sixty children sent there to be educated only eight bear names which have any suggestion of Ireland or Catholicism about them,[130] and these, no doubt, were from families which had conformed earlier in the century. Even the water-rate collectors and the very charwomen employed by the Corporation have English and Protestant names. If we turn to Limerick the preponderance is not quite so marked, and Irish names, though seldom met with when anything financially advantageous was in question, do appear very frequently in the minutes of the Assembly. All the butchers who combined to take a lease of a plot for the new shambles had Irish names, as had several of the gate-keepers, though as I mentioned in Chapter IV, names cannot be taken as a very reliable guide to religious denomination. When subscriptions were required for the new cathedral bells, only two out of the nine collectors appointed were of English extraction. A donation towards these bells was evidently regarded as a sign of grace, for we find a man of the very Irish name of Managh O'Grady admitted a freeman in 1674 because he gave a guinea to that fund. This was done at the request of the mayor.

The mayor of a city was in no sense a figure-head. The Mayor of Limerick in the 'seventies and 'eighties was paid £200 a year and his out-of-pocket

---

[130] Viz.: Sweetman, Dillon, Lea, Kennedy, Carey, Geoghegan, Ward, Fennel.

expenses. In Dublin he received a salary of £500. The money was well earned for the post was no sinecure. The duties undertaken by the Mayor of Limerick, as revealed by the minutes of the Assembly, were not unlike those discharged by a city manager under the system introduced into Ireland since the dissolution of the Union. Nominally it was not a whole time job ; but he had little time or energy to give to his own business after he had finished making detailed arrangements with tradesmen for carrying out works, big and small, from the setting down of a public seat to the building of a new Exchange, when he had finished negotiating with the dean of the Cathedral about land and with the butchers about the " noisomeness " of the shambles, had attended to the extensive routine business of his office and presided over meetings of the Assembly, to say nothing of such tasks as looking after the judges at the assizes, entertaining distinguished and not always perhaps too welcome visitors, or pouring oil on the troubled waters stirred up by his somewhat tactless Recorder. It may certainly be allowed that he fairly earned his salary.

The Town Clerk was available to do the secretarial work. The way in which his writing, at the best a rather slovenly hand with all the abbreviations and peculiarities of the period very much in evidence, deteriorated towards the end of the minutes of a long meeting of the Corporation gives life to this rather dry old manuscript and suggests that, like other clerks, he sometimes rushed his work in order not to be too late home to tea. The Town Clerk, however, was more than a mere secretary. It was he, for example, who in 1677 was instructed to go to

Dublin in order to retain and consult counsel in the important lax-weir case to which I have already referred.

To go from Limerick to Dublin : a matter of three and a half hours in the train to-day. We will consider in the next chapter what such a journey meant two hundred and fifty years ago.

CHAPTER VIII

Communications: Their Difficulties and Dangers

WHEN the Town Clerk of Limerick received instructions to go to Dublin in connexion with the lax-weir case he felt, no doubt, that this was an event of considerable importance in his life, for it meant that he would probably be away for at least a fortnight and that he would be visiting a city where he could really enjoy the atmosphere of up-to-date urban civilization for the few days his business kept him there. The journey, however, even though it was between the two principal towns in the country and therefore easier than most, was arduous enough, not to mention the cost which was heavy.

The customary travelling expenses allowed to a government " messenger in ordinary " were as much as £30[1] for the return journey between Dublin and London, plus ten shillings a day.[2] These officials were allowed sixpence per mile on posting journeys, plus two shillings for every stage of ten miles. The ordinary rates were less than this. Macaulay gives 3d. per mile, with 4d. per stage to the guide, as the customary charges in England in the reign of James II, and the fares by the new fast coaches as 2½d. to 3d. per mile. The accomplishment by these of a journey of 50 miles on a fine summer's day was then regarded as an almost incredible sign of modern progress and was an impossibility on Irish roads.

[1] Lord Orrery estimated £50 to £60 as the cost of the journey from London to Castlemartyr when undertaken by a member of his family, *circ.* 1676. *Orrery Papers*, pp.157, 160, etc.
[2] This was reduced to 6s. 8d. per diem in 1695. Cal. Treas. Papers, 1557 to 1696, Vol. XXVIII., p.378.

In point of time the journey from Limerick to Dublin would occupy as a rule four days. Travelling by Silvermines, Roscrea, Kildare and Naas, the distance was little more than 120 English statute miles. Though that was the shortest road, other considerations, such as congenial company, accommodation for the night, the latest rumours about the activities of rapparees, and the condition of the roads themselves at the time, might easily influence a traveller to take a longer way, the usual alternative between Limerick and Dublin being by Pallas and so to the east of the Slieve Phelim mountains.[3]

Ireland, with its smaller population and less settled conditions, lagged far behind England as regards travelling facilities. If the Town Clerk of Bristol or Liverpool had been ordered to proceed to London he had nothing to do but to book his place in one of the stage coaches which already ran fairly regularly between the more important centres in England[4]; or, if the traveller had plenty of money to spend, he had no difficulty in hiring a private coach in which he could do the journey in long or short stages as best suited his own convenience and temperament.

[3] Dineley, *Observations*, p.76, *et. seq.*
[4] See Belloc, *The Highway and its Vehicles*, London, 1926, in which there are a number of valuable illustrations of coaches, litters, sedan chairs, etc. Much valuable contemporary information on the coaching arrangements in England in the second half of the seventeenth century is to be found in the pages of the early English novelists such as Defoe. The use of glass windows in coaches was a novelty in Dublin in the time of Charles II. Dr. George Clarke refers in his autobiography to "the new glass coach which had just come into fashion " in London in 1666. It was introduced after the Restoration from France which was ahead of England in such matters. Dr. Clarke spent four years in Ireland (1690-94), and his correspondence covering that period is preserved in the Trinity College Library (K. 5. 1-13). His autobiography has been published: H.M.C., Leyborne-Popham MSS. Its interest, as regards Ireland, is mainly political, but it also throws light on social conditions after the Boyne.

In England the main roads were bad enough to cause serious delays to coaches, which in wet weather not infrequently sank almost to the axle in soft patches or were overturned as a result of the unevenness of the surface.[5] In Ireland they were so bad that, even on the main routes, hardly any public coaches were in existence and wheeled traffic was in constant difficulties ; most men indeed preferred to travel light on horseback.[6] Pack horses were much used, and in the remoter parts of the country these represented the normal and indeed almost the only form of transport. Transport between the principal cities on the sea-coast was mainly carried on by sea, but inland, where suitable rivers were available, water-carriage was used and is frequently mentioned by Dineley, Molyneux, and in replies to the questionnaire sent out by Sir William Petty.

It requires something of an effort to-day, especially to the younger generation, to realize the importance of the horse in the everyday life of the seventeenth century, and indeed of the eighteenth and early nineteenth also. Then to be able to ride a horse was as much a matter of course as it is to be able to ride a bicycle to-day. Not only men, but women also, except those in the lowest station of life who seldom if ever had occasion to leave their own cabins, were more or less at home in the saddle, though when making a journey

---

[5] For English roads, Webb, *English Local Government : The Story of the King's Highway* (London, 1913) is valuable ; but references to Ireland in it are few. See also Defoe, *Tour in England and Wales*, Appendix to Vol. II. of 1st edition and *passim*.

[6] Ladies and invalids were often carried in litters. Rinuccini, who was in bad health when he arrived in Ireland, though he was able to ride into the city on horseback, accomplished the greater part of his journey from Kenmare to Kilkenny in a litter. Hynes, *The Mission of Rinuccini*, p.32 ; J.R.S.A.I., Vol. II., p.224.

on horseback it was quite usual for them to ride pillion behind a man, while children were perched on the horse's withers in front of the rider.

Owing to the state of the roads, which in many places were little more than ill-defined tracks, progress was always quicker on horseback than by a carriage of any kind. If our Town Clerk had been in a hurry no doubt he could have ridden from Limerick to Dublin in less than three days but that would have meant more hours in the saddle than the average townsman relished. In the 'forties, when of course war conditions rendered the roads even worse than they were in peace time, three days was regarded as the normal length of time occupied by the journey from Limerick to Cork,[8] just half the distance of that from Limerick to Dublin.   Sir Thomas Molyneux, in his descriptions of his tours through the country in 1709, usually states the exact length of time it took him to go from point to point. When he rode, and had no occasion to tarry by the way, he generally did about seven miles per hour, but when he and his friends travelled by chaise they moved much slower. The standard Irish mile was and is considerably longer than the English statute mile, the proportion being 14 to 11.[9] This leads to some confusion on the part of English writers on

[8] La Boullaye le Gouz, p.26. Le Gouz actually only took two days to do it.
[9] Being based on this difference in long measure, i.e., on a perch of 7 not 5½ yards, the acre which was adopted as the standard in Ireland was correspondingly larger than the English acre. This measure, known as the Irish Plantation Measure, came into general use at the time of the Cromwellian settlement, and since the Irish acre was equal to approximately 1⅗ statute acres it created the illusion that the allotments made to the English soldiers and adventurers were much less than was really the case. It is ironical to reflect that this now distinctively Irish acre, which has survived the general process of anglicization, was actually popularized by Cromwell ! The Irish long measure, however, as we know from Ware (Vol. II., p.224), was in use before Cromwell's time.

Ireland, especially as in practice the length of the mile varied in different parts of the country: as Molyneux remarks in his diary of his journey to Connacht—" the further from Dublin the longer the miles." The standard Irish mile remained in general use until the introduction of motor cars, and among other places the old milestones, spaced according to that measure, are still to be seen on the main road from Dublin to Naas. It was on this very road, which was better than the average, that Molyneux did one of his longest day's runs by chaise. They started at 10 a.m. and reached Naas (20 English miles) at 3 p.m.[10] After resting there they proceeded to Kildare, passing across the Curragh, taking 2½ hours to cover that 12 miles; and finally on reaching the less frequented country approaching Monasterevan, although it was midsummer, took 2 hours to do the last 7 miles.[11] And so it was throughout his journeys which brought him through a great part of the midlands and as far afield as Kerry and Connacht. In the wet winter probably their chaise could not have travelled at all.

As he went he described the nature and appearance of the countryside through which he travelled. To him there was nothing singular or specially remarkable about the absence of fences and enclosures, though he recorded it as John Stevens did in northern France, but that is the fact which strikes

---

[10] Later in the year, on Nov. 8th, he did the journey to Naas in four hours, but he does not specify whether he rode or drove. He was probably on horseback, as the following day he went off the main road and made for Blessington.

[11] MS. T.C.D. I. 1. 3. pp. 71 to 129. This MS. is paged and is more easily referred to than the originals in Molyneux's hand which are also in T.C.D. Library.

the present-day reader most forcibly.[12]   Open unenclosed country, champaigne country as Molyneux calls it when describing the eastern part of Co. Galway, was a normal condition in England and France as well as in Ireland. Here and there a certain amount of corn was grown, but the area devoted to tillage was as a rule only fenced off temporarily, and for the most part extensive sheepwalks stretched away on each side of the open road. All the cattle he saw were black,[13] a fact constantly noted by John Stevens, and by every seventeenth century writer who mentions the subject.

René Mézandiere, whom we noticed in the last chapter as getting the concession for the licensing of hackney-car drivers in Dublin, made a half-hearted attempt in his original petition to obtain also a monopoly of the inter-town coach services throughout the country, but as far as my researches go I can find no evidence that his activities ever extended beyond Dublin and the adjacent seaside places. All the parties concerned probably realized that the roads were too bad to allow of any regular coach services.

References to coaching in Ireland in the seventeenth century are rare.   Molyneux, under date April 8th, 1709, mentions that he went by coach from Moate to Athlone in three hours, adding that the " coach roads " in those parts were " in-

---

[12] The land, however, adjacent to the larger towns was less open. Stevens, for example, remarks on the well-enclosed land on the Clare side of Limerick, and Begley in his description of the Siege of Limerick and Sarsfield's famous exploit at Ballyneety refers to the network of hedges in the district on the east side of the city. At the beginning of the next century Lothian was the only shire in Scotland where the practice of enclosing fields with permanent fences had been adopted. (P. Hume Brown *Hist. of Scotland*), III., p.46. For lack of hedges in England, see Ogilby, *Itinerarium Angliae* (e.g. pp.2, 6, 12, 17. Brit. Mus. MS. pagination). The pictorial page-headings of this rare work, showing contemporary sporting and farming scenes, are of considerable interest.

[13] See Chapter VI., note 3.

different " ; the previous day he had described them as " mighty bad". It must be remembered that in those days the word ' coach ' was not restricted in its meaning. Mrs. Freke in her diary, the principal value and interest of which lies in her descriptions of travelling in England and Ireland and between the two countries, uses the word to denote a private carriage as well as a public conveyance, the expression ' stage coach ' being employed to indicate the latter,[14] a distinction also observed by Defoe in *Moll Flanders* and his other novels of the period. Dunton tells us that he took a coach, meaning a hackney carriage, from Drogheda for a mile or two to the place where he had left his horse ; we read of Lord Ossory paying £41 1s. 6d. for a new mourning coach for his lady,[15] and again of the Countess of Ossory being escorted into the City of Dublin by sixty coaches, most of them with six horses.[16]

John Stevens, whose marches as an officer in the army of King James brought him over a large number of roads in the south, the west and the midlands, and as far north as the Boyne, frequently describes their condition in his journal. As long as the weather was fine the main roads seem to have been good enough for wagons and carts, but in very few places were they more than barely passable after heavy rain. " The great rain," says John Stevens in his *Journal*, writing of the country near Drogheda, " has made the ways almost impassable, the horse road which is most old cause way being broken up and quite out of repair and the footway in the fields very boggy with abundance of ditches

[14] Her diary covers the years 1671 to 1714.
Cf. Narrative of Adrian Adornes, MS. Bodl. Rawl. c.439, fo. 250.
[15] J.R.S.A.I., Vol. I., p.418.
[16] *London Gazette*, 14 June, 1670.

at that time full of water." No doubt even a year or two of war conditions causes the state of the roads to deteriorate greatly, and at any rate as far as the more remote places were concerned, not much improvement occurred for nearly a century. "Even at this period [A.D. 1771]," says Very Rev. P. White, writing of County Clare, "so long after the Williamite subjugation the country had scarcely yet begun to recover from the prostrate condition into which it had been flung. The means of communication between the people were of the worst kind. Roads were few and bad and badly kept. They were run invariably against the hill-tops for the purpose of securing at little cost a solid foundation. Produce was carried to fairs and markets or dragged on rude sleighs over the ill-constructed narrow roads. Eugene O'Curry mentions[17] that his grandfather, Melaghlan O'Curry, a large farmer, employed his men, horses and *sledges* in burying the victims of the famine of 1741.[18] The almost equally rude and inconvenient block-wheel carts began to be used first about this time. The wealthiest of the gentry owned heavy four-wheeled carriages, but seldom used them, because of the difficulty of drawing them up and down the steep and dangerous roads. Spring cars were totally unknown. Pillions upon which the gentleman's or farmer's wife sat behind her husband on horse-back took their place and were much used far into the present [nineteenth] century."[19]

The war, of course, disorganized such rudimentary system of road-making as existed in the

[17] Fr. White here refers the reader to O'Curry's *Ordnance Survey*, p.369.
[18] As late as 1837 in a Donegal parish there was no wheeled car and carrying was done by slide-cars and creels. Evans, *Irish Heritage*, pp.50, 110.
[19] White, *History of Clare and the Dalcassian Clans*, p.312.

country. Rudimentary it was, with no standard common to different parts of the country, or even to adjacent parishes, so that an important main road might be quite good for a stretch and then you would meet an almost impassable patch, due as a rule not to the nature of the land but to the incompetence or laziness of the local people charged with the responsibility of repairing it.

In earlier times the chiefs had been able to maintain such highways as there were by calling upon the clansmen for men and horses to repair roads as well as to build bridges.[20] It was not until the roads began to be regarded as through routes for long distance travellers that this system became intolerable. Up to the latter end of the seventeenth century the vast majority of the people did not look upon roads as performing this function, and felt no grievance so long as they offered well defined and fairly safe tracks, upon which they could ride over to a neighbour's house or visit the nearest small town. Although the Romans never came to Ireland, the conception of a road as a means of easily bringing people and goods from one distant place to another was familiar to the ancient Irish, who had their great highways converging upon Tara from every province ; but such ideas were lost sight of in the general chaos of the Middle Ages when no central authority held sway in the country. No doubt roads were often deliberately destroyed by the Irish themselves to hamper the movements of invading troops, and it is as a military measure that the idea of making good roads reappears at the beginning of the seventeenth century. " It was part of the plan of the English to build roads in

[20] Green, *Making of Ireland*, p. 101.

Ireland with the object of facilitating the passage of troops ; and in 1614 provision was made for the maintenance and repair of all existing highways by the forced contribution of labour and materials by the inhabitants of each parish. The repairing of bridges, causeways and toghers was further provided for twenty years later, when the imposition of a tax for this purpose in each county was authorized. The roads, however, do not seem to have been satisfactory ; Boate complained of the scarcity of bridges ; and in 1662 ' the general defect in the highways of the kingdom ' engaged the attention of the House of Commons. As late as the beginning of the eighteenth century the Irish roads continued to be wretched and frequently impassable."[21] On some of the principal highways, however, good bridges, existed in the middle of the century, such as the " fair stone bridges " at Trim and Drogheda,[22] and at Golden.[23] By the end of the seventeenth century something approaching a nation-wide system of road maintenance was in operation, though it was far from being effective in its results. " The roads were maintained by the joint effort of the landowners and labourers of each parish : the former were obliged by law to furnish horses and vehicles for six days per annum and the latter to labour for six days. When this proved insufficient the Grand Jury[24] of the county could raise a sum sufficient to complete the work."[25]

[21] O'Brien, *Economic Hist. of Ireland in the* 17*th Century*, p.68. He gives references for his statements which I need not repeat here. Boate in another place refers to the frequent cases of persons being drowned while attempting to cross fords. See *Natural History of Ireland*, p.54.
[22] *Analecta Hibernica*, No. 8, p.424.
[23] Dineley, *Observations*, p.92.
[24] Cf. Co. Cork Grand Jury Presentments in *Analecta Hibernica*, No. 15, p.190, *et seq.*
[25] O'Brien, *Ec. Hist.* 18*th Century*, p.359 *et seq.* Cf. Clarke MSS., cccx. (T.C.D. K. 5. 4.)

Such a plan, of course, was bound to lead to abuses, and in 1720 it was found necessary to pass an Act prohibiting the raising of money for roads and bridges unless two responsible and credible persons swore that the work was necessary. Not until 1760 did labourers receive any pay for road work, and it was ten years later before the contract system was inaugurated, which in turn led to the even more flagrant abuses so graphically described in Dutton's *Survey of Co. Clare.*[26]

Some landowners undoubtedly did more than was actually required of them by law and regarded road-making as a regular item of estate work. In the description of Co. Antrim by R. Dobbs, in the general chorographical survey of the country initiated by Sir William Petty, to which I have referred in earlier chapters, he says : " all the highways within 8 or 10 miles of Lisburn are very good not only from the nature of the soil which generally affords gravel but from Sir George Rawdon's care." The same writer remarks that Rawdon " is I believe the best highway man in the kingdom." Rawdon's beneficent activities, to which reference has been made in Chapter IV, were principally connected with the estate of Lord Conway and Killulta, whose agent he was. Some landlords were ruthless in their methods and swept aside anything which stood in their way with a lack of humane feeling remarkable even in an age when to show any sign of sensitiveness was to be effeminate and the rights of the poor were championed only by poets like O'Bruadair, who ascribed to the old dispossessed proprietors virtues which they too often

[26] Though not within the period under consideration Mr. George Pakenham's opinion of Leinster roads in 1737—" the finest I ever saw "—should be mentioned in this connexion. See *Analecta Hibernica*, No. 15, p.120.

did not possess. One landowner, indeed, who was no Cromwellian but was " a great improver " of his estate in Leix, planting many trees and making double ditches set with thornquicks,[27] included the making of several roads in his activities. His disregard for the rights of the poor and defenceless made this man, whose name was Gerald Fitzgerald, notorious and long remembered. He employed hired labour to do his work—Ulstermen, paid in cattle—and when making these roads he yoked a team of bullocks, drew a strong chain around some widows' cabins that stood in the way and pulled them down. That is the story as Hardiman relates it.[28]

The work of tracing the exact positions of the roads belongs rather to the local antiquarian than to the general historian and, fascinating study though it is, cannot be pursued here.[29] We have now considered briefly the nature of those roads and the kind of traffic that made use of them. Returning to our Town Clerk, the next question which arises is what sort of accommodation would he be likely to meet when he stopped for his dinner or his night's lodging. Here again, as in everything connected with travelling, Ireland was greatly inferior to England. In a word, the accommodation was bad. Travellers in fact were not catered for as they were in England, perhaps because they were too few. The

[27] See lease 25 May, 1680 in *An. Hib.*, 15, p.396.
[28] *Irish Minstrelsy*, Vol. I., p.189.
[29] The sources mentioned in this chapter are themselves a mine of information on this subject. There is a large collection of seventeenth century maps in the National Library ; but until after the Down Survey (prior to which Irish cartography was largely guesswork) roads were not shown. Several maps published towards the end of the century, however, do show them. (See Bibliography, Section III) though, as might be expected, these vary considerably in their delineation of the exact course of the roads. A small book entitled *The Geographical Description of Ireland* was published in 1720. Based on Petty and Pratt it consists of a " prefatory description " written in the reign of Queen Anne, and a number of maps on which the roads are shown.

inns in the inland towns were but wretched
pot-houses.

Even at a place like Holyhead, where passengers
for Ireland constantly required accommodation,
sometimes (when strong westerly winds were blow-
ing) for many days or even weeks, travellers were
liable to find themselves without shelter. In 1660
and 1661, for example, the garrison at Holyhead,
which had been placed there " for the safety of
the Irish packets," occupied all the regular inns
and lodgings for several months, and the resultant
confusion was only obviated by quartering the
troops in the church.[30]

At the beginning of the century inns providing
beds were so scarce that in the cities lodgings were
appointed by the urban officials for travellers[31] ;
and, as we saw in the last chapter, even in Dublin
nearly a hundred years later, visitors like Dunton
stayed in lodgings, not in public inns. Bourchier
in 1623 remarks on the scarcity of inns, especially in
the Pale, adding that travellers had to find accommodation in gentlemen's houses. Travellers enjoyed the prescriptive right of demanding accommodation at inns where such existed. William
Edmundson describes in his journal how he arrived
one evening at Mullingar and, being refused shelter
and refreshment by the innkeepers on the ground
that he was a Quaker (and so a potential cause of
disturbance on their premises), he repaired to the
constable[32] and insisted on that official finding him

---

[30] C.S.P. Dom. Dec. 16, 1660, and April, 1661 (p.579).
[31] Fynes Moryson, *Description* (ed. Falkiner), p.227. He mentions that inn-
keepers did not hang out signs as in England, but this practice was fairly
widely adopted some fifty years later. See p.217, *supra*.
[32] Constables were appointed from among the civilian population. Their
duties included the making of arrests. Thus William Penn, another famous
Quaker, was arrested by several constables, backed up by soldiers, as we
know from a letter written by him to Lord Orrery. (See Wight, p.101).

lodging, "for I was a traveller and had money to pay for what I should have." The constable got him a room with a fire, and hay for his horse. This was in 1656. Quakers were comparatively well treated under the Cromwellian régime.

Most of the travellers who have left a record of their experiences, having no doubt been warned beforehand what to expect, trusted to the hospitality of the resident gentry from whom, of course, they almost always received a welcome of which they had no cause to complain : Dineley went from place to place armed with letters of introduction : Molyneux had friends and relations all over the country ; Bishop Dive Downes stayed with the parochial clergy of his diocese ; and Archbishop Brenan could always find some faithful Catholic gentleman or farmer who was proud to entertain so eminent an ecclesiastic ; but others, like le Gouz, and indeed Dunton at times, took their chance and were seldom much worse off for that. Dineley mentions two inns in Limerick[33] not unfavourably, but it is their claret[34] he praises ; he had no occasion to sample their beds. Writing sixty years later, Pococke says all the inns in Limerick were bad.[35] Let us hope that the Town Clerk of Limerick had friends on the way to Dublin, or at least the temerity to ask a night's lodging from some person of standing, for if not he must assuredly have slept ill for three nights.

[33] *Observations*, p.122. Writing to Orrery in 1672 the Mayor of Limerick remarks that hardly one of the eighty or so alehouses in the city was capable of finding two beds besides those required for the proprietor's family. *Orrery Papers*, p.101.
[34] Much of the wine sold was adulterated.   17/18 Ch. II., c.19 prescribes severe penalties for adulterating it with cider.   Sir Patrick Dun in 1698 states that wines were adulterated with spirits. *Analecta Hibernica.* No. 2, p. 10.
[35] *Tour*, p.113.

The sort of accommodation which might be expected by a traveller in the more remote parts of the country, where coach roads were unknown and strangers seldom seen, is shown by Dunton's letters. A hundred years after Dunton's time there was little change. The Rev. Caesar Otway's entertaining descriptions of Mayo might, but for his greater refinement of speech, have been written by Dunton in 1698. Otway often had to eat his dinner without a knife and to drink from a wooden noggin, there being no cup in the house.[36] Dineley notices the use of ' sliogáin ' (shells) for spoons, and that only of comparatively recent introduction among the poor. Forks were, of course, quite unknown except in up-to-date establishments since they were not used at all for their present purpose, even in England, until the reign of James I.[37] This, like many other fashions in the seventeenth century, came to England from Italy ; Ireland, though politically, and to some extent intellectually, in touch with the Continent, took its domestic fashions—slowly enough—from England, not from Italy, France or Holland.

Irish people were not accustomed to regular meals and it was not to be expected that the inn-keepers would be any less casual than their neighbours. Many of the inns of which we read such dismal accounts were in fact little more than cabins, and differed hardly at all from the ordinary dwellings of the cottiers and scollogues. It is easy to err on the side of emphasizing the aspects of life which seem to us the most extraordinary from our twentieth century viewpoint, and we must not allow the

[36] See *Sketches in Erris and Tyrawley*, p.29 and *passim*.
[37] Wright, *Domestic Manners*, p.457.

pictures drawn by Dunton, and other travellers to
the back of godspeed, to lead us to take too unfavourable an estimate of the country as a whole.
All inns were not so primitive as to offer no forks
or to provide wooden platters and drinking vessels.
Pewter mugs, we know, were to be found in the
public-houses frequented by O'Bruadair[38] ; and
beds were not all so lousy as those described by
Fynes Moryson.

The food supplied at the small inns was no doubt
the same as that in use every day among the poorer
people. The question of the diet of the people is one
which has already been dealt with very thoroughly
by other writers, so that it would be superfluous to
quote at length from contemporary sources. Professor O'Brien in his *Economic History of Ireland in the
Seventeenth Century*[39] has made an admirable selection
from Petty, Stevens and others, and it would be
difficult to improve upon his summary, though
perhaps the fairly general use of vegetables (often
contemptuously dismissed as " roots ") has not
been sufficiently realized.[40] " Their diet generally,"
says a contemporary writer, " is very mean and
sparing, consisting of milk, roots and coarse unsavoury bread." This bread was the oaten cake
so frequently mentioned by writers on the food of
the Irish ; and by roots he means potatoes. This
use of the word ' roots ' was quite common in the
period under review.[42] In the absence of sugar

[38] In the seventeenth century, before glass and china came into general
use for domestic purposes, pewter largely took their place.
[39] *Op. cit.*, pp.107, 139-140, 146, etc. See also Dr. Murray's Introduction
to John Stevens's *Journal*.
[40] Dr. McAdoo (see note 10, p.85 *supra*) mentions beetroot, cabbage,
peas and beans as well as potatoes as among the commonest articles of
food of the poorest section of the community.
[42] Cf. *The Western Wonder*, p.31. There is a reference in that book (p.20)
to what was evidently " Irish stew," though not so called.

A · TRAVEL SCENE

GALWAY

in the form in which we now use it[43] honey was an important article of diet in the seventeenth century and for the same reason metheglin or mead was a popular drink. Milk and milk products, such as " troander " and the " bonnyclabber, mulahaan and choak-cheese " mentioned by Dunton, had long been the basis of Irish diet,[44] and gargantuan feasts such as that described by Moffet in his *Irish Hudibras* must be regarded as occasional. Indeed, the Irish people have always been fonder of drinking than of eating. The greatest disparagers of their food all praise their usquebagh or whiskey[45] ; and while there is not the same unanimity about the beer it is as often praised as condemned : no doubt the varying opinions expressed were due to the multiplicity of brewers,[46] large and small, throughout the country, and the consequent variation in the standard of the beer brewed.[47] Le Gouz, who as a Frenchman might be expected to have a fairly critical palate, found the brandy he got in gentlemen's houses excellent and the beer very good. Francis Rogers met very good French claret in the taverns, but considered the malt liquor not so good as in most parts of England.[48] Almost anywhere you stopped in the country you could get whiskey, milk and potatoes, and perhaps the boxty bread

---

[43] Some West Indian cane sugar was, however, refined in Ireland. See C.S.P.I. 1666/69, p.338, and other references in the State Papers.
[44] Cf. Fynes Moryson, *Description* (ed. Falkiner), p.424 *et seq.* ; *Advertisements for Ireland*, p.9 ; Capt. Cuellar's *Narrative*, p.61 ; and indeed every sixteenth and early seventeenth century writer who touches on the subject at all.
[45] From 1664 distillers were subject to regulations prescribed by Statute.
[46] Home brewing was a regular feature of the domestic economy of the Big House. Cf. *Orrery Papers*, p.177 and *Kenmare MSS.*, pp.97, 98.
[47] The use of gutter water in brewing was quite common. In Kinsale, for example, a Presentment of 6 Sept., 1714, prohibits the practice except between Nov. 1 and Feb. 28 of each year.
[48] *Three Sea Journals of Stuart Times*, p.196. Cf. Dineley's view, p.254, supra.

which was made from potato flour. Considering the conservatism of the people and their retention of age-old customs, the rapidity with which the potato became popular in Ireland is remarkable. Dr. Salaman states that potatoes were the ordinary food of the people as early as 1630[49] : this is perhaps an overstatement, but it was increasingly true as the century advanced, especially so far as the poorer parts of the country were concerned.[50] The ease with which a poor family could be kept alive on a small plot of potatoes must have been the cause of the rapid increase in their cultivation, and probably, as Professor O'Brien suggests, the fact that they could be left in the ground and only dug as required was another reason for their popularity, since people did not easily forget the days when their stocks of food in the form of cattle and corn were liable to be commandeered or destroyed by military forces.

However, if we are considering travellers on the more frequented routes, it is not the food of the very poor majority which need concern us, but that of the more well-to-do. We know that the gentry kept good tables[51] with abundance for any stranger who might claim their hospitality. The more these approximated to English ideas the more regularity was observed in the hours of meals. Breakfast

[49] *Influence of the Potato on Irish History*, p.5. Professor O'Brien, says they were the staple food by 1657.
[50] Cf. MS. T.C.D. I. 1. 2. (R. Leigh's description of Co. Wexford) ; Stevens's *Journal*, p.47 ; *The Western Wonder*, p.31. Petty in his *Political Anatomy* mentions potatoes as an article of diet, but only from August to May. (*Tracts and Treatises*, 1692 to 1769, Vol. II., p.59). Q'Bruadair in a poem written about 1664 mentions potatoes, but Father McErlean, in an editorial note, draws attention to the fact that this is the earliest reference to potatoes in literature written in the Irish language. (Irish Texts Edn., Part II., p.67). W. D. Davidson, Journal of the Dept. of Agriculture, Vol. XXXIV., No. 2, discusses this question very fully.
[51] Rawdon, however, in his letters frequently complains that the Irish are bad cooks : e.g. C.S.P.I. 1666 /69, pp.703, 710, 712.

hardly counted as a meal[52] and throughout the seventeenth century the custom was to dine at noon[53] and have supper about seven o'clock. Before that even earlier hours were kept: dinner was taken at eleven o'clock; and in the fifteenth century the man who was still in bed at six o'clock in the morning was counted lazy, whether he were simple or gentle.[54] As time went on there was always a tendency to dine at a later hour. Thus by the middle of the eighteenth century the customary time was three or four o'clock, but already this was regarded by some as old-fashioned, and we read of Lord Trimblestone, a Catholic peer, who returned to his home at Trim in 1754, after having lived abroad for some time, dining at seven o'clock, and even later in the evening.[55]

Dunton, like all his age, was a good trencherman; he tells us about his meals, but he does not tell us at what times he was accustomed to take them. He often dined at a cook-shop in Dublin, which he selected not only because the proprietress was an obliging woman but on account of her reasonable tariff, for he remarks that though flesh and fish were very cheap in the markets, the " ordinaries " were dearer than in London.[56]

Such conveniences as cook-shops were only to be found in Dublin and perhaps one or two of the

[52]   In one of his long descriptive letters to Viscount Conway Sir George Rawdon mentions that at breakfast the Duke of Ormond drank his (Conway's) health " in a great glass of claret." (C.S.P.I. 1666/69, p.125). Robert Lye, also an interesting letter-writer prominent in the same volume, gives a picture of another well-known public figure enjoying his glass of Xeres, i.e. sherry. (*Ib.*, p.468).

[53] Dr. Arthur Bryant states that breakfast, " usually a morning draught," was taken at any time from dawn to 11 o'clock, and dinner from 12 to 1.30 p.m. He tells us that it was customary in the 17th century to eat less often than the English now do and to drink much more. (See *The England of Charles II*, p.104).

[54] Wright, *Domestic Manners*, pp.451 and 438.

[55] R. L. Edgeworth, *Memoirs*, p.34.

[56] *Dublin Scuffle*, pp.319, 320.

larger towns, all of which, if we except Kilkenny, a place hardly to be described as a large town, were on the sea-coast. Thus travellers arriving by sea saw Ireland at its best so far as the conveniences of civilization, such as they were, were concerned. Nor were the means of communication between Ireland and the outside world so backward as those inside the country itself.

Even nowadays the daily life of every dweller in the country is influenced more by the weather than by anything else : in the seventeenth century the traveller was as much dependent on the weather as the farmer or the tennis-player is to-day. Inland heavy rains made the roads almost impassable : some organization and hard work could remedy that and eventually did ; but no human effort or ingenuity could make the wind blow from the east when the laws of nature ordained that it should be from the west, so travellers by sea had to wait another century before they could hope for anything like a regular service across the Irish sea.

In spite of the difficulties created by adverse winds, the government constantly attempted to make communication between Dublin and London as regular as possible. The stage coach from Chester to London made this easy, once the sea voyage was accomplished.

The establishment of postal services first drew the attention of those in authority to the importance of regular communication between the two countries and the State Papers from the viceroyalty of Falkland down to the last days of Ormond are full of references to this question, most of which are concerned with delay in delivery.[57]   After the Restoration, when public affairs became more settled, the posts between Dublin and London were dispatched regularly, and when weather conditions were favourable, letters were expected to take from five to eight days, though there are cases on record when they were actually delivered three days after being posted.[58]   Adverse winds, however, delayed the post to such an extent that even important government dispatches, which could if necessary be sent by special ship, were frequently not received till three weeks after they were sent out ; and we find the suggestion seriously made by the Irish Postmaster in 1662 that at times when bad weather "made a month's delay possible," correspondents should write their letters in duplicate, sending one copy by the newly-established Dublin-Edinburgh mail, and thence to London or vice versa.

The post office services in Ireland were somewhat disorganized by a long drawn out dispute between rival claimants for the place of Postmaster.[59]   Public positions which carried the control of public services, as we have seen in dealing with those under the control of the city Corporations, were usually sold to the highest bidder—unless they were given to some person of influence as a reward for services rendered.   In either case they were looked upon as a negotiable asset which might be sold or sublet to

[57] The majority of these references can be found in the indices of the volumes of the Cal. of State Papers, Ireland, dealing with the 17th century. As early as 1656 there were, weather permitting, weekly packet boats between Dublin and Holyhead, Waterford and Milford and also between Carrickfergus and Scotland.   Commonwealth State Accounts, *An Hib.*, No. 15, pp.260, 299, 305.

[58] Sir Geo. Lane to Jos. Williamson, 25 June, 1663 : " It is admirable that I should receive yours of 21st on the 24th." His use of the word ' admirable ' (i.e. remarkable) shows that such quick delivery was quite unusual.

[59] See C.S.P. Irel. 1663 /65' p.295, *et seq.* This controversy really began in 1658 : see C.S.P. Irel., 1660 /62, pp.683, 684 ; and *Analecta Hibernica*, No. 1., p.24.

another person without regard to his fitness for the position, and were even sometimes the subject of litigation. The policy of farming the General Post Office came to an end in 1677, though local farms were continued till the middle of the eighteenth century. The G.P.O. was established by Cromwell in 1657, the object, judging from the preamble of the Act, being largely to legalize the interception of correspondence. A Royal Proclamation soon after the Restoration laid down the principle of the secrecy of the post, but later on it was found necessary to tighten up the regulations to this end and an Act was passed in England with that object in 1711. In Ireland complaints were made from time to time that letters were lost or opened en route, but on the whole, considering the looseness of organization and control, they are hardly as numerous as might be expected. There was perhaps a disinclination to use the public post for comparatively short distances, but men like Orrery and Rawdon constantly employed it when writing from their places in the country. The former in a letter to Arlington, or Bennett as he was then, writing from his country house in Co. Cork, remarks that " the post from Dublin sets out every Tuesday and comes hither every Friday and is back at Dublin the Monday following. The post also from Dublin comes thence every Saturday and is back at Dublin the Friday following."[59a] It would thus appear that there was a bi-weekly post to Charleville, taking only six days to do the double journey of about 280 miles. Lisburn,[59b] we learn from another letter in the State Papers, had only one post a week, but there was a

[59a] C.S.P.I. 1663/65. p.29.
[59b] Nevertheless it was a place of some importance: it, not Belfast, was the centre for revenue collection for that area. (MS. quoted p.78, n.87 *supra*).

regular day appointed for delivery. Orrery was not a man to allow slackness to go uncomplained of if it affected his own interests in any way: he is definite enough in his statement which he does not qualify, and I quote it as evidence that normally the roads were quite passable at least for a man on horseback. The controversy over the Postmastership was essentially political, but if we can judge by an affidavit made by a post office official, which was certainly confirmed by a petition of influential Irish merchants to the King, Vaughan, who was before the Restoration accused of having Royalist sympathies,[60] was much more efficient than his rival the Cromwellian Anabaptist, Bathurst, who is accused of opening and holding up letters, including those of Mrs. Vaughan, as well as of nepotism and incompetence. Vaughan, on the other hand, is said to have arranged matters so that gentlemen could ride post in all parts of Ireland, and letters were delivered carefully into safe hands instead of the packets being left by post-boys at ale-houses of no repute.[61] With regard to the actual delivery of letters to their destinations the practice varied. Of course people living at a distance from towns had to call themselves for their letters. Even in large towns there was no recognized machinery for house to house delivery up to 1772, except in London, Dublin and Edinburgh. In some places the local postmaster delivered them himself or employed his own messenger to do so, and it would appear that in some English towns at any rate this was done free, while in others the fee for delivery was quite arbitrary and depended on the postmaster him-

[60] *Analecta Hibernica*, No. 15, p.287.
[61] C.S.P.I. 1660 /62, pp.683, 684. See also *An. Hib.* No. 1, p.24, *et seq.*

self."² The rates of postage, of course, varied with the distance and the size of the packet, but were on the whole not very high."³ Thus we find the postage on a letter written by a steward of Lord Conway and Killulta's in the north of Ireland to him " at Regley, in Warwacksheare in Eangland " made up as shown by the following superscriptions :

" Post Paid to Dublin 4d." (in one hand).

" Forward to London 2d." (in another hand).

" From London 2d. in all 8d." (in yet another hand).

The rates of postage for letters to the Continent were, by the standard of the time, not exorbitant, but when the volume of a man's correspondence was considerable, postage amounted in the aggregate to a very formidable sum. Bl. Oliver Plunket complains that out of his scanty income he had to provide no less than £25 every year under this head.

There were, of course, very few regular sea mail routes, and letters and parcels were conveyed by any convenient ship which offered. Thus we hear of them being sent from Galway to Scotland in a French frigate ; and William Bolton's business correspondence sometimes travelled from Madeira to Liverpool via Ireland."⁴ Inland, too, the regular post was not always used even by government officials : the Deputy Vice-Admiral of Munster, for instance, anxious for quick delivery of his dispatches, might prefer to avail himself of the services of an Irish footman rather than his Majesty's mail, as

⁶² Sir G. E. Murray, *The Post-Office*, London, 1927.

⁶³ For examples of internal rates of postage see *Orrery Papers, passim.* The usual rate from Co. Cork to Dublin and from Co. Wexford to Limerick was 4d.

⁶⁴ *Dublin Intelligence*, Nov. 4, 1690 ; *Bolton Letters* (ed. Simon) : e.g. on 25th March, 1698.

we may see from this entry in the memorandum of
his accounts, preserved among the Irish State
Papers : " To messenger (Dermot McOwen) who
on foot carried the news of the sale of ships, etc.,
at Cork, Youghal, Waterford and Limerick—
14 shillings."[65]

Prepayment of postage was not encouraged, as it
was felt there was no guarantee that a letter would
reach its destination if there were no fee to be
collected on delivery.

A great deal of considerable interest might be
written on this subject if we pursued it in further
detail, but to do so would, I think be tedious in a
general survey of everyday life. We may note,
however, before leaving it that the mail, as it was
already sometimes called, went from Dublin to
Holyhead. In 1661 the two vessels which had been
appointed for the cross-channel mail service were
diverted to coast-guard work. Two specially
designed ships were then put in hand, pending the
building of which " three barques " were sent to
maintain the service. M. Jouvin de Rochefort
tells us that in 1666 when he visited Ireland,
Chester was the point of departure of the ordinary
packet boat, that there were large store-houses in
that town devoted solely to merchandise for and
from Ireland, and that travellers frequently got a
passage in ordinary merchant vessels when such
happened to be sailing at a time convenient to
them. He states that a more or less regular monthly
service existed for cargo, apart from the intermittent
sailings of private owners. Chester was the port
at which Irish cattle were usually landed. Holyhead, however, was used for letters and by messen-

[65] C.S.P.I. 1663/65, p.665. Cf. *An. Hib.*, No. 15, p.314.

gers on urgent business. " We saw the post arrive," he says, " who gave his packet to the Captain of our ship." It would appear that there were one or two vessels running direct between Dublin and Holyhead, for he mentions that " a boat commonly sets out for Ireland " from the latter place.

The road from Holyhead across North Wales was in the seventeenth century, like those in Ireland, in places little better than a mountain track, " in mountainous country and wide and rapid ferry ways " especially inconvenient for baggage,[66] and more suitable to riders than carriages, so that in spite of the risks of delay ordinary passengers found Chester a much more convenient port of disembarkation. Carriages travelling to Ireland were normally dismantled on arrival at Conway and carried thence to Holyhead in pieces, the passengers completing that stage of the journey on horseback. When in 1685 the Viceroy's coach accomplished the journey on its own wheels this was considered a great feat.[67] On the Irish side Ringsend had superseded Howth and Dalkey as the regular landing place for Dublin passengers. Not always, however, did a passenger land where he intended to : a change in the wind and a passenger bound for Cork might wake up to find himself heading for Waterford ; or if a ship were obliged to make a certain port the length of time sometimes required to do this is almost incredible. Imagine a man " taking shipping " at Chester on August 15th, 1698, and hoping, of course, to reach Dublin in a couple of days, who " affter haveing bin neer seven week cast up and downe (and putt in

[66] Bush, *Hibernia Curiosa*, p.3.
[67] Macaulay, *History*, Vol. I. (ch. iii.), p.374.

to Five several harbours) . . . every Howre expecting the fate of A Mercyless sea,"⁶⁸ eventually landed safe in Dublin on September 25th. Such was the experience of Mr. Freke and his son. It was, of course, exceptional, and they had something worse than the customary bad crossing, but it serves to show how slow and perilous travelling between the two countries was. The Freke family were particularly unlucky in this respect. Mrs. Freke, who made the crossing a good many times in her life, hardly ever accomplished it without some mishap. She was a woman who revelled in lamentation, but, though she may have exaggerated somewhat, her diary does not bear the stamp of a liar. On the rare occasions when she found the weather not too unfavourable she was forced to embark on " a crazy ship," or was lost in the dark when disembarking in a small boat, or barely escaped capture by a French privateer. She was often delayed for weeks waiting to find a ship, and on one occasion, when she had succeeded in getting a passage, another week was wasted " to mend up their ship which was fired by green hay and all the passengers like to be smothered."

This occurred at Bristol, then the leading port for the West Indian and Virginian trade and also the usual point of departure for ships plying between the south of England and the south of Ireland. These ran to Waterford and also to Youghal, Cork, Kinsale and several other places on the south coast. Waterford is described as having the finest quay in Ireland, and further up the river the port of New Ross, where ships of 500 tons, a considerable size

⁶⁸ Eliz. Freke, *Diary*, p.48. Cf. Crofts to Southwell, 11 June, 1688. Southwell MSS., T.C.D., I. 6. 11.

in those days, could ride at low water,[69] also did a thriving trade.

Mrs. Freke was consistently unfortunate. Her clothes were stolen at Billingsgate ; she was set upon by highwaymen between Deal and London ; and only once does she record a fairly quick and uneventful cross-Channel passage when in July, 1683, she crossed from Bristol to Cork in less than three days. In this year, as also in 1677, she took a risk of a different kind and travelled without first obtaining the necessary official permit, " it being the custom of this kingdom not to depart without leave."[70]

As might be expected, in an age when scientific discoveries and inventions were just beginning to touch everyday life, some attempts were made to eliminate the delays and dangers which beset the traveller by sea, but the most ambitious of these, which resulted in the building of Sir William Petty's double-bottomed vessel, was doomed to complete failure, for his ship foundered under conditions which would have been easily weathered by one of ordinary design. Some improvements were made in rigging, and the first sign of the disappearance of the high poop, which had been a feature of all sea-going sailing ships, was to be seen in the introduction of a new type of small ship, known as the yacht[71] ; but no real progress was made. On one occasion the first Earl of Cork left Youghal

[69] MS. T.C.D. I. 1. 2. (Descriptions of Waterford, 1683). Dineley (*Observations*, p.51) says, " where can ride ships of four hundred tons and upwards before the very quay." Limerick was inferior in this respect and the largest ships did not pass Bunratty (Dineley, *Observations*, p.112).
[70] *Desiderata Curiosa*, Vol. II., p.124. See also *Analecta Hibernica*, No. 1, 83, etc. Two original "passes" are preserved in MacGillycuddy MSS., folios 50 and 51.
[71] See Quennell, *History of Everyday Things in England*, 4th edn., p.102, and *Three Sea Journals of Stuart Times*, Roch's illustrations of yachts in 1677 and 1678, p.90.

early one morning and, helped by a fair wind and good horses, supped in London the following night.[72] At the end of the century, seventy years later, it would have been impossible for anyone to do the journey quicker.

The second half of the seventeenth century was the period in which the Virginian and West Indian trade was being rapidly developed by England. Ireland, however, had at first no great part in this beyond her melancholy interest in the transportation of human cargoes to those parts.[73] Although as we saw in the previous chapter[74] an export trade to the West Indies and America was gradually built up, till by 1700 it was considerable, Ireland's intercourse with the great world lay in the direction of the Continent of Europe whither her trade was diverted from Britain by the English Cattle Acts of the sixteen-sixties. The prosperous export trade in provisions and wool, which grew up as a result of the short-sighted policy responsible for these Acts, could only be carried on by means of direct shipping and the vessels so engaged usually brought wine, lemons and oranges from the Continent and tobacco or sugar across the Atlantic on their voyages to Ireland.[75] Passenger traffic, too,

[72] Townshend, *Life and Letters of the Great Earl of Cork*, p.27. Cf. C.S.P. Ire., 1663/65, p.640: on 2nd Sept., 1665, Ormond embarked at Milford Haven at 6 p.m. and at 10 o'clock the following morning his ship was at anchor in the river off Duncannon.

[73] Some made the journey voluntarily—see Chapter IX for example. The Calendars of State Papers, entitled " West Indies & America," describe a vast quantity of documents, among which there are many references to the Irish there in the seventeenth century. Most of them appear to have had little love for the English, who in turn disliked and distrusted the Irish. A very full collection of documents bearing on the question of transportation of Irish men and women as slaves to Barbadoes and other places and the hardships they there endured has been made by Prof. A. Gwynn, S.J., and is printed in *Analecta Hibernica*, No. 4, October, 1932.

[74] P.225 *et seq.*

[75] A contemporary (1691) bill of lading is printed in J.R.S.A.I. Vol. III., p.135.

between Ireland and Spain, France and the Low
Countries increased steadily as the century advanced.   Beginning with the young men who,
following the abolition of Catholic schools in Ireland,
went abroad to the continental universities to
complete their education or to be prepared for the
priesthood, the stream was swelled, after the
Cromwellian campaigns and again after the Treaty
of Limerick, when great numbers of dispossessed
gentry and unemployed soldiers emigrated and
took service in foreign armies but sometimes still
returned from time to time on a visit to their native
land.   There was intercourse, too, of a diplomatic
nature : Rome kept in constant touch with Archbishops Plunket and Brenan, while at times of inter-
national crisis envoys were frequently on the move
between Dublin and the continental capitals.
All such travellers had necessarily to make their
voyages direct without calling at any English port.
Passes issued by some person in authority were
needed to cross the seas,[76] though the regular
formal passports to which we are now accustomed
were not yet in use.   The ships in which they sailed,
though the cabin accommodation for passengers—
especially for " persons of quality "—was remarkably comfortable, were very small, and no
modern landsman would venture on the high seas
in one of them without feeling that he was taking
his life in his hands.

Owing to the commercial policy of England
embodied in the Navigation Act there was very
little Irish-owned shipping ; however a great many

[76] See, for example, C.S.P.I. 1660/62, p.387 ; *ib.* 1669/70, p.432.   A
proclamation issued in March, 1688, which uses the word " passport "
as well as " pass " made the regulations relating to passes to Ireland much
stricter than theretofore.

Irishmen were to be found not only in the British Navy, some joining voluntarily others as victims of the press-gang, but also in the royal and merchant navies of several European nations, particularly Spain, where many of them rose to considerable eminence in their profession.[77]

Small ships of 200 tons and less still sail all over the world, and they have to contend with storms as terrible as those which harassed the mariners of the seventeenth century ; but the navigators of to-day can provide themselves with reliable nautical instruments and with accurate charts of the seas for which they are bound where the skippers of the past had to depend on a compass and the stars. Nor were the dangers of an ocean voyage confined to tempests and uncharted shores,[78] or the discomforts to shortage of water and the disorders produced by stale and half-rotten food. The press-gang was at work.[79] Mutiny was not uncommon, wreckers lurked on desolate coasts[80] and pirates infested the high seas, even in European waters. These were not confined to professional marauders like the notorious Algerian rovers. Many cases of piracy towards the end of the century are recorded in contemporary documents: one for example occurred in 1675,

[77] Lawlor, *Maritime Survey*, p.42.
[78] The coasts of Ireland, Great Britain, France and most of Europe were marked with tolerable accuracy on the maps of the time—which is not to say that ships were provided with maritime charts—but lighthouses were only beginning to be erected in any numbers towards the end of the Stuart period. A few in Ireland are mentioned by Dineley, Robt. Leigh and others who have left their observations on record. See also O'Brien, *Ec. Hist. 17th Cent.*, pp.197 and 199. Lighthouses were established at Dublin, Cork, Waterford, Wexford, Kinsale, Carrigfergus and Youghal between 1660 and 1667. (C.S.P.I. 1660 /62, pp.487, 488 and *ib.* 1666 /69, p.332).
[79] See C.S.P.I. 1666 /69, p.586, C.S.P. Dom. 1697, p.124 and an interesting letter on the subject in C.S.P. Dom. 1702 /03, pp.54, 55.
[80] Wreckers, or wreckmongers as they were often called at the time, were active even near the larger ports and carried on their nefarious trade long after the close of the seventeenth century. Cf. *Alexander the Coppersmith*, p.112.

when six Irishmen embarked as passengers on a
Dutch ship bound from Hamburg to France,
murdered the master and the crew and brought
their prize to Glandore harbour in Co. Cork.
Their enterprise, however, was a failure : though
the leader managed to escape, the heads of the
other five were set up in prominent positions at the
towns along the southern coast to remind Irish
seamen that piracy did not always pay.[81] A remarkable instance of the fidelity of an Irish crew to the
owners of their vessel is to be seen in the strange
adventures of the ship, " Ouzel Galley." They at
length succeeded in turning the tables on the
Algerian corsair who had captured them and, years
after the claim for her total loss had been paid by
the underwriters, they returned to Dublin with the
ship, laden with a cargo far exceeding in value that
seized by the pirates.[82] The Algerians were driven
away from these coasts by Wentworth in 1632, but
it was not long before they returned ; and there is
a very graphic account extant, written by the Rev.
Devereux Spratt, a Protestant clergyman of Co.
Cork, describing his capture by Algerian pirates
in 1641 and his adventures in North Africa
after he had been sold into slavery there.[83] Mr.
Spratt was captured just off Youghal on his way,
as he thought, to England. The very next year
these same pirates captured the ship in which Dr.
Edmund O'Dwyer was sailing to Ireland as the
confidential agent of the Vatican. He was eventually
sold as a slave, being purchased for £40 by a French
Calvinist minister who kept him in La Rochelle,

[81] *London Gazette*, Aug. 20, 1675.
[82] Chart, *The Story of Dublin* (Mediaeval Towns Series), p.300 and Falkiner,
Illustrations of Irish History, p.203.
[83] Printed in J.C.H.A.S., Vol. XII., New Series, p.90.

until after much delay he obtained from Father Luke Wadding the sum—£60—agreed upon as his ransom.[84] They were still operating as late as 1687 : Capt. Henry Boyle in a letter to his mother in June of that year refers to their temporary absence and his hopes of crossing from Minehead to Youghal without encountering any " Algerines."[85]

The pirates of the sea had their counterpart on land in the rapparees of Ireland and the highwaymen of England ; the road had its dangers as well as the ocean. Highwaymen, even more than pirates, were nearly always made, not born, and it was dire necessity—a crushing burden of debt or the shadow of the gallows—rather than mere love of adventure, which made them adopt their dangerous calling. In Ireland there had long been reasons for men to take to the woods and hills and live " upon their keeping," and at no time were there more recruits to the profession of rapparee than at the period we are considering. It was indeed almost an aristocratic profession, and its best known exponents, such as Capt. Dudley Costello in the west, and Count[86] Redmond O'Hanlon in the north, were men of ancient and once powerful family. Not every man of spirit whose family fortunes had been ruined by the Cromwellian confiscations, and the ruin confirmed by the Acts of Settlement and Explanation which followed the Restoration, was content to try his luck abroad. After years of waiting in Dublin in increasing poverty and steadily diminishing hope of obtaining what he not unnaturally considered just

[84] Begley, *Diocese of Limerick*, II, p.444.
[85] *Orrery Papers*, p.330.
[86] He was always known as " Count " in Ireland after his return from France but I have met no evidence that this title was ever formally conferred on him.

treatment,[87] many a penniless gentleman whose sword had been constantly and faithfully at the service of Charles II during his exile on the continent was faced with the alternative of renewed and permanent exile or a life—so long as it might last—on the road, if he were to avoid complete destitution or menial labour : 'and the latter the proud gentry of Ireland would not accept, particularly in the service of men whom they regarded as upstarts and interlopers, and perhaps within sight of their own ancestral lands.

In the uncertain times after the Restoration, one great encouragement of toryism was " the foolish ancient way of hospitality to receive and give food to all comers of their nation, not enquiring the cause of their coming or business ; so that they continue wandering about from house to house as long as they will[88] . . . alleging themselves innocents, but necessitated to do so, having not wherewithal to pay the fees of their trial or acquittal in the Court of Claims . . . One design of these men is that thus terrifying and discouraging the British, having nothing certain, but all at their mercy, they will induce them by degrees to leave those places of danger and recede into those more secure, which they daily begin now to do ; and so the lands will be laid waste, none else daring to take them, whereby the natives will rent them at such mean

[87] The difficulty of the King's position, owing as he did his Restoration largely to men like Broghill and Coote, must be recognized, but the discussion of that question belongs rather to political than to social history.

[88] This " coshering " on the peasantry was discouraged by Archbishop Oliver Plunket. One of the statutes of the General Synod of the Irish Church summoned by him in 1670 ordered all priests and preachers to warn their people against giving aid to tories. But the tories were strong and dangerous, while the church was weak and disorganized, and the hospitality continued to be given, whether the guests were welcome or not. Speaking of Dudley Costello, whom no informer could be found to denounce, Bagwell remarks that all the native population sympathized with him. (*Ireland under the Stuarts*, Vol. III., p.92).

values as they please, and thereby embody themselves, and grow numerous and opulent."[89] A little
later on when these men finally realized that their
attempts to regain their land were hopeless they
settled down to their adventurous life in fairly well
defined districts. It was the custom for the country
people to pay the tories for a pass to go unmolested :
Prendergast illustrates this by a story of how
Redmond O'Hanlon punished another band of
tories for molesting three Scotsmen who were
tributaries of his in this way.

The allusion to tories in the document given in
Appendix A, written in the year 1683, is one of many
examples of contemporary references to this state of
affairs, and the point of view of the tories or rapparees of the next generation is to be seen in the
numerous pamphlets purporting to report their
" last speeches " on the gallows.

There is no doubt that the roads all over the
country were unsafe. In 1665 travellers on the
main road from the north to Dublin were not considered immune from attack. Rawdon writes to his
employer about the arrival in Dublin of £900 which
he had sent " well guarded." Such a large sum
necessitated a special convoy, but even when
travellers had nothing of much value with them
they were glad to fall in with others going the same
way, not only for company but for mutual protection
also. This was of little avail in the remoter parts of
the country if they should encounter one of the
larger bands of rapparees. So large were these that
there was one party in Co. Clare consisting of no

[89] Sir Geo. Acheson : Carte Papers, Vol. XIV., p.309, quoted by Prendergast in *Ireland from the Restoration to the Revolution.*

less than 28 horsemen and 20 foot[91] : and this was in 1685 after over 30 years of peace and with no prospect of another war yet upon the horizon. The traveller's only hope in such a case was that he might be considered too small game to be worth molesting.

The ordinary peaceful citizen was in fact thoroughly scared. The dangers he feared were by no means imaginary and they were probably exaggerated by sensation-mongers. Though there was no halfpenny press to disseminate stories of tory frightfulness, rumours did the work, and it was fed by the printed word. The newspaper in Dublin did its part—a mangled corpse was " good copy " then as now[92]—and the pamphleteers were not silent. Most of the latter deal with the close of rapparees' careers : trials, last speeches, and some-times when, as in the case of Redmond O'Hanlon, the gallows was cheated of its prey, a description of the actual " downfall " in the field of the " arch-traytor and tory."[93] Not all, however, dealt with this theme, in which there was an element of reassurance for the law-abiding citizen. One, longer than most, gave a terrifying description of the lawless conditions obtaining in north-west Kerry. The author, Richard Orpen, recounts how in a district where the Papists outnumbered the Protes-

[91] Prendergast, *op. cit.*, p.80. See also Burnet, *History of My Own Time*, 1897, Oxford edn., p.449.
[92] For a newspaper account of alleged horrible mangling of a victim by rapparees, see the *Dublin Intelligence*, No. 21, Feb. 10-17, 1690/1.
[93] The best collection of trials and last speeches is probably that in the Cambridge University Library. A copy of the pamphlet describing the death of O'Hanlon and the events which led up to it is in the collection of the Royal Irish Academy (Box 94, Tract 11), which contains several others of interest on this subject. A good account of the career of Redmond O'Hanlon is that by Prof. T. W. Moody in the Proceedings of the Belfast Natural History and Philosophical Society, 2nd Series, Vol. I, part 1 (1935-6). For a contemporary description of one of his exploits which shows him in a favourable light see letter from Archbishop Boyle, *Orrery Papers*, p.203.

tants by 900 to 1, a band of 20 or 30 or even sometimes a hundred tories[94] moved up and down the
country, and at the approach of any considerable
part of the army dispersed and concealed themselves
in the glens and fastnesses. If any of the inhabitants
were suspected of giving information against them,
they were lucky, if we are to believe Orpen, when
they suffered no worse fate than the burning down
of their houses, for such " discoverers "[95] often had
their ears cropped, or their tongues cut out and
" sometimes they were kept prisoners whole nights
stark naked in the open fields." In reading such
statements as this due allowance, of course, must be
made for the violent anti-Irish and anti-Papist
feelings which were rampant at the time. The
bitterness which was always simmering and had
been intensified by the war had not died down in
1694 when this work, which was published under
the curious title of *The London Master or the Jew
Detected*,[96] was written. Perhaps the Rev. James
Alexander, of Raphoe, was one of those who read
this pamphlet. At any rate he was appointed in
May of that year, in the course of his duties as a
Presbyterian minister, to visit Sligo. He failed to
do so ; and four months afterwards his excuse, that
the road was so infested with rapparees that he
dared not do so, was accepted.[97]

Prendergast says that Munster was not so full of
tories as the other provinces. Sir Richard Cox

[94] This was no exaggeration. A fight with 200 Tories near Longford is
reported in the *London Gazette* of 19 July, 1666; and the next year, when
Dudley Costello was killed he had a party of forty with him. (*Ibidem* 12
March 1666[7].)
[95] The Act of 7 Wm. III. c. 21 introduced the principle of compensation
for malicious injuries by the inhabitants of the area in which the crime was
committed.
[96] It was reprinted in J.C.H.A.S., New Series, Vol. VIII., from the original
pamphlet preserved in the T.C.D. Library.
[97] R.S.A.I., Vol. XXIX., p.411.

declared in 1684 that the Co. Cork was free of them,[98] but in an interesting letter dated 19 April, 1681, Lord Shannon describes how he and others were " very busy playing the judge's part by a Commission under the Great Seal to rid the prison of a great many tories" they had taken, and he adds that though they condemned all but seven he has no taste for hanging people.[99]   There is ample evidence, too, that a few years later Cox's statement was far from true of the Co. Cork, for the presentments at the assizes of 1691 and subsequent years, recorded in a manuscript now in the library of Trinity College, Dublin,[100] include a number of references to rapparees.   " We present that the sum of one hundred and seven pounds in lieu of 69 cows and 6 heifers taken by rapparees since the 19th Dec. [1690] be levied on the Popish inhabitants of the Barony of Killnataloon, etc. "; " The widow Jeffer's house " in Bandon, of all places, is presented as dangerous to passengers ; tories are repeatedly named and rewards allowed for those engaged in reducing and destroying them, and there are presentments against other persons of failing to appear upon the High Sheriff's " summons to pursue the tories."   There is no sign here of Co. Cork being free of rapparees ; and the private letters contained in such collections as the Clarke and MacGillycuddy MSS. are full of nervous references to their dangerous activities all over the country.[101]

[98] MS. T.C.D. I. 1. 2, p.256.
[99] *Orrery Papers*, p.243.
[100] MS. T.C.D. N.320. See also Kinsale Presentments in *An. Hib.*, No. 15.
[101] The seventeenth century documents printed in *Analecta Hibernica*, No. 15, abound in references to tories and highwaymen, e.g. pp.232, 237, 265, 267, 273, 285, 290, 291, 301, 304, 361. They were usually dispatched out of hand but occasionally got off with transportation to the West Indies.

It was not until the eighteenth century, when the aristocratic element of the first generation had died out, that such unwholesome figures as the notorious Freney and his gang appeared upon the scene. These were mere robbers.[102] Their forerunners, the rapparees, while not surrounded by the atmosphere of romance associated with Claude Duval, or Dick Turpin and his mare Bess, were capable of chivalrous actions and of great bravery, even though, as we have seen,[103] they occasionally suffered from the treachery of their followers who were encouraged by the government to save their own skins by selling their fellows and their leaders.

---

[102] They were gradually stamped out, and Luckombe, writing in 1779, says that there were no highwaymen or footpads left in Ireland, (*Tour*, p.39).
[103] See p.84 *supra*.

CHAPTER IX

The Clergy and the People

I REFERRED in the last chapter to the efforts of the government to put down the rapparees, and the most successful of the methods they employed is said to have been the origin of the common phrase, " to set a thief to catch a thief." [1] It is a principle which is essentially mean. We must not, of course, judge the seventeenth century by the standards of the twentieth, but this encouragement of the sort of treachery that schoolboys call sneaking, by appealing to the most sordid side of men's natures, would be called unsporting nowadays by the average Englishman whose forbears employed it : employed it not against outlaws only, for that principle was the very basis and foundation of the Penal Code.

That complete system of oppression in all its mean ferocity did not come into force until after the final debacle of the Catholic cause in 1691. The penal laws enacted against Irish Catholics in the eighteenth century may be regarded as the worst in the annals of religious intolerance,[2] not only because they were devised at a date when the world had freed itself of mediaeval ideas, but also because in themselves they were infamous, relying as they did on treachery and dishonour for their execution and being imposed on a majority by a minority, powerful only by reason of external backing. The

[1] J.R.S.A.I., Vol. IV., p.53.
[2] It is not necessary to adduce authorities for this statement. Notwithstanding the rather feeble attempts which have from time to time been made to justify the penal code (e.g. T. D. Ingram, *A Critical Examination of Irish History*, London, 1900), historians of repute since Lecky are unanimous in their condemnation of it.

appalling persecution and degradation of Irish Catholics under Anne and George I has obscured the popular view of the religious situation after Luther and Henry VIII between them broke up the old uniformity of creed. Nowadays we are accustomed to regard people in Ireland as being almost immutably Catholic or Protestant. In actual fact the position, particularly of the laity, before Cromwell's time, was entirely different from that existing in what are usually called the penal times. While many individual Catholics suffered severely, they were not yet frankly penalized as such to any extent: they could hold land and enter the professions, and enjoyed other elementary rights of the citizen of which they were later deprived. The process of subjection of the Catholic population to a state of absolute degradation and humiliation was a gradual one, and the period with which this book deals represents an intermediate stage in their descent.

References have inevitably been made in previous chapters to the efforts of the clergy to influence the conduct and habits of the people, and even to the character of the clergy themselves.[3] Any detailed examination of ecclesiastical affairs, already exhaustively treated in works devoted solely to that subject, would be outside the scope of this book ; but at the same time religious questions vitally affected the everyday life of the ordinary citizen and a brief consideration of them cannot be omitted.

The origin of the Penal Code is to be found in Tudor times, when the first attempts were made to bring Ireland into line with England. It was quite

---

[3] See Index under Brenan, Clergy, Plunket, Religious Affairs, etc., etc.

in accordance with the spirit of that period that the enforcement of religious uniformity should seem as important as the introduction of English law and language.

The passionate and exemplary attachment of the Irish nation to the Catholic faith dates from a later time, and was in fact the direct result of the penal laws which were designed to uproot it. At first the opposition to Protestantism was mainly political: men changed from one denomination to the other with as little disturbance of conscience as would have been involved a generation or two ago in England, when the English were still a church-going people, in a transfer from High Church to Low. In 1553 we read of Desmond " in accordance with the spirit of the age reverting to the old religion "[4] after having conformed for a while, and in 1573 the citizens of Dublin itself were described by the Jesuit, Dr. Wolfe, as almost all Catholics, especially the natives, " though they were forced to go to the communion and preaching of the heretics."[5] Before organized persecution had re-aroused the spirit of the Church in her priests, and crystallized the half-hearted and vacillating beliefs of various families, there was nothing unusual, especially among the well-to-do classes, in two members of a family professing different creeds. Again, a man might attend a Protestant church for some reason of policy, while sending his wife and children to Mass the same day. Religious tests, for example, were imposed on men before they could fill certain offices like that of sheriff, but such oaths were taken quite carelessly

[4] Begley, *Diocese of Limerick*, Vol. II., p.13.
[5] See description of Ireland, by Fr. David Wolfe, S.J., printed in the original Italian in Begley's *Diocese of Limerick*, transcribed from the document in Vatican Archives.

and were regarded as a rule almost in the light of political formalities, except at certain times, such as during the famous Battle of the Mayors in Limerick, when one Catholic after another was elected as mayor and deposed for refusing to take the oath. This exciting controversy, which convulsed the Corporation of Limerick in the years 1611 to 1615, blew over in due course, and ten years later the mayor and sheriffs were going publicly to Mass.

The Catholic practice of outwardly conforming, so prevalent in the time of James I, was the occasion in the following reign of the issue of a Bull by Pope Urban VIII in which the people, who in spite of previous Papal condemnation, had hitherto attended Anglican services without scruple, were exhorted to suffer death rather than continue to do so.[6]

The political aspect of the question gradually receded into the background, and, as the cause of Church and nation became ever more closely identified and the idea of nationality grew up in Europe, the stereotyped division which has lasted till our own time developed. In Ireland the words Catholic and Irishman became almost synonymous, and the word ' English ' was often used to denote a Protestant, even though his family might have been in Ireland for several generations. Thus the Protestant Dean of Cork, writing in his Journal in 1689, uses the expression " English gentlemen " to include Irish Protestants[7]; Francis Rogers a few years later remarks that the Protestants " are not pleased to be called Irish at home,"[8] and to this day the Irish-speaking population of the Decies have no

[6] Lecky, *History of Ireland*, Vol. I., p.36.
[7] *Journal of Rev. Rowland Davies*, Camden Soc. Journal, 1857, p.9.
[8] *Three Sea Journals of Stuart Times* (London, 1936), p.197.

other word for Protestant but " sasanach." The
Protestants of Gaelic stock were very few, and those
to whom I referred in Chapter IV were confined to
the wealthy landed classes. In England, on the other
hand, Catholics who, it must be remembered, were
a severely persecuted minority, were not by any
means well disposed towards Ireland. D'Avaux,
writing to Louis XIV in April, 1689, remarks :
" Les Irlandois reconnoissent aussi que les Anglois
qui sont auprès du roi, même les Catholiques, sont
leurs plus grands ennemis." A letter of Bishop
O'Molony's, which Archbishop King thought
worth quoting, supports this view. He says : " nor
is there any Englishman, Catholic or other, of
what quality or degree soever alive will stick to
sacrifice all Ireland for to save the least interest
of his own in England ; and would as willingly see
all Ireland over inhabited by English of whatsoever
religion, as by the Irish."[9] Mr. Philip Wilson
considers that by the time of Charles II the feeling
that the real contest was between Englishmen
and Irishmen rather than Protestants and Catholics,
had already grown up.[10]

Catholicity in Ireland was thus greatly strength-
ened by its association with what we now call
patriotic and national feelings : it became the proud
heritage of a people steeped in tradition, and it was
immensely intensified by persecution, since it
happened that the people persecuted had and have
an innate dislike to brooking any tyranny imposed
by strangers.

Another tributary which fed the main stream
must not be overlooked : the existence of real piety

[9] *State of the Protestants of Ireland,* 3rd Edn. (1692), p.357.
[10] *Studies in Irish History,* p.110.

and religious faith among a very considerable
proportion of the population. The people generally,
according to Dr. Brenan, as we have already noticed
in Chapter III, led a Christian life without great
faults or many scandals. Religion was a reality in
the seventeenth century : it had not become just an
aspect of life, a mere interest which, like literature
or gardening, appealed to a certain type of person
only. This was true even of England, that land of
successful compromise. " For one without faith "
says Dr. Arthur Bryant, " it is difficult to understand seventeenth century England. For faith was
part of the air the men of that day breathed . . .
It was this which gave the men of that age their
courage and their content. They were afraid—but
they were afraid only of a divine mystery. They did
not fear, as we do, poverty, discomfort, pain and
death. They disliked these evils, but when they
came they accepted them as marks of God's intention, to be borne with courage and good cheer . . .
Such faith supported our forefathers in every crisis
of life, nerved them to bear pain worse than modern
science permits most of us to know, and buoyed
them in the frequent hour of deprivation which the
heavy mortality of the day made their lot."[11]

This does not mean that many, even most, men
may not have been careless in attending their
religious duties and as prone to sin as any other
generation. Nothing is more clearly revealed by a
study of the past than the fact that human nature
is essentially the same in all ages : civilized men
have behaved in a civilized way, and barbarians
have been barbarous, since human records were
first preserved. In Ireland in the seventeenth

[11] *The England of Charles II*, p.77.

century there was faith and there was religious zeal in plenty, but the martyrs it produced were nearly all priests : the Irish laity were still for the most part only passively and traditionally Catholic, and had not yet been roused to that passionate devotion to their religion for which they were remarkable during the next two centuries.

The missionary priests in Ireland kept the light of faith burning at the time when the devastation produced by the almost continuous warfare of Elizabethan times had completely disorganized the activities of the church, and the story of the work they did during that dark time and throughout the seventeenth century is one to which we can look back with undiluted pride. For these men whom we term missionaries were all Irishmen who returned to follow their perilous calling in their native land after distinguishing themselves at Rome or in the various universities of the Continent. In my chapter on morals I referred to the labour of certain saintly and hard-working Jesuits. The recognition of the devotion of those priests is not confined to members of the Catholic Church, as may be seen by the following appreciation written by a distinguished Protestant historian : " We must render a most sincerely cordial tribute of admiration and respect to the perfect zeal and self-devotion of the Jesuits and priests who co-operated with the faithless lords of the Catholic league. These men, animated only by religious principle, faced all dangers, endured all hardships. Whoever else were time-servers, waiters on events, diligent worshippers of the main chance, these priests and Jesuits were in deadly earnest. Hunger and cold, the dungeon and the scaffold, had no terrors for them. We shall meet some of them in the progress of this tale, notably James Archer, the Jesuit, and the Papal Legate, MacEgan, but of such noble and devoted servants of religion there were hundreds whose names we shall never hear."[12]

The belief of these men in the work they had to do was as intense as that of the early Christians ; their courage and self-sacrifice were no evanescent enthusiasm stimulated by the Counter-Reformation, for the same faith that urged them on sustained their successors in every subsequent generation till the cessation of the persecution. When after the breathing space afforded in the reign of Charles I priest-hunting[13] again became general under the Cromwellian regime, such men as Fathers William O'Kelly and Cullen, O.P., and other priests, as well as some lay brothers, bravely suffered martyrdom[14] ; while thirty years later, when anti-Catholic prejudices were again inflamed by the deliberately engineered " Popish Plot " scare, Oliver Plunket, the best known and most saintly of all the long list of Irish victims, was put to death with a show of legality which was more disgraceful than the out-of-hand executions of the martyrs who went before him.

We can form a good idea of the problems with which he and the clergy of his day had to deal by a perusal of the decrees adopted by the National Council of 1670 and by the Provincial Synods which he and Dr. Brenan of Cashel managed to hold.

[12] Standish O'Grady, *Pacata Hibernia*, preface, p.lxi.

[13] Several specific instances of rewards (usually £5) paid for taking priests between 1653 and 1656 will be found in "The Commonwealth State Accounts " (*An. Hib.*, No. 15, pp.227-322). The names of the " apprehenders" prove that renegade Irishmen as well as Cromwellians engaged in this occupation.

[14] This subject, so far as it relates to the Diocese of Limerick, is fully dealt with by Canon Begley, *Diocese of Limerick*, who cites a number of works of an ecclesiastical character from which further information can be obtained.

More than half of those are devoted to purely ecclesiastical affairs, but a number, of which the following are perhaps the most interesting, related to the conduct of the ordinary everyday life of the laity. The priests are commanded to prohibit drinking at wakes and the holding of wakes at night ; to put down certain abuses connected with funerals, particularly excessive keening[15]; "to warn the faithful against aiding or countenancing the bodies of lawless bandits, who were called Tories, and under the pretence of defending the national rights, infested the country." They were also ordered to keep baptismal and marriage registers,[15a] never to omit publication of marriage banns, and to resist the tendency of parents to impose unusual names in baptism. They were to condemn superstitious practices such as the offering of children with certain spells and incantations at Holy Wells, under pain of excommunication if persisted in.[16]

Only a few years earlier Dr. Lynch summarized the type of morality inculcated by priests and preachers thus : " The grand object of all the instructions given from our pulpits, and confessionals, by the priests of our church, was, that unlawful marriages should be either contracted

[15] Keening in itself was not, of course, regarded as an abuse though frequently the subject of unfavourable comment. Brereton, writing in 1635, was astonished to hear the wife or sister of an Irish merchant, who lay dead in his house in a busy Dublin street, " roaring out as though she were violently distracted" until he learned that this was the normal Irish custom. Sir William Brereton *Travels*, p.142. See also *ibidem*, p.155.

[15a] Dr. King (p.27 of MS. *cit.* Ch. VII, n.2 *supra*) says in 1691 that the Protestant clergy were then urged to keep proper parochial registers.

[16] The decrees of the National Synod of 1670 are printed in Cardinal Moran's *Memoir of Dr. Plunket*, pp.116 *et seq.* Those of the Provincial Synods held at Clones and Ardpatrick in 1670 and 1678 are given in the same work, Chapters XI., and XII., while those of the Synods convened by Dr. Brenan in 1676 and 1677 are ably summarized by Canon Power in his *Bishop of the Penal Times*, pp.49 and 50.

anew, according to the laws of the Church, or be completely dissolved ; that adulteries and all crimes against purity be repressed ; that theft, rapine and robbery be prevented ; that usurious contracts be annulled ; that enmities be forgotten ; disputes adjusted amicably ; that children be obedient to their parents, servants to their masters, and all to the magistrates." [17]

The conduct of the priests themselves, as well as of the laity, was the subject of some of the decrees adopted by the synods I have referred to. For example, they were forbidden to drink whiskey in public, to attend fairs and markets, or to take a female (even a relative) with them on horseback, besides, of course, receiving instructions on many matters relating to their office, such as the giving of religious instruction to the young on Sundays, the recovery of sacred vessels from the laity to whom they had formerly been given for safe custody, and so on. One personal prohibition addressed to the clergy is of particular interest : they were ordered not " to admit those pupils who are called Dallas." This is explained in a letter written by Archbishop Oliver Plunket to the Internuncio at Brussels. " Some wicked priests," he says, " becoming *nutritors* [fosterers], took to their care the children of Protestants, that thus they themselves might be defended against their ecclesiastical superiors : these children were called *dallas*."

All Irish priests, as may be seen from the necessity of some of these decrees, were not made of the same fine stuff as Archbishops Plunket and Brenan, as Dr. Lynch, and as the many brave and devoted men who lived and died for the faith. It was the

[17] *Cambrensis Eversus*, Chapter XXVII., p.117.

missionary priests, men who had nearly all been educated abroad, who formed this zealous *corps d'élite* inspired by a burning faith, and every one of them a potential if not an actual martyr. On the other hand, as Froude, always hostile to Irish Catholics, has emphasized, there was another type of priest, of the kind occasionally satirized by the poets, O'Bruadair and O'Rahilly, ordained from among the rank and file of Catholics at home,[18] to whom, of course, a proper education was denied by law, and who had to obtain it as best they could more or less clandestinely ; yet even these men, the majority of whom were Franciscan friars, numbered among them at least one author of considerable repute.[19]   It would seem that the members of this Order in Ireland, who now enjoy a reputation for learning enhanced by their famous library in Dublin with its wonderful collection of books and manuscripts of historical interest, were for the most part rough and uncultured men in the second half of the seventeenth century—though this was far from the case on the Continent, or indeed in Ireland before the Cromwellian conquest when it was still possible for the monks to travel frequently as they did, from Ireland to France and thence to Brussels, Rome and elsewhere. In fact the period 1615 to 1650 has been described as the golden age of the Irish Franciscans[20]. Nevertheless, for the reasons already given, they undoubtedly deteriorated for a while. Cardinal Moran, although he is always guarded

---

[18] In the diocese of Raphoe, at the time of Archbishop Oliver Plunket's visitation, he found that only one out of fourteen priests had been abroad. This diocese, of course, lies in a remote part of the country. In 1669 he found that there were eighty secular priests in the diocese of Meath, " learned and exemplary men."

[19] Viz. Father Anthony Bruodin.

[20] *Measgra Mhichil ui Chléirigh*, pp.21 to 33.

in his censure and repeatedly emphasizes the better side of the Franciscan Order in Ireland, admits that some of its members led vicious lives.[21] Although instances of the abduction of heiresses with a view to marriage are met with in the reign of Charles II, priests of the notorious " couple-beggar" type were as yet almost unknown.[22] Degradation of that kind belonged to the next century when the organization and the discipline of the Church was quite destroyed by the severity of the penal legislation.

The regular clergy were almost as numerous as the secular.[23] Dr. Brenan tells us that in 1673 for one secular priest he ordained ten friars, often of a very rough and uneducated type.[24] Having regard to the character of the bishop himself and to the confidential nature of his letters and reports, he is perhaps the most valuable individual witness of all those whose testimony is available, not only indeed on questions of religion and public morals, for his correspondence throws much light also on everyday customs and conditions of life. His reliability is exemplified by the scrupulous fairness of his judgements, and when, for instance, he informs the Vatican in 1672 that thanks are due to the Protestant gentry of his diocese for their helpful attitude, we know that this is the genuine

[21] *Op. cit.* p.281 *et passim.*

[22] See, for example, the interesting case of the abduction and rape of Mary Ware, C.S.P.I., 1666/69, pp.566, 567.

[23] The total number of secular clergy was approximately 1,000. This figure is given both by Dr. Plunket and Peter Walsh. The latter reckoned the regulars as 800, 400 of whom were Franciscans and 200 Dominicans. The Archbishop's estimate of the regulars was somewhat less than this. Incidentally I may mention that he overestimates the Catholic population at two millions. (Moran, *Memoir of Dr. Plunket*, p.26).

[24] *Op. cit.*, pp.22 and 39. The ignorance of the candidates for ordination was of course, due to the suppression of Catholic education under Cromwell. This fact is too obvious to be emphasized. For an interesting non-Catholic reference to it, see Rousele's *Irish Villainy* (Lambeth MS. 711, No. 4) partly quoted by Murray. (J. Stevens's *Journal*).

expression of a personal opinion and is not said with his tongue in his cheek for the sake of effect."

There is nothing very remarkable in this reference to a tolerant spirit among the Protestant gentry, for we know from the poems of O'Rahilly and Carolan that there were many kindly folk among them, even if the Coopers and Blennerhassetts were less typical of their class than the Dawsons and Temples[25] ; and of course before 1641 there was little or no religious discord among neighbours, however acute political controversy might be on the subject. Father Strong, another distinguished Franciscan, writing to that illustrious member of his order, Father Luke Wadding, in Rome, even at a time when anti-Papist proclamations were being read everywhere, can tell him: "The Master of the Rolls is a most worthy man . . . he is my most intimate friend. I keep up a good correspondence with the Primate Ussher," who, he remarks, allowed him access to his library.[26] It is necessary to remember that a few years after that letter was written the majority of Peter Walsh's adherents were Franciscans, and of course any priest who might be a supporter of the Remonstrance would be regarded favourably by Protestants in important official positions.

Dr. Brenan shows few prejudices, but he may have been slightly biassed against the Franciscans and the

[25] The letters in the *Orrery Papers* often reveal an anti-Catholic bias but this is frequently actuated by fear of invasion rather than by religious bigotry, and occasionally even by fear of personal danger as when Sir Francis Foulkes writing to the Countess of Orrery in 1672 says: "Indeed, Madam, I think it is dangerous in these times to keep a Papist butler, though he is a good serviceable man, for the Papists are so wicked that they would be glad to have my Lord out of the way on any terms." Indeed, so real was the fear of foreign invasion that a clause allowing an extension of the term of the tenancy in the event of foreign invasion was sometimes inserted in leases. See, for example, a Co. Kerry lease of 1673 calendared in *The Kenmare MSS.*, p.143.

[26] H. O'Grady, *Strafford*, p.440.

Dominicans, since he had frequent trouble with them in his attempts to make them submit to episcopal discipline. The friction was not confined to his diocese[27] or his time.[28] The bishops' reports before the war tell the same tale.[29] Rinuccini, when he was in Ireland, regarded the regular clergy with disfavour and showed himself definitely pro-secular ; understandably so indeed, for—apart from the abuses already noticed—in the words of Canon Begley, " the regulars, for the most part, by using privileges and faculties they received during times of persecution, greatly hindered the reformation of the clergy, for in the very safest places in the kingdom they went about in secular dress, with long hair, in military fashion, celebrated the divine mysteries in private houses where churches were open, and even twice in the same day without necessity." The same authority speaks highly of the work of the Franciscan fathers a generation later in ministering to the spiritual needs of the poor scattered Catholics on the hillsides and lonely valleys at home, as well as of the brilliance of their achievements on the Continent.[30]

We have already glanced in Chapter III at the tendency of the clergy to be somewhat given to intemperance, and judging by Archbishop Oliver Plunket's remark, it would seem that this weakness was not confined to the more bucolic whose uncouth behaviour disgusted Rinuccini.[31]

[27] See Order made by Warden and Vicars of Collegiate Church of St. Nicholas, Galway, in 1684. (*Analecta Hibernica*, No. 14, p.36).
[28] See Moran, *Memoir of Dr. Plunket*, chap. XX., for controversy between Franciscans and Dominicans and the Archbishop's decision thereon.
[29] O'Grady, *Strafford*, p.612, where references to MS. sources on this subject are given.
[30] *Diocese of Limerick*, pp.448 and 488.
[31] Cf. Ode composed by an unknown bard in the latter part of the 17th century in praise of drinking, in which he says, " agus gaol ro-mhór ag eagluis Dé leat." Hardiman, *Irish Minstrelsy*, Vol. I., p.152.

A number of the parochial clergy were absentees, but those who were courageous enough to remain at their posts continuously were assiduous in their arduous duties, riding long distances to attend sick-calls, celebrating Mass in hovels with the rain beating down on them through holes in the roof, not once in a day but twice, at places separated from each other by many miles of the roughest road or track, striving to keep the light of faith burning among a people whom tradition made exceedingly superstitious and English policy doomed to illiteracy. They led as a rule exemplary lives, especially in the observance of their vows of celibacy, though it was an age when sexual morality was generally lax, when the Catholic clergy were usually obliged to wear lay attire and the discipline exercised over them by their ecclesiastical superiors was necessarily less strict than it now is. Any evidence to the contrary is either from very prejudiced persons like William Moffet, or relates to apostate or insubordinate regulars not engaged in parochial duties. The very absence of charges of this nature by responsible men who were not very well disposed towards Catholics tends to confirm this. Bishop Dive Downes records as a rule the names of the Catholic priests of the various parishes of the diocese of Cork and Ross, and we may perhaps believe that Rev. Charles MacCarthy, who had been in charge of a parish near Dunmanway for many years, was exceptional in being neither sober nor chaste, since this Protestant bishop was not in the habit of speaking disparagingly of his rivals, if indeed he regarded as rivals men living on sufferance, yet looking after ninety per cent. of the population, while his own clergy ministered to the small well-to-do minority, nearly all strangers of comparatively recent introduction. Bishop Downes made his visitation of the diocese in 1699. Exact dates, which can be ignored in considering social conditions generally, are of more importance where we are concerned with the Church and religious affairs. The daily life of an Irish farmer, country gentleman, shopkeeper or servant would not have been very different in 1669, 1679, 1689 and 1699. Yet how different was the lot of Catholic priests in each of those years. In '69 they were enjoying comparative freedom from daily anxiety, though the brief lord lieutenancy of Lord Robartes, which began at the end of that year, marked a temporary tightening up of the regulations[32] ; 1679 saw two Archbishops prisoners in Dublin[33] ; in '89 James was still King and the brother of one of these archbishops was Lord Deputy ; while ten years later the Jacobite cause was irretrievably lost and militant Protestantism firmly, and apparently permanently, in the saddle.

The ordinary Irish layman did not, of course, experience such sudden vicissitudes as did the clergy : he was liable, no doubt, to arrest on a trumped-up charge when a scare like that produced by the " Popish Plot " occurred ; his heart was filled with new hope when Charles II died, as it had been at his restoration twenty-five years earlier, and sank with the defeat and flight of James ; but

---

[32] Even Archbishop Oliver Plunket was constrained at that time to pass himself off for two or three months as a military officer, calling himself Capt. Brown, " with my sword and a wig and pistols " (Moran, p.185), but the very next year under Berkeley, Dr. Dowley, recently appointed as Vicar-Apostolic to the diocese of Limerick, of which he became bishop in 1677, found religion in a flourishing condition and Catholic schoolmasters teaching in nearly every parish (Begley, p.479). Cox and Hammond were the pseudonyms used by Dr. Plunket in signing his correspondence with Rome. The use of the name Brown was only a temporary expedient.

[33] Archbishops Oliver Plunket and Peter Talbot. The latter had long been living openly and unmolested in his brother Richard's house (Bagwell, Vol. III., p.134).

it was not until the very end of the century that he
was faced with the alternative of emigration from
the land of his fathers or real misery if he stayed at
home. The ever increasing difficulties and dangers
surrounding the priesthood naturally reacted on the
people to whom they ministered. The extent to
which the Catholic religion was openly practised
in the reign of Charles II varied from year to year :
reasons of state policy sometimes dictated an increase of energy in its repression, as at the time of
the alleged " Popish Plot," and at other times
allowed a greater degree of toleration, as under the
Berkeley regime, or when Ormond wished to encourage the efforts of Peter Walsh in the hopes of
creating a division in the ranks of the clergy.

Catholic laymen suffered certain disabilities, but
even after 1650 they could hold land and most of the
professions were open to them still : Sir Nicholas
Plunket, perhaps the ablest lawyer in Dublin in the
reign of Charles II, was a Catholic. The disabilities
were of two kinds. Politically the Catholics were
unmistakably the under-dogs : they were virtually
excluded from parliament ; they had no part in
municipal government, and as time went on even
the humble artisan in the city was penalized for his
religion, particularly in Limerick, where Orrery's
influence was strong. The subordinate position
which Papists[34] were doomed to occupy was more
evident in the towns than in the country. There
they were not allowed to forget it. In Limerick,
for example, the billeting of soldiers on the citizens
was made to bear most heavily on the Catholics[35] ;

[34] The word ' Papist ' was officially used by the Dublin Corporation after
the flight of James II. Henri Misson says in 1698 that it was used in London
" without designing it as an affront." (*Memoirs*, p.204).
[35] Nat. Lib. MS. 89. (Under date 26 Sept., 1679).

and in Waterford in the 'seventies no Catholic was allowed out of doors on Sundays while the Protestant service was going on ; Mass was permitted but had to be over before the hour of the Protestant service.[36] Hence Mass was often said in the houses of the gentry, who indeed often went rather too far in demanding this privilege.

It was, in fact, in the exercise of their religion that ordinary Catholic laymen were most affected by oppressive legislation in their everyday life. It was not only often difficult to attend Mass, and when it was possible it usually meant much discomfort in bad weather ; there were pecuniary disadvantages under which the Catholic laymen laboured too, and these pressed heavily on the poor. Catholics were compelled to contribute towards the upkeep of bells and organs and repairs generally to Protestant churches. The Protestant ministers were legally entitled to insist on all fees due for baptisms, marriages, etc., being paid to them,[37] and in practice the Catholic priests were not often allowed to perform these rites unless this were first done. Catholics had therefore to pay twice over, because their own clergy were dependent principally on such fees for their livelihood.[38]

In theory Protestant dissenters also suffered great disabilities, but in practice, as Macaulay says, " the

[36] Brenan, *op. cit.* p.26. Galway was always an exception. Dunton found it " almost entirely Papist " in 1698, and noticed the church bells of St. Nicholas as something remarkable. Armagh Cathedral had a fine organ and bells, and also glass windows, in Cromwell's time. O Mellain (6 May, 1642) MS. R.I.A. 23. H.7.

[37] The predominantly Catholic Parliament which sat under James II in 1689, though politically it showed little moderation in its treatment of the new Protestant landed class, has at least to its credit the passage of a measure providing that tithes should be paid by Protestants and Catholics to their own clergy. The relief thus afforded to the majority was, however, shortlived, for two years later Catholic Ireland was once more a conquered nation.

[38] Brenan, p.28, Moran, *Plunket, passim*, etc.

Protestant nonconformist endured with more patience than could have been expected the sight of the most absurd ecclesiastical establishment the world has ever seen." In Ireland religious divisions were subordinate to national divisions ; and the Presbyterian looked on the hierarchy of that " monstrous institution . . . with a sort of complacency when he considered it as a sumptuous and ostentatious trophy of the victory achieved by the great race from which he sprang." Macaulay does not mention another cause for complacency on the part of the northern Presbyterians, and that was the fact that they were numerous and strong enough to curb the pretensions and demands of the established Anglicans in their own province.[39]

One section of the community, numerically negligible but already coming into prominence in the commercial and financial life of the country, was heartily disliked by all and systematically subjected to the exactions of the Protestant clergy and the officers of the law. These were the Quakers. At this early stage of their history they combined with the amiable characteristics of their present-day successors a fierce intolerance of anything savouring of Popery and a persistence in fighting injustice which was at once patient and pugnacious. Their persistence, as is well known, eventually resulted in achieving many reforms which brought relief to others besides themselves. Their immoderate methods not unnaturally influenced popular feelings against them and they suffered rough handling in the stocks and elsewhere as well as the legal punishments which were meted out to them by the magistrates. An example of their outrageous

[39] Carte, *Life of Ormond* (1851 edn.), Vol. IV., pp.15, 16.

behaviour is given by the contemporary Quaker historian, Wight. No doubt it was an extreme case, but he evidently related as an example of laudable courage what now appears to us to have been the act of an insolent meddler in other people's affairs, if not that of a madman. Stripped to the waist this man entered a Catholic church during the celebration of Mass, carrying a dish of burning coals and brimstone on his head, violently disturbing the devotional quietness of the building by his loud cries as he denounced the supersititous idolatry of the congregation upon whom he had thus dramatically intruded. He was imprisoned for this performance[40]—this was in 1669, at the end of one of those short periods during which the Catholics were allowed to hear Mass unmolested by the authorities. Wight tells us that there was no persecution of Quakers for several years before this except by the " priests " on account of tithes. He always refers to the Anglican clergy as " priests."

The Catholic clergy were miserably poor. We have already noticed the case of the priest mentioned by Richard Head, whose income was so small that he had perforce to work all the week at manual labour to keep himself alive—an imaginary case, no doubt, but one quite true to life. Head uses the words ' parson ' and ' priest ' indiscriminately, and were it not for the context his description might have referred equally well to a poor Protestant minister. In Connacht, where conditions were worst

[40] Wight, *History of Quakers in Ireland*, p.101, *et seq.*
    In 1670, this same Quaker, Eccles, was expelled from Cork after having been whipped though the streets and receiving 90 stripes in the process. Edmundson and other prominent Quakers often found themselves in the stocks, and even William Penn, despite the protection of Orrery, who was invariably lenient to the Quakers, was frequently in trouble with the authorities. For examples of typical Quaker activities and consequent persecutions see C.S.P.I., 1669/70, Index. For Penn in Ireland see article by Eila Buckley, Dub. Hist. Rec. VI. 3. 81.

and Protestants fewest, the vicar (who did the work) commonly got but 40s. and sometimes only 16s. per annum.[41] Dr. Brenan reported to Rome, after his arrival in his diocese in 1671, that his clergy had to supplement their meagre incomes by farming and cattle dealing.[42] Previous to the Cromwellian war they had been in comparatively comfortable circumstances, but they were by this time reduced to the direst straits. The income of the Archbishop of Cashel, for example, derived as it was from the voluntary offerings of the priests of the diocese, had fallen in 1678 to £20 from over £1,000 per annum. At the same time, according to Dr. Brenan, the Protestant See had a revenue of £1,750, largely derived from Catholic sources, though no service, of course, was rendered to them in return.[43]

The bishop's estimate was not far wrong. A contemporary report made for Ormond's information gives the incomes of all the dignitaries of the established Church. Having regard to the value of money at the time, most of these were excessive. Archbishop Margetson actually received £3,500 a year. The many plums of the Anglican Church were reserved for ecclesiastics of British birth or parentage. On the other hand, their inferior clergy[44] were in even worse case than the Catholics, who could at least feel that the pittances they lived on were well

[41] Bagwell, III., p.323. Archbp. King estimated that only one-sixth of the established clergy were in comfortable circumstances. MS. Nat. Lib. S.1. (See p.184 *supra*) p.31.

[42] *Bishop of the Penal Times*, pp.10, 15, and 28.

[43] From 1641 to 1649 Dr. Arthur paid rent due on a lease from the Rector of St. Lawrence, near Limerick, to the Catholic rector ; previously and afterwards to the Protestant rector. Incidentally it may be observed that the Protestant rector's name was Donnoghow (O Donoghue), a typical Gaelic Catholic name.

[44] For the poverty and inferior social position of the rural clergy in England at the same period, see Macaulay's *History*, Chapter III., but this should be read in conjunction with Sir Charles Firth's criticism in his *Commentary on Macaulay's History*. (London, 1938).

earned and voluntarily given. The Protestant
Church in Ireland in the seventeenth century was
not without its illustrious men—Bedell, Taylor,
Ussher and King, for example—but if after the
Restoration the Protestant clergy no longer deserved
to be described as " a set of very profane and
drunken fellows "—which was Sir John Bingley's
considered opinion of them in 1629[45]—they were for
the most part little credit to their calling[46] ; though
the frequent complaints of their neglect of their
churches and manses must be ascribed more to their
poverty and to the selfishness of their superiors.

The most serious disability which directly affected
the native population was the almost total suppression of Catholic education. The practice of
sending young men destined for the priesthood to the
continental universities at Salamanca, Louvain,
Paris and elsewhere,[47] arose from their inability to
obtain it at home. If we accept the view that the
old Irish culture, which had produced men like
Pierce Ferriter[48] and Geoffrey Keating, was doomed
to extinction as a result of the English conquest,
then no doubt this practice had a beneficial effect,
inasmuch as it preserved some cultural standard
in Catholic Ireland, even though it was cosmopolitan rather than national. Students for the priesthood could not, of course, go to Trinity College,
Dublin, but prior to 1641 a considerable number of

[45] C.S.P. Ire. *An. cit.* p.442. Sir J. Bingley was markedly anti-Catholic.
[46] The constant disputes between Lord Orrery and the Rev. Christopher
Vowell, culminating on one occasion in the use of violence by the parson's
exasperated patron, are graphically described in letters printed in the *Orrery
Papers*, p.245 *et seq.* The English and Scots ministers introduced under the
Cromwellian regime had a proportion of worthier men (see *An. Hib.*,
No. 15, p.279 *et seq.*).
[47] For list of students and historical details about these, see *Irish Colleges
on the Continent*, by Very Rev. J O'Boyle. (Dublin, 1934).
[48] It is interesting to note that Pierce Ferriter's son, Major Dominick
Ferriter, was restored to his estate. (C.S.P.I. 1660/62, p.193).

Catholic laymen were educated there. In 1615 this new seat of learning, which was then just beginning to develop from a mere school into a real university, numbered among its students Thomas, son of Maurice Fitzgerald, and Fergal O'Gara, the patron of the famous Four Masters. As late as 1640 it was not unusual for the sons of chiefs to go to Oxford.

The leading Protestant school in Ireland in the second half of the seventeenth century was Kilkenny College which, in contrast to England with its many ancient foundations, if we except the King's Hospital[49] and one or two of the Erasmus Smith schools, is the only public school of any great antiquity still flourishing to-day. It had been founded in Tudor times by a Catholic Butler, but soon adopted, perhaps half-heartedly, the principles of the Reformation. Apart from penal legislation the influence of its patron, the Great Duke of Ormond, would have been enough to change its religious complexion. Early in the eighteenth century it became one of the recognized places of education for the Anglo-Irish aristocracy. Before that time, though it was less fashionable, it had many pupils who afterwards became famous: Swift and Congreve, for example, and George Berkeley,[50] the bishop and philosopher, all of whom entered it between 1677 and 1695. Orrery also founded and controlled a school at Charleville,

[49] See *Analecta Hibernica*, No. 15, pp.325-330 for documents relating to this (" the Bluecoat ") school in the seventeenth century. One of slightly later date (p.329) records that two boys, having first been whipped, " were stripped and ran the gauntlet through all the boys and made a public acknowledgement of their faults."
[50] For an account of Bishop Berkeley's schooldays at Kilkenny College see Hone and Rossi, *Bishop Berkeley*, London, 1931.

which he modelled on Winchester College,[51] but
it was not a success.[52]

During the war of 1641-52 several Catholic
schools were flourishing, at least in those places,
such as Limerick,[53] where resistance to the invader
was stoutest, but with the establishment of peaceful
conditions and with them the complete supremacy
of Protestantism, such schools could not be carried
on, and Catholic education in Ireland was confined to
what could be given by obscure laymen in out-of-the
way parishes where religious persecution was not
much felt except at times of exceptional activity.[54]
These men taught the children of their neighbours,
more or less clandestinely, and were the precursors
of the hedge-schoolmasters who became an integral
part of the " hidden Ireland " of the eighteenth
century.[55] O'Bruadair wrote a poem to one
Seán O Criagáin, who evidently carried on a school
and was a member of one of the courts of poetry
which were a not yet moribund survival of the old
Irish cultural system.[56] A similar revival followed
the accession of James II when many new Catholic
schools were opened [57] but with the downfall of
his cause these were suppressed and even in the
remotest parts of the country " all Popish recusants

[51] *Orrery Papers*, p.70 and *passim*. These letters give some glimpses of
school life which are interesting. See also C.S.P.I., 1666/69, p.367.
[52] One of the difficulties in the way of success was the fact that about this
time a number of schools were established (*ib*. p.251). One of the most
successful of these, though too far from Charleville to have an adverse
effect on Orrery's, was the Latin School at Athlone, conducted by the
Thewles family from 1660 to 1725, a description of which will be found in
J.R.S.A.I., Vol. XXI., p.214.
[53] During the viceroyalty of Lord Berkeley, when more tolerance was
shown than at any other time in the reign of Charles II, several quite
flourishing schools existed in the diocese of Limerick (see Begley, p.479),
but at no time did they enjoy a sense of security and their precarious existence was not longlived.
[54] Cf. *Short Study of a Transplanted Family* p.63.
[55] See Dowling, *The Hedge Schools of Ireland*, Chap. I.
[56] viz. Eachtas uaim ar amus Oide—24 June, 1675.
[57] Cf. *Orrery Papers*, p.353.

keeping schools in manifest contempt and opposition to the laws of this Realm " were to be apprehended, brought before a Justice of the Peace and punished according to law.[58]

The small gentry and the professional classes were the most severely hit, since the rich could send their sons abroad, and the labouring masses, Protestant as well as Catholic, regarded schooling as the luxury of the few. Dr. Brenan reported to Rome that " a great part of the youth of the country wastes its time in idleness through want of means of education, so that many who would be desirous of embracing the ecclesiastical state are delayed, the penal laws not allowing Catholics to keep school, and though some do keep school for half a dozen lads, that is only in secret and at some risk. Hence the Catholics are obliged to send their children to the public schools of Protestant teachers, not without some danger of perversion. Even if it were permitted to our people to keep school, few of them have ability to do so. The pastors teach the children the catechism and instruct some of them in reading and writing, but they are weak in the humanities and other sciences. In the diocese of Armagh there is great toleration in the matter of public schools, and the Catholics of that province have a great advantage of which they happily avail themselves, and may God grant them the continuance of the favour. There is almost similar toleration in the diocese of Ossory, but here we have not been able to break the ice."

[58] Proclamation by J. Coote, Justice of the King's Bench, 16 June, 1696, addressed to the " mayors, sheriffs, bailiffs, high and petty constables, and others whom it may concern to execute " concerning sixteen Catholic schoolmasters of Cos. Leitrim and Roscommon, whose names and abodes are given. Lane Papers, MS. in Nat. Lib., not yet catalogued.

This report accompanied a letter dated September 6th, 1672. His pious wish that God might grant the Catholics of the province of Armagh a continuance of their favoured position was not realized, for, in spite of the fact that Blessed Oliver Plunket was so much respected by Protestants as well as Catholics that he enjoyed the protection of the Earl of Charlemont[59] and other powerful persons in Ulster, nevertheless these schools referred to by Dr. Brenan were closed after three and a half years, when the measure of toleration associated with the viceroyalty of Berkeley had been superseded by the more oppressive regime of Essex. The success of these schools, to the establishment of which Oliver Plunket devoted so much earnest effort and to their maintenance the last halfpenny of his small and ever-dwindling income, shows how anxious the people were for education if it was available. His principal school, in charge of three Jesuit fathers, was at Drogheda, and this soon had not only 150 Catholic pupils, but even 40 sons of Protestant gentry as well.[60] "You can imagine," says Blessed Oliver, in a letter to the General of the Jesuits, "what envy it excites in the Protestant masters and ministers to see the Protestant children coming to the schools of the Society."[61] Just a year later he was writing to the Secretary of Propaganda in Rome:

"Matters here have been very severe . . . so that I am in concealment, and Dr. Brenan is with me.

[59] The Earl gave the Archbishop for his life a good house with garden, excellent orchard and two fields. See his letter of 23 Feb., 1671, printed, Moran, p.186.
[60] Another at Dundalk, also under the Jesuits, is referred to in a memorandum written on 17 Aug., 1670, by the Protestant Archbishop of Armagh (C.S.P.I., 1669/70, p.226).
[61] This letter, dated 22nd Nov., 1672, is preserved in T.C.D. and is quoted in Moran's *Plunket*, p.100.

The lay Catholics are so much afraid of losing their property that no one with anything to lose will give refuge to either ordinary or regulars, and although the regular clergy have some connivance to remain, yet the Catholics dread almost to admit them to say Mass in their houses. The priests give nothing to the bishops or ordinary ; I sometimes find it difficult to procure even oaten bread, and the house where I and Dr. Brenan are is of straw, and covered or thatched in such a manner that from our bed we may see the stars, and at the head of our bed every slightest shower *refreshes* us, but we are resolved rather to die of hunger and cold than to abandon our flocks . . . There is nothing that occasions me more inward grief than to see the schools which were instituted by me, now destroyed after so many toils. Oh ! what will the Catholic youth do, which is both numerous and full of talent? "

A few years later, when the complete extinction of the Irish Hierarchy had been determined on, we find him still firm in his resolution to remain at his post at the risk of his life. " We shall not," he wrote, " abandon our flocks till we are compelled by force to do so : we will first suffer imprisonment and other torments. We have already suffered so much on the mountains, in huts and caverns, and we have acquired such a habit, that for the future suffering will be less severe and troublesome."[42] That these were not idle words is proved by his death on the scaffold.

Thus sadly but gloriously ended the life of the finest character produced by Ireland in the seventeenth century, indeed I may almost say in any

[42] Brenan, *Letters*, p.18.

century. Though an aristocrat by birth, though a
distinguished personage in Rome and the holder
of the highest ecclesiastical position in Ireland, he
was no Olympian standing aloof and above his
countrymen and, more than Owen Roe O'Neill,
Patrick Sarsfield or any other national hero of
those days, Oliver Plunket was closely in touch with
the everyday life of the people. The fact of his being
often on his keeping—" on the run " as it would be
less picturesquely phrased nowadays—did much to
establish that intimate contact ; but it was the
character of the man himself which made him
loved by all who knew him, made him respected by
his opponents and hated by a few who had experienced the fearless courage which was as much
part of him as were his unselfishness and his
exemplary private life, and his human weaknesses,
too.

From one of his letters, dated August 2nd, 1678,
we learn that he was accustomed to preach in the
Irish language as well as in English. In the diocese
of Waterford we are told that " the mass of the
people speak nothing but Irish, but the educated
speak English and Irish," and this was probably
true of the country as a whole.[63] Petty remarks
that no English was used in at least 100,000 poor
houses.[64] Sir Henry Piers, who evidently knew Irish,
says that it was commonly used in Co. Westmeath
in 1683, though much adulterated with English
words.[65] The upper classes, of course, required

---

[63] A knowledge of Irish was considered essential for revenue officers in
Co. Waterford in 1675 (*Analecta Hibernica*, No. 1, p.178). Some of the
witnesses produced by the Crown in the trial of Archb. Oliver Plunket
spoke no English. (*Ibidem*, No. 2, p.91). Interpreters were, of course,
necessary in the Court of Claims. (*Ibidem*, No. 15, p.312, etc.).
[64] *Petty Papers*, ed. Lansdowne, Vol. I., p.58.
[65] MS. T.C.D. I. 1. 2, p.337. O'Bruadair complained that nothing but
colloquial Irish was understood.

a knowledge of the native language in order to communicate with their dependants, but it was evidently not regarded generally as a mark of inferiority, for it was much spoken by Irish gentlemen resident in London at least in the first half of the seventeenth century, and Father MacErlean states that it was from associating with them that James, Duke of Ormond, learned to speak it in the year 1629.[66] He evidently lost it again, though he understood it, as we know from the account of his bilingual conversation with the Irish priest, who could understand but speak no English.[67]

English, however, was undoubtedly beginning to be more generally used in Ireland. By the beginning of the seventeenth century, in the remoter parts of the country as well as in places where alien influence was strongest, English had almost superseded the language of the people for such purposes as leases and other legal agreements, and Gaelic documents of this kind of a date later than 1620 are almost unknown.[68] Even wills in Irish were the exception. The increasing use of English in everyday life was to be expected in the north. William Brooke, of Portadown, reported in 1682 that " most of those few Irish we have among us " spoke English,[69] and twenty years later Molyneux found " everybody understanding or answering you in English in the small cabins on the road in Co. Monaghan."[70] Irish, however, must have still been largely spoken as the vernacular in the north, because it was used

---

[66] Note by Fr. MacErlean in Irish Texts Edn. of O'Bruadair's Poems, Part II., p.65.
[67] D. Coffey, *Douglas Hyde* (1st Edn., Dublin, 1917), p.19.
[68] Some leases, etc., in Irish are preserved at Dromoland Castle, Co. Clare (Inchiquin Papers). The latest of these is dated 1618.
[69] MS. T.C.D. I. 1. 2, p.223.
[70] MS. T.C.D. I. 1. 3, p.106.

by an open-air preacher in 1678, not to convert the Papists of some remote glen but in the public market place of Lisburn. It is interesting to note that the preacher on this occasion was a woman— one Katherine Norton (née McLoughlin). She had been brought up an Irish-speaking Catholic at Derry, sailed to Barbadoes at sixteen, married there and was " convinced " by George Fox, the Quaker. On her return to Ireland she set to work to " convince " Irish men and women in their native language, but apparently with indifferent success.[71] In the south, too, the invading language seems to have been making some progress : Sir R. Cox, at any rate, was pleased to be able to tell the Dublin Philosophical Society so, and, though we must always somewhat discount the evidence of people with whom the wish is father to the thought, we must believe that he had some basis for his statement that the English language was altogether used in Co. Cork except by the poorer sort.[72] That it was used by people of position is proved by the fact that as late as 1697 it was in Irish that Rev. Dr. Coleman wrote a lengthy homily[72a] for his pupil, the nine year old son of Sir James Cotter, who, though a Catholic, continued to hold a place in County Cork society. The " poorer sort " only spoke English very unwillingly if they could do so at all. Francis Rogers may be regarded as an entirely unprejudiced observer, and after his visit to Co. Cork in 1703 he wrote in his journal : " The poor people ... seem to love their ease or idleness, or else are care-

---

[71] Wight, *op. cit.* p.123. Other Quakeresses are also mentioned as having preached publicly.
[72] MS. T.C.D. I. 1. 2, p.256.
[72a] Cotter MS. (Nat. Lib. No. 711), p.67. Young Cotter developed into a militant Catholic. He was executed in 1720, ostensibly for inciting riots. *Ibid.* p.127, *et seq.*

less and become stupid, by seeing themselves slaves as it were to the English, to whom they are very sullen, and will rarely understand them or speak English if they can, unless forced."[73] David O'Bruadair cannot be classed as one of the poorer sort, for all his temporary periods as a manual worker, and he certainly did not speak English if he could help it, even if it meant foregoing the chance of a good glass of beer. He tells us himself that though the minister at Croom kept " beoir slachtmhar seannda so-óla " he will not call in for a glass of it because of his inability to speak English fluently.[74]

The Protestant clergyman of Croom would seem from this to have been either disinclined or unable to speak Irish, but the idea that the language of the people might be used as a means of weaning them away from their allegiance to the old religion occurred to several influential Protestant ecclesiastics. Dr. Brenan describes in one of his reports the steps he took in Cashel to counteract the efforts of the Protestant bishop who proposed to preach a proselytizing sermon to Catholics there in Irish.[75] In 1655 a preacher was officially appointed to give sermons in Irish in St. Bride's Parish, Dublin.[76] The Bible, which Bedell had had translated into Irish, was published under Protestant auspices, the New Testament in 1681[77] and the Old in 1685.

[73] *Three Sea Journals of Stuart Times.* (London, 1936), p.197.
[74] *Dúanaire*, Part I., p.112. It will be noticed that just as Richard Head uses the words " priest " and " parson " as synomymous, so O'Bruadair in Irish describes the minister whose excellent beer he did not drink as both " ministir " and " sagart."
[75] This Bishop, Dr. Thomas Price, was very active in this way. Cf. his letter to Ormond of 13 June, 1680, in which he speaks very hopefully of the efforts of one of his clergy who preached open-air sermons to Papists in Irish ; he takes the opportunity of thanking the Duke for his encouragement of proselytism by this means. H.M.C. Ormonde Papers. New Series. Vol. V., p.334.
[76] Commonwealth State Accounts (*Analecta Hibernica*, No. 15, p.281).
[77] A translation of the New Testament, which was the basis of Bedell's edition, appeared in 1603.

Trinity College, indeed, gave considerable encouragement to the native language at this period ; Dr. Marsh, the founder of Marsh's Library, as well as his successor in the Provostship, doing much to promote it in the University,[78] while even in the less liberal generation which preceded his we find the College authorities giving an annual grant of £120 for Irish lectures.[79] " The belated work was perhaps more useful," says Bagwell, " in the Scotch highlands than in Ireland, for the time had long passed when the Reformation might have appealed to a Roman Catholic people in their own tongue."[80]

The Catholic clergy continued to employ the Gaelic language effectively, not to disseminate the Scriptures, but as the medium of their preaching, and even in Dublin itself the Dominicans preached in Irish every Sunday evening in 1708 and for some years afterwards.[81] The regular orders did their share in keeping the Irish language alive as the living speech of the people. Dr. Lynch expressed the hope " that the labours of the Rev. Fathers of St. Francis in Louvain College would once more revive the Irish language."[82] His remarks on the subject in 1662 have a familiar sound, so like are they to what was being written and said by workers in the same cause thirty or forty years ago ; he deplores its decay and recognizes a deliberate intention on the part of the government to obliterate interest in Irish history by destroying the language, and he applauds the efforts of some Irishmen who were resolved not to let it perish. No doubt his

[78] W. McN. Dixon, *Trinity College, Dublin*, p.56, *et seq.*, London, 1902.
[79] Commonwealth State Accounts (*An. Hib.*, 15, p.233).
[80] *Ireland Under the Stuarts*, Vol. III., p. 324.
[81] Gilbert, *History of Dublin*, Vol. I., p.334.
[82] *Cambrensis Eversus*, Vol. II., p.379.

reason for writing his own great vindication of the Irish nation in Latin was his desire that it should be widely read outside the shores of his own country. He cannot have been really seriously concerned at that time about its survival as the vernacular, but rather as a language of culture and education.

Irish, in fact, remained the vernacular throughout the greater part of Ireland until after the great famine of 1847. The effects of that national catastrophe on the Irish language were intensified by the establishment of the national schools system, which was the principal direct instrument in bringing about the decay of Gaelic, and its decline in turn affected the religious life of the people.

The Irish language, more even than Latin, is the medium of all that is sincerest and most beautiful in the religious literature of the country, and unquestionably its decay deprived Catholicity in Ireland of one of its strongest supports. We have witnessed in our own time a determined attempt to revive the old language in face of the all-powerful cosmopolitan influences of press, cinema and radio —an attempt which after fifty years of effort has had only a partial success. How far this will help to save the Church in Ireland from the dangers which have beset it in other countries, till recently considered as Catholic as Ireland, we do not know. We do know that the destruction of that language was one item in the penal system which was devised to destroy the Irish and their religion. The effects of that code, which culminated in the ferocious Acts passed under Queen Anne and George I, though falling far short of the intentions of its authors, have lasted for centuries and, however happy a termination to the long struggle between the two races may lie in the future, are likely to last for generations more. We can let incontrovertible and well-attested facts speak for themselves ; and rather than succumb to the temptation to indulge in diatribes and invective let us thank God that the results of this evil thing have not been themselves entirely evil.

INDEX

References are not given in this Index to the names of writers when such appear in the text or notes merely as the authority for a quotation or statement.

A

Abductions : 289

Absence, leave of : 266

Acres, Irish and English measure : 242

Actors : 214

Adornes, Adrian : 169

Advertisements : 141, 213 *et seq.*

Agriculture : Chapter VI *passim* and see Bettimore, Booley, Cattle, Creaghting, Crops, Dairies, Enclosures, Fairs, Hay, Herdsmen, Horses, Land tenure, Labour, Lime, Orchards, Oxen, Ploughing, Potatoes, Sheep, Wages

Alexander, Rev. James : 275

Algerians : see Pirates

Almshouses :- 204, 224

Anglesey, Arthur Annesley, Earl of : 192

Anglicization : 8, 34, 117 *et seq.*, 242 , and see Assimilation

Animals, diseases of : 142, 178

——, domestic : see Cattle, Horses, etc.

——, love of : 140

——, wild : 134, 138,

Antrim, County : 249

——, Randal McDonnell, 2nd Earl of : 220

Apothecaries : 224,

Apprentices : 213, 224

Archer, Rev. J., S.J. : 285

Architects : 98

Arlington, Henry Bennett, Earl of : 55, 80, 129, 260

Armagh, Archdiocese of : 302, 303

—— Cathedral : 295

Armorial bearings, use of : 24, 412

Armourer, Sir Nicholas : 35, 145

Army, discipline : 82, 133

——, drilling of : 234

——, general refs. to : 224, 247, 251, 294,

Arran, Earls of : 145

Arthur, Dr. Thomas : 12, 32, 56, 98, 219 *et seq.*, 298

Arthure, Robert : 411

Assemblies, City : see Corporations

Assimilation of races, extent of : 12, 59, 87, 93, 111, 122, 123

Aston, Henry : 193

Athenry : 327

Athlone : 189, 301

Auctions : 211, 213

Axtell, Col. : 415

B

Bagnall, Col. : 206

Bagpipes : 164

Bagwell, Richard : 11

Ballingarde (Co. Limerick) : 97

Ballybay (Co. Offaly) : 108

Ballybough : see under Dublin.

Ballycar (Co. Clare) : 94

Ballyclough (Co. Clare) : 97

Ballykitt (Co. Clare) : 97, 101

Ballyluddane (Co. Clare) : 94

Ballyneety (Co. Limerick) : 244

Bandon : 59, 189, 190, 276

Bankers and banking : 231-232

Banshee : see Superstition

Barber-chirurgiens : 116, 224

Barbers : 116, 143, 217,

Bards : 18, 32 ; and see O'Carolan

Barlone (Co. Cork) : 110

Barry, Miss, of Monanimy : 94

Bathing : 100

Baths : 29, 100

Bathurst, Samuel : 261

Bawns : 108, 168

Beargardens : 147

Beaulieu (Co. Louth) : 98

Bedell, Wm., Bishop of Kilmore : 299, 308

Beds : see Sleeping accommodation

Beer and Ale : 41 ; and see Brewing

Beggars : 66, 72, 205 ; and see Poor Relief

Belfast : 183

Bells, church : 199, 236, 295

Belton, Dr. : 219

Benburb, battle of : 43

Bennet : see Arlington

Beranger, Gabriel : 141

Berehaven : 114, 138

Berkeley, John, Baron : 294, 301, 303,

——, George (afterwards Bishop of Cloyne) : 300